In Praise of What Counts

Touted by many sector leaders worldwide, here's what some of them have to say about *What Counts: Social Accounting for Nonprofits and Cooperatives, Second Edition:*

In Canada

"The research upon which this book is based has proven to be a powerful tool to our organization, in enabling us to fully articulate to our stakeholders and potential donors the significant impact of our added value, the social capital generated as a result of our work. We have integrated a range of the principles and practices outlined in the book, incorporating an annual assessment of our 'value added' as part of our series of benchmark indicators that both guide us internally and help tell a more accurate story externally. We applaud the innovation offered by Mook, Quarter, and Richmond in practice and principle and recommend this resource to other nonprofits seeking to demonstrate leadership in their work."

Sharon Wood, Executive Director, Canadian Breast Cancer Foundation, Ontario Chapter

"Generally, books about accounting are not exciting to read. However, *What Counts* is an eye-opener and raises issues that have the potential to change practice for nonprofits, cooperatives, and other organizations with a social mission."

Eric Plato, Director of Finance and Administration, Frontier College, Toronto

"This book makes a strong contribution to nonprofit organizations and cooperatives as well as accounting as an academic field. The work of Laurie Mook, Jack Quarter and Betty Jane Richmond is innovative, original, brilliant and provocative. Social accounting is a social innovation that is worthy of dissemination among social enterprises as well as large corporations."

Denis Harrisson, Centre de recherche sur les innovations sociales, Université du Québec à Montréal

"Social accounting is just as important as financial accounting. This book is very useful for studying and teaching in the field."

Dr. Greg MacLeod, Professor Emeritus, Tompkins Institute, Cape Breton University

"This is a path-breaking book that has in a short time become a standard text for students and scholars of the social economy. Those who manage and govern nonprofit and cooperative organizations will benefit tremendously from the practical guides for incorporating systematic and analytical reports of social value in regular statements to stakeholders. The book's contribution goes well beyond a call for social organizations to begin assessing and communicating the true impact of their activities on communities, however, by presenting a major challenge to policy makers and the accounting profession to develop new systems of standard reporting that facilitate greater accountability of all organizations through an assessment of their social, environmental and economic value. This is a wonderful book—clear, practical and insightful—and destined to become a classic in the fields of management, accounting and nonprofit studies."

Brenda Gainer, Royal Bank Professor of Nonprofit Management, and Director, Nonprofit Management and Leadership Program, Schulich School of Business, York University, Toronto

"As more people become concerned about the social impact of economic activities, communities want to understand what the social economy does for them in creating social cohesion. This book makes a central contribution for people wishing to meet these needs. It belongs, its pages turned and reflected upon, in the board rooms and among memberships of all cooperatives and, indeed, all like-minded institutions."

Dr. Ian Macpherson, Director, British Columbia Institute for Co-operative Studies

"The book is illuminating and will be useful for people involved in social organizations, either as staff, donors, or board members."

Harvey Schachter, Managing Books Columnist, *Globe and Mail*, Toronto

"At a time when our economy is making the rich richer and the poor poorer, when we are mining our ecology and when we are realizing that economic democracy is tied to political democracy, we are in great need of the tools that help us understand and measure the impacts of economic activity. *What Counts* contributes usable tools to measure what we do as a major contribution to our society and our world. We cannot manage what we cannot measure. This book is a must for anyone serious about making this world a better place for our children and grandchildren."

Tom Webb, Program Manager, Master of Management: Co-operatives and Credit Unions Program, Saint Mary's University, and President, Global Co-operation Inc.

"As a participant in the research for this book, the Jane/Finch Community and Family Centre has had a firsthand opportunity to apply the Expanded Value Added Statement to our organization. Knowing the value added that we create has helped our funders to appreciate our contribution and has had the same effect for our staff and our volunteers. We have to come to realize that we don't simply use resources, but that we also add value to society through our services."

Margarita Mendez, Executive Director, Jane/Finch
Community and Family Centre, Toronto

In Israel

"The originality of this book is its integration of the discussion of theoretical topics with the presentation of case studies and with detailed analysis of accounting systems. This mixture might be problematic for some readers; it has however the advantage of bridging theory and practice and offers important tools to the practitioners of social and economic organizations."

Professor Menachem Rosner, University of Haifa

In Sweden

"The insight that social undertaking and economic activity are two faces of one and the same coin is voiced by many, but concretely measured only by few. *What Counts* is perhaps the most prominent example of this latter group. The book argues for, and develops, workable quantitative measurement tools for the elusive field in which economic and social inputs shade into, and are converted and reconverted into each other. In doing this, it actually manages the rare feat of being both a no-nonsense undergraduate textbook, and a substantial contribution to case study research method. The standards it sets for the measurement of social and voluntary inputs' *economic* impact—a sphere that is all too often overshadowed by traditional fund-raising (or, in the European case, grant-raising) deserve particular attention, and have the makings for becoming highly useful management tools as well."

Dr. Yohanan Stryjan, Professor of Business Administration,
Södertörns högskola, Stockholm

In the United Kingdom

"This is an intriguing book written at the interface between theory and practice in social accounting by three individuals who operate on the boundary of academe and the applied world of the third sector organizations in Canada."

Rob Gray, Professor of Social and Environmental Accounting, The School of Management, St Andrews University, Scotland

"The need for organizations to assess impact and demonstrate value is growing. Most, however, are grappling with exactly how to go about it. *What Counts* provides a valuable framework and guide for organizations. It offers insights and practical suggestions for how organizations can get to grips with social accounting and moves us on considerably in our thinking."

Dr. Angela Ellis Paine, Assistant Director, Institute for Volunteering Research, London, England

In the United States

"For years, I collected examples of social accounting practices and developed a thick folder of materials. Thankfully, it has now been replaced by a detailed and effectively written reference—*What Counts.*"

Elizabeth K. Keating, CPA, Senior Research Fellow, Hauser Center, Harvard University

"This book is very significant in providing the beginnings of an alternative social accounting that can actually be described conceptually with procedures spelled out in a 'how-to-do' manner. I cannot rave enough about the significance and value of this book."

Thomasina Borkman, Professor, George Mason University

"*What Counts* is impressive for the depth of scholarship and astonishing wealth of detail. I am excited about this fine contribution to the literature on social accounting. The book can be utilized by professors as a teaching resource to complement general nonprofit management and finance courses in schools of social work, public administration, and business. Agency accountants and external consultants will also find that the case materials described in this volume can be used to develop social accounting statements for the benefit of board members, managers, volunteers, and funders."

Karun K. Singh, Faculty of Social Work, Hunter College, New York

"With new questions arising every day to challenge the contributions that nonprofits make to our communities, it is essential that we have the tools to clearly demonstrate our worth. This book holds out the promise that we can meet this challenge. For those of on the firing line, Mook, Quarter, and Richmond give us the ammunition we need to answer the communities' questions."

**Bill Benet, Ph.D., Director, Community/University
Partnership Project, Rochester, New York**

"*What Counts* focuses on the crucial issue of fully valuing the contributions of nonprofit organizations, in particular their volunteers, to the larger society. Conventional accounting practices tend to overlook these aspects, even though they are among the most important effects of nonprofit organizations. Building from sound theory and principles of accountancy, the authors present novel approaches to address this oversight that advance the field. At the same time, they write with a view to application so that the new approaches are equally valuable for nonprofit practitioners and academic researchers."

**Jeffrey L. Brudney, Ph.D., Albert A. Levin Chair of Urban Studies and
Public Service, Cleveland State University**

"This important book shows us how to rethink the way in which nonprofits do their accounting. By ignoring social accounting, nonprofits at their own peril ignore the value they add to society. I highly recommend this book to all practitioners and academics in the field of nonprofit management."

**Femida Handy, Associate Professor, University of Pennsylvania and
York University**

"As the authors point out, conventional accounting statements are internally focused reports that emphasize financial dimensions of the organization and market-based measures. By contrast, the methodology of social accounting that is developed in this book casts a wider net, giving a fuller picture of the net contributions, resource usage, liabilities and assets, of an organization. It is especially relevant to nonprofit organizations, whose missions are explicitly social, which engage multiple important stakeholder groups, and which productively employ large quantities of volunteer effort. The net effect is that social accounting potentially provides a much fuller, more accurate, and very likely a more positive picture of the social and economic contributions that nonprofit organizations make to society."

**Dennis Young, Bernard B. and Eugenia A. Ramsey Professor of Private
Enterprise and Director of the Nonprofit Studies Program,
Georgia State University, and President of the
National Center on Nonprofit Enterprise**

WHAT COUNTS

SOCIAL ACCOUNTING FOR NONPROFITS AND COOPERATIVES

SECOND EDITION

Laurie Mook
  Ontario Institute for Studies in Education,
  University of Toronto

Jack Quarter
  Ontario Institute for Studies in Education,
  University of Toronto

Betty Jane Richmond
  York University

Sigel Press

Sigel Press
51 A Victoria Road
Cambridge CB4 3BW England

4403 Belmont Court
Medina, Ohio 44256 USA

Visit us on the World Wide Web at:
www.sigelpress.com

First edition published by Prentice Hall, a division of Pearson Education, Inc., Upper Saddle River, New Jersey, 07458, USA, Copyright ©2003

Second edition published by Sigel Press, London, England, E17 6RD, Copyright ©2007

Second edition, second printing published by Sigel Press, Cambridge, England, CB4 3BW, Copyright ©2007

ISBN: 1-905941-01-3
ISBN: 978-1-905941-01-8

British Library Cataloguing-in-Publication Data
A catalogue record for this book is available from the British Library

Typeset by Professional Book Compositors, Lorain, Ohio, USA
Printed and bound in England by CPI Antony Rowe, Eastbourne
Printed and bound in the USA by Standard Printing Company, Canton, Ohio

The publisher's policy is to use paper manufactured from sustainable forests.

To the many dedicated staff, volunteers, and members of nonprofits and cooperatives who are doing work that counts

About the Authors

Laurie Mook is director of the Social Economy Centre of the University of Toronto. She has degrees in accounting, international development, and education. During her Ph.D. studies she was a Social Sciences and Humanities Research Council of Canada doctoral fellow at the Ontario Institute for Studies in Education of the University of Toronto. As part of her research, Mook has taken the lead in designing accounting statements that are appropriate for organizations with a social mission. One such adaptation is the Expanded Value Added Statement (EVAS), a statement that illustrates the impact of the organization upon the surrounding community and the effects of the organization on an array of stakeholders. In her Ph.D. thesis, Mook applied this framework to environmental accounting.

Jack Quarter is a professor at the Ontario Institute for Studies in Education of the University of Toronto, specializing in the study of nonprofits, cooperatives, and the social economy. He is one of the first researchers in English Canada to undertake a comprehensive study of the social economy, published in his 1992 book, *Canada's Social Economy*. Quarter is the author of 12 books and over 100 journal papers and book chapters addressing a broad range of social issues. He is the principal investigator for large number of research projects funded by the Social Sciences and Humanities Research Council of Canada (SSHRC), including the research currently being undertaken through the Social Economy Centre, but his more recent work has, together with Mook and Richmond, focused upon social accounting and its application to nonprofits and cooperatives.

Betty Jane Richmond (B.J.) is a professor in the Faculty of Education, York University, specializing in inclusive education, adult and community education. Richmond has extensive experience in the nonprofit sector including work with a large Ontario-wide funder of nonprofits. For her doctoral thesis (under the supervision of Jack Quarter) at the Ontario Institute for Studies in Education of the University of Toronto, Richmond developed the Community Social Return on Investment model and applied it to a community-based training agency for people on social assistance because of various forms of disability. Richmond won the outstanding dissertation award for 1999 from ARNOVA (Association for Research on Nonprofit Organizations and Voluntary Associations), the leading learned society in this field.

Brief Contents

Contents

List of Tables and Figures

Tables

Figures

Foreword

What Counts: Social Accounting for Nonprofits and Cooperative, Second Edition, by Laurie Mook, Jack Quarter, and Betty Jane Richmond, raises an important issue for nonprofits. Those of us who care about the nonprofit sector have long recognized that conventional accounting does not count many important contributions of nonprofit organizations.

Also, as we know, many nonprofits rely heavily on volunteers and because they are not paid, their contributions normally do not find their way onto accounting statements. These uncounted contributions are significant: The most recent figures on volunteering from the Independent Sector indicate that for the year 2000, 44 percent of adults over the age of 21 (83.9 million) volunteered a total of 15.5 billion hours, or the equivalent of over 9 million full-time positions.

For these reasons, *What Counts* is a very timely analysis of a major challenge facing nonprofits today—how to properly assess social impacts and the important contributions of volunteers. In an era of resource constraints and increased demands for accountability, creating accounting procedures that highlight the social impacts of nonprofits is critical. *What Counts* tackles this issue by presenting actual social accounting statements that allow nonprofits to do just that: Four models are presented using seven case studies. Among the issues that are addressed within these accounting statements are the value of volunteer contributions, the impact of the organization on the personal growth and development of its volunteers, the impact of the organization on the recipients of its services, the impact on the community, and the impact on the environment. In other words, these statements address issues that are of importance to nonprofits.

The field of accounting has traditionally evolved in response to the needs of the business community. While this is an important constituency, nonprofits are different in that they do not have shareholders and they serve many stakeholders. Therefore, new accounting models are needed that speak to the uniqueness of nonprofits. While going a long way in demonstrating how volunteer contributions and unpaid services to the community can be included in accounting statements, *What Counts* acknowledges that this work represents only a beginning. Nevertheless, it is an important beginning!

Alan J. Abramson
Director, Nonprofit Sector and Philanthropy Program
The Aspen Institute
Washington, D.C.

Preface

This second edition of *What Counts* coincides with the release of *VolunteersCount*, an online software program that allows nonprofits and other community organizations to keep records of their volunteers. This online program attributes an estimated value to volunteer contributions and produces social accounting reports that present the volunteer contributions as a percentage of human resources and of financial resources. The online program also produces an adaptation of a Value Added Statement called an Expanded Value Added Statement, which is discussed in detail in this book.

At this point in time, it is not uncommon for nonprofits, under increasing pressure from funders, to justify the impact of their expenditures and to keep records of volunteer contributions to their organizations. Even though an increasing number of nonprofits record their volunteer contributions, most do this work manually. A national survey of 661 Canadian nonprofits we undertook in 2004 indicated that 41 percent kept records of volunteer contributions through their organization, but about 80 percent of that group did so manually—that is, without a computerized system. *VolunteersCount* should help such organizations; even more so because, as an open source program, it is available without charge.

Embedded within *VolunteersCount* is an electronic workshop that explains social accounting in basic terms and that discusses strategies for including volunteer value within a social accounting system. This workshop, like this book, helps participants obtain an understanding of the reports in *VolunteersCount* as well as an understanding of social accounting more generally. While there is a growing body of research and writing about social accounting, most of it represents a critique of conventional accounting (see Chapter 3). Relatively little of this work presents alternative accounting frameworks, and even less is applied to nonprofits and cooperatives, or to what we label as the social economy (see Chapter 2).

The accounting statements used for organizations in the social economy are identical to those applied to businesses oriented to generating profits for their owners. However, accounting statements for nonprofits and cooperatives miss an important feature of their activities—these are organizations with a social mission and, as such, their social impact is a vital part of their performance story. In addition, nonprofits rely in varying degrees on volunteers, yet ironically the value of this service normally is excluded from accounting statements. In other words, for organizations with a social mission conventional accounting misses critical aspects of their operations. This book begins the process of rectifying this oversight by including within accounting statements the contribution of volunteers and other forms of unpaid labor (unpaid member contributions in a cooperative and nonprofit mutual association) and social outputs that normally are not exchanged in the market. This is a challenging task because it involves making appropriate market comparisons for items normally not involving any market exchange. We locate this work in the emerging field of social accounting, which attempts to broaden the domain of accounting by analyzing the impact of the organization on society and the natural environment. In this book we define social accounting as a **systematic analysis of the effects of an organization on its communities of interest or stakeholders, with stakeholder input as part of the data that are analyzed for the accounting statement.** This definition is developed in detail in Chapter 3.

The predominant tradition in social accounting is the creation of qualitative reports that systematically organize feedback from stakeholders on how well the organization is meeting its mission. In general, social accounting has bypassed financial statements and limited itself to supplementary reports, also referred to as social or ethical audits. We depart from this tradition and utilize actual accounting statements but with a difference—we broaden the domain that is considered and attempt to tell a more complete story of the organization's performance.

Three social accounting statements are presented in this book:

➢   the Socioeconomic Impact Statement, an adaptation of an income statement;
➢   the Socioeconomic Resource Statement, an adaptation of a balance sheet; and
➢   the Expanded Value Added Statement, an adaptation of a Value Added Statement.

In addition, a fourth approach—the Community Social Return on Investment model—was created specifically to measure the social impact of nonprofits. While not a formal accounting statement in the same sense the Socioeconomic Impact Statement, the Socioeconomic Resource Statement, and the Expanded Value Added Statement, the Community Social Return on Investment model is a relatively simple framework that social organizations can use to measure their social impact.

With each of these approaches, volunteer contributions and other forms of unpaid labor are included as are some social outputs that are not exchanged on the market. These approaches are applied to seven different organizations—nonprofits and one student-housing cooperative. For each application, there are illustrations and detailed explanations of how the calculations were arrived at. In addition, one chapter presents the data collection devices used in the book—these are useful for preparing social accounting statements and for organizations wanting to systematize their record keeping of volunteers and social impacts and to place a market value on them.

This second edition of *What Counts* serves as an explanatory text for *VolunteersCount* and also presents a theoretical rationale for this work. We view the book also as a supplementary text for persons in such programs as nonprofit management, cooperative management, and accounting. In addition, we feel that it is written in such a way as to be of use to managers of nonprofits and cooperatives in such activities as:

➢ annual reports, to more accurately reflect to supporters, members, donors, and other audiences the value the organization returns to the community;

➢ volunteer recognition programs, to demonstrate to volunteers their value to the organization and to those served by the organization;

➢ funding proposals and in reports to funders, to show how the impact of funder dollars was stretched by voluntary efforts; and

➢ to demonstrate to policymakers the value of investing in community-based organizations.

This book is an outgrowth of each of our diverse but related experiences. Betty Jane Richmond (B.J.) has served in management and on the board of directors with various nonprofits and worked with a large nonprofit foundation. Currently, she teaches in the Faculty of Education at York University. Through her experiences with nonprofits, she began to realize that the ways of evaluating how well a nonprofit organization is doing are limited and unbalanced. The costs of nonprofits are all too evident, but the value they contribute to the community is not easily assessed. She concluded that the evaluative mechanisms for nonprofits, including the accounting systems, are missing something critical—the impact of their services on their clients and the community.

For her doctoral thesis (under the supervision of Jack Quarter) at the Ontario Institute for Studies in Education of the University of Toronto, Richmond developed the Community Social Return on Investment model and applied it to a community-based training agency for people on social assistance because of various forms of disability. That perspective looked at part of the social return that these organizations create. Within this work, Richmond utilized the social economy framework that had been developed in Western Europe and had been applied to a Canadian context by Quarter, and written up in his book, *Canada's Social Economy*, and subsequent research. Unlike most frameworks for nonprofits, the social economy casts a broader net and includes all types of organizations formed primarily for a social purpose, including nonprofits oriented to the public and often with a charitable status, nonprofit mutual associations serving a membership, and cooperatives. All of these are referred to as social organizations. Richmond won the outstanding dissertation award for 1999 from ARNOVA (Association for Research on Nonprofit Organizations and Voluntary Associations). ARNOVA, based at the University of Indiana, is the major international association for researchers of nonprofits.

Through a fortuitous contact, Richmond met Laurie Mook, and together they began extending this work. With funding from the Canadian Co-operative Association, Ontario Region (now the Ontario Co-operative Association), they conducted research into how a student-run housing cooperative participated in the social and economic life of its community. In this research, Mook (a researcher who completed a Certified General Accountant's degree and who has a related set of social interests that led to degrees in International Development and in Educational Policy Studies) adapted a

Value Added Statement to illustrate both the social labor contributed by members to the cooperative and the effects of the organization on an array of stakeholders. This adaptation was named an Expanded Value Added Statement (EVAS). Mook undertook her Ph.D. program at the University of Toronto with the support of a prestigious doctoral fellowship from the Social Sciences and Humanities Research Foundation of Canada (SSHRC). Mook's thesis extends her research on the Expanded Value Added Statement and applies it to environmental accounting. She too was under the supervision of Jack Quarter.

After the completion of the project with the student housing cooperative in 2000, the three of us were fortunate to receive an International Year of the Volunteer grant from Human Resources Development Canada and the Canadian Centre for Philanthropy (the forerunner to Imagine Canada and the apex organization for nonprofits in Canada). The International Year of the Volunteer project with the Canadian Red Cross, Toronto Region, Canadian Breast Cancer Foundation, Ontario Chapter, Canadian Crossroads International, and the Jane/Finch Community and Family Centre, as well as a related project with the Junior Achievement program in Rochester, New York, allowed us to apply the Expanded Value Added Statement in different contexts. The project also permitted us to address more specifically the issues of attributing a comparative market value to non-monetary items, including volunteer contributions, within such a statement. As part of the work with Junior Achievement of Rochester, an income statement has been adapted to a Socioeconomic Impact Statement and a balance sheet to a Socioeconomic Resource Statement. These adaptations better suit the social purpose of this organization and take into consideration its important stock of intellectual capital.

In writing the book, it was also important for us to make accessible knowledge about suitable approaches to accounting for nonprofits and cooperatives to current and future managers and directors of these organizations. Through the International Year of the Volunteer project, we developed hands-on experience in how to help nonprofits track their volunteer tasks, hours, and non-reimbursed out-of-pocket expenses, and how to research the skills that they develop from volunteering. In addition, we have conducted workshops on social accounting with more than 700 staff and Board members of nonprofits and cooperatives. Instruction and examples illustrating how to proceed with social accounting can be found in our how-to chapter (Chapter 8).

We view the models that are presented here as a beginning rather than a final point. As will become apparent from our discussion in the chapters that follow, developing appropriate accounting systems for social organizations requires creating practical and replicable procedures for measuring the effects on key stakeholders, including society. Doing this requires time-consuming research on the creation of appropriate benchmarks or social indicators that become the standards for interpretation and also requires general agreement among professionals who account for the performance of social organizations. For example, measuring the contributions of volunteers is a complex labor-intensive process that social organizations often are reluctant to become involved with, in part because of a lack of human resources. Part of the solution is practical (establishing the know-how) and part is political (establishing the agreement of the profession about standards that should be applied for estimating the dollar value of particular volunteer tasks).

In addition to the financial support already mentioned, some of the research flowing into this manuscript was supported by a grant from the Kahanoff Foundation, 1998–99, through the Queen's University School of Policy Studies, that permitted some development of the social economy framework. More recently, our research has been supported by grants from the Social Sciences and Humanities Research Council of Canada (SSHRC), including a Public Outreach grant, which includes the development of *VolunteersCount* and its related electronic training tutorial. For this latter work, we are working closely with Imagine Canada, the umbrella organization for nonprofits in Canada.

We are also indebted to a number of people with whom we have worked with these models. These are the staff and board of directors of the Waterloo Co-operative Residence Incorporated (WCRI); Cathy Lang, former Ontario Regional Director of the Canadian Co-operative Association; Kunle Akingbola, former Manager of Employee and Volunteer Resources, and Maria Harlick, Director, Service Support & Development Services, at the Canadian Red Cross, Toronto Region; Margarita Mendez, Executive Director, and Clare Blythe, Volunteer Coordinator, at the Jane/Finch Community and Family Centre; Karen Takacs, Executive Director, Ian McNeil, Director of Finance, and Mario Gagnon, National Program Manager, at Canadian Crossroads International; Sharon Wood, Ontario Chapter Executive Director, and Beth Easton, the Ontario Community Programs Director, of the Canadian Breast Cancer Foundation; and Andrew Portanova, President, and Rebecca Sherman, Program Manager, of the Junior Achievement program of Rochester, New York.

To undertake this research, we were fortunate to have the assistance of some highly skilled and motivated graduate students: Dorothy Aaron, Anne Dimito, Michelle Hamilton-Page, Jorge Sousa, and Shannon Wall. Jorge also put together the index of the book and generously assisted with formatting. His support was invaluable in making the manuscript camera ready.

Professor Daniel Schugurensky helped us to formulate the discussion questions at the end of each chapter and Hugh Oliver gave generously of his unique skill in the use of the English language. We would like to thank those who have commented on earlier versions of this manuscript, and in so doing have provided feedback that has helped us to move the ideas forward: Professors Thomasina Borkman and Patricia Lewis of Nonprofit Management Studies at George Mason University; Professor Roger Lohmann of West Virginia University; Professor Ian MacPherson, University of Victoria; Professor Leslie Brown of Mount St. Vincent University; Professor Emeritus Hugh Oliver of the Ontario Institute for Studies in Education of the University of Toronto; and Bill Benet, Director of the Community/University Partnership Project. Angela Ellis and Kathy Gaskin were helpful in passing on their work on the Volunteer Investment and Value Audit (VIVA).

In particular, we would like to extend our appreciation to Professor Femida Handy (University of Pennsylvania and York University) with whom we have collaborated on the SSHRC-funded research and who has been a great support in developing and promoting this work. Michael Hall, Vice-President of Research for Imagine Canada, has provided ongoing support for our work. We give a special word of thanks to Thomas Sigel, the former Acquisitions Editor (Accounting) of Prentice Hall, for believing in our work. Thomas, as is probably apparent from the front matter, is now our publisher.

On a personal level, we would like to thank Daniel Schugurensky, who went well above and beyond the call of parenthood while Laurie worked on the manuscript, Robert Paskoff along with B.J.'s family and friends for their support while her many duties called, and Dale Willows, who was there at all times for Jack.

Laurie Mook
Jack Quarter
B.J. Richmond

Chapter 1

Introduction

The United Nations Human Development Report (1995) estimates that worldwide non-market work (that is, work that does not receive a payment in the market) should be valued at $16 trillion and would add about 70 percent to the officially valued global output of $23 trillion. While this estimate covers a broad range of activities and focuses on marked gender inequalities in the payment of work, it does highlight an issue that is central to this book: Accounting involves the counting of and analysis of some types of contributions and excludes others. *What Counts*, the title of this book, refers to the fact that many types of economic contributions do not count.

The focus of the book is to give greater recognition to items that are not counted by creating accounting statements for nonprofits and cooperatives that illuminate the impact of such organizations. As will be discussed in Chapter 2, these organizations have some distinctive features—for example, their volunteer labor and many of their key outputs are non-monetized (that is, do not involve monetary transactions). As a result, these items normally do not appear in accounting statements, even though they are critical to the mission of the organizations.

In an international study of 36 countries, Lester Salamon and associates of the Johns Hopkins Comparative Nonprofit Sector Project (Salamon, Sokolowski, and List 2004) estimate that volunteers contributed the equivalent of 20.2 million full-time equivalent jobs and that the value added of this volunteer contribution amounts to $316 billion. For these countries, this represents an invaluable, sustaining contribution to local communities; but neither this contribution nor any additional social impact finds its way onto conventional accounting statements.

Although the Johns Hopkins study presents its analysis at the level of the nation, it has direct implications for the accounting of nonprofits, as these are organizations that depend in varying degrees on volunteer contributions. At minimum, volunteers form the board of directors, and in many organizations they are the primary service providers. Yet because their contributions do not involve market transactions, normally they are not counted in accounting statements.

This same point pertains to cooperatives. Their members contribute labor that reduces the market cost of goods and services and also contribute unpaid services to their governance through participating in committees and on the board of directors. Without these services, the costs of operation would be greater.

Social accounting, the subject of this book, endeavors to broaden the range of contributions and outputs that accounting statements consider. There is already a well-established field of financial accounting and related branches of managerial and government accounting, but social accounting is more recent and much less developed with fewer practical working models. As will be discussed in Chapter 3, social accounting is based on a critique of the limitations of financial accounting, particularly the limited range of items that it considers, its exclusion of items that do not result in a market transaction (non-monetized), and its focus on shareholders and other financing providers.

What Counts broadens the domain of items that are included in financial statements so that nonprofits and cooperatives can better tell their story. This is the point of departure between this book and many other texts on accounting—for example, financial accounting (Larson et al. 2003; Meigs, Lam, and Mallouk 2002; Larsen and Jensen 2005), managerial accounting (Garrison, Chesley, and Carroll 2006; Kaplan and Atkinson 1989), or government and nonprofit accounting (Finkler 2005; Garner 1991; Razek, Hosch, and Ives 2004). In order to broaden accounting statements, it is necessary to address the contentious issue of assigning an appropriate value to items that do not involve market transactions. As will be discussed in Chapter 2, there is a tradition for making market comparisons for volunteer contributions, but this is generally done in relation to volunteer surveys (Hall, McKeown, and Roberts 2001; Independent Sector 2001a) and not in a broad sense within accounting statements. One of our primary objectives in *What Counts* is to present procedures for integrating within financial statements volunteer contributions and social outputs that do not involve a market exchange. Integrating the important non-monetized items into actual accounting statements—social accounting statements, as we label them—is the unique feature of this book.

Human resource accounting also involves a critique of the limited number of variables considered in financial accounting—a critique that overlaps with social accounting (Flamholtz 1985). Human resource accounting argues for a fuller accounting of human capital issues such as the treatment of employees—for example, a full costing by a corporation of the effects of layoffs. Such a costing would include not just apparent considerations like expenses related to replacement and training but also a costing of the effects on employee morale and motivation. While a fuller costing of human capital is compatible with social accounting, the latter goes further and addresses impacts that are external to the organization. Using the layoff example, the costs that society has to pick up to support the laid-off workers would be included within a social accounting framework.

The definition of social accounting used in this book is "**A systematic analysis of the effects of an organization on its communities of interest or stakeholders, with stakeholder input as part of the data that are analyzed for the accounting statement**." This definition, which is discussed in detail in Chapter 3, has similarities to others (Estes, 1976; Gray, Owen, and Adams, 1996; Gray, Owen, and Maunders, 1987; Institute of Social and Ethical AccountAbility 2001; Mathews and Perera 1995; Ramanathan 1976; Traidcraft 2000) in that all involve the consideration of a broader set of variables than are typically included in conventional accounting. Whereas conventional forms of accounting focus on one primary stakeholder, the shareholders, social accounting addresses the impact of the organization on an array of stakeholders including the employees, users or consumers of the service, providers of financing, society, and government. For nonprofits, volunteers are often included as a stakeholder, and for cooperatives and nonprofit mutual associations, members are also a key stakeholder.

Social accounting is also referred to as social and environmental accounting in that a primary concern is the impact of corporations on the natural environment (Bebbington, Gray, and Owen 1999; Gray, Owen, and Adams 1996; Mathews 1997). The early work in social accounting was referred to as environmental accounting, but gradually the concerns have broadened to include a wider array of social issues. Normally, those impacts are excluded from corporate accounting statements in that they are non-monetized and, if included, would often reduce the net income. Although this book does not focus on environmental impacts, Chapter 5 presents a Socioeconomic Impact Statement (a variation of an income statement) that utilizes data from an environmental program in California to account for its environmental impact.

Whereas the approach to social accounting presented in this book utilizes accounting statements to integrate social and the economic data, the most common model does not attempt such integration. That approach, originally referred to as social or ethical auditing, uses qualitative data and descriptive statistics to assess the extent to which an organization is meeting the expectations of its stakeholders in executing its mission (Co-operative Union of Canada 1985; New Economics Foundation 1998; Sillanpää 1998; Zadek 1998). Although it is more common in the literature to refer to this approach as social auditing than as social accounting (Gray 1998; Zadek, Pruzan, and Evans 1997), we have chosen to use the term social accounting—specifically, qualitative social accounting.

There is, however, a limitation of qualitative social accounting in that it has a status secondary to the financial accounts. At best, qualitative reports are viewed as supplements to the financial accounts. Within conventional accounting frameworks, it is quite common to report or disclose additional information, but this is seen as supplementary to the accounting statements (Financial Accounting Standards Board 1978). The integrated approach to social accounting that is used in this book broadens the financial accounts by building in variables that are typically viewed as "social" and, in addition, by rethinking how financial statements should be organized. There is a catch, however, to labeling a particular approach as social because it gives tacit credence to the viewpoint that conventional accounting practices are asocial or socially neutral. Within that perspective, concepts such as profit and loss are viewed as reality rather than a particular way of constructing reality (Tinker 1985). Although we are conscious of the difficulty in labeling only particular accounting phenomena as social when all are deserving of that characterization, the label *social accounting* is used in this book because it places emphasis on the inclusion of social variables such as social outputs and volunteer labor.

NONPROFITS AND COOPERATIVES

The case for social accounting is applicable to all organizations, including profit-oriented businesses; however, this book focuses on social organizations—primarily, nonprofits and cooperatives—because their impacts have been the most neglected by conventional accounting. As well, relatively little of the writing on social accounting is related to nonprofits and cooperatives. However, as seen through the framework of the social economy (Chapter 2), nonprofits and cooperatives are prime candidates for social accounting. As will be developed in Chapter 2, nonprofits and cooperatives have characteristics distinct from the public and private sectors (Defourny and Monzon Campos 1992; Quarter 1992; Snaith 1991). Although organizations in the social economy are engaged in economic activity, they are distinguished from those in the other two sectors by the emphasis on their social mission. Within this framework, nonprofits and cooperatives are created to serve a social purpose rather than to earn profits for shareholders. As such, the accounting practices applied to profit-oriented businesses are not ideally suited for nonprofits and cooperatives, and these organizations (also referred to as social organizations) require their own accounting models.

Throughout most of the twentieth century, accounting theory and accounting standards have largely ignored social organizations (Skinner 1987). There has been some recognition within the accounting profession of the limitations of applying to social organizations financial statements that were created for profit-oriented businesses, but without developing a distinct approach. Most of the concern has focused on nonprofits, and particularly those that do not sell their services on the market (Macintosh 1995, 2000). Conventional approaches to accounting may be the most problematic for that particular type of organization, but as will be discussed in Chapter 2, all social organizations—including those that sell their services either on the market or derive their revenues from a membership—have a social mission and require forms of accounting that measure their social impact. The predominant trend in accounting has been to extend the statements of profit-oriented businesses to these organizations.

One of the earlier critics of this trend (Henke 1972, 53) argued that "the financial statements for most not-for-profit organizations show little more than where dollars came from, for what they were expended and the extent to which the acquisitions and expenditures were consistent with the budgetary plan." Income statements, which were created for profit-oriented businesses, indicate the net gain or net loss for the accounting period. This information is of benefit to the owners of these enterprises because they are able to see the return on their investment; but for organizations that do not have shareholders in the same sense as profit-oriented businesses, an income statement has a more limited role.

To some extent, the accounting profession has recognized these limitations and has considered adaptations of income statements; but generally, the profession has avoided departing from that framework and has ignored approaches that recognize the unique features of social organizations. In 1980, the U.S. Financial Accounting Standards Board (FASB), in its Concepts Statement No. 4 (Objectives of Financial Reporting by Non-business Organizations), stated that the measurement of performance for private not-for-profit organizations should take on a different character (Financial Accounting Standards Board 1980). The FASB concluded that measurement of performance of not-for-profit organizations required information about the service efforts and accomplishments of the organization, together with information about the amount and nature of net resources. It went on to state: "financial reporting should provide information about service efforts (how resources are used to provide different services) in the financial statements" (cited in Fountain 2001, 2). The FASB also recognized that, ideally, if a nonprofit organization reported on performance, information about service accomplishments should be provided as part of financial reporting. This pronouncement recognized the difficulties organizations face in measuring and reporting program accomplishments and acknowledged the need for more research to determine whether service effort and accomplishment measurements could be developed that met the characteristics necessary for inclusion in nonprofits' financial statements.

The FASB ruling was influenced by a Statement of Position from the American Institute of Certified Public Accountants (1978) that attempted to address the thorny issue of the circumstances under which volunteer contributions ("donated services") could be monetized and included within financial statements (Gross and Warshauer 1979). The statement enunciates four criteria for inclusion: The amount is measurable; the organization manages the volunteers much like its employees; the services are part of the organization's normal work program and would be paid for otherwise; and the services of the organization are for the public rather than its members. These criteria were quite restrictive and excluded the services that members donated to nonprofit mutual associations such as religious organizations, clubs, professional and trade associations, labor unions, political parties, and fraternal societies. Nevertheless, the criteria did provide some recognition that volunteer labor had a market value that ought to be included in financial statements. A 1993 update (FASB 116) has the same restrictive character: "Contributions of services are recognized only if the services received (a) create or enhance non-financial assets or (b) require specialized skills, are provided by individuals possessing those skills, and would typically need to be purchased if not provided by donation" (Financial Accounting Standards Board 1993, 1). The Canadian Institute of Chartered Accountants (CICA) has followed the pattern established by FASB and suggested in 1980 that volunteer labor should be recognized in financial statements but with similar restrictions.

However, for a variety of reasons (especially the difficulties in keeping track of volunteer hours and in assigning a fair value to them), most volunteer contributions still go unreported in financial statements or, at best, are included as a footnote (Canadian Institute of Chartered Accountants 1980; Cornell Cooperative Extension 1995). Where volunteer labor is noted, it is in the Summary of Significant Accounting Policies included in the notes to the audited financial statement reports. For example, the American Association of Retired Persons (AARP) includes this note in its financial statements: "AARP and its members benefit from the efforts of many volunteers. These in-kind contributions by volunteers are not recorded in the consolidated financial statements as they do not meet the requirements for recognition under generally accepted accounting principles" (AARP 2000, 9).[1]

The FASB and CICA statements came at a time when there were already many examples of cost-benefit analyses undertaken by economists that accorded a market value to non-monetized social outputs (see discussion in Chapter 3) and other reports from major accounting associations on this issue (for example, see the American Accounting Association [1971] report of the Committee on Non-Financial Measures of Effectiveness). In an interpretation of the FASB ruling, Gross and Warshauer (1979, 309) stated that "nonprofit reporting will become more similar in appearance to reporting by profit-oriented entities." This statement is prophetic of what has transpired. For example, by March 1996, the Canadian Institute of Chartered Accountants released a special set of accounting standards for nonprofits (Sections 4400–4460), effective for fiscal periods beginning on or after April 1, 1997. These standards were largely adaptations of those applied to business enterprises, focusing on profit and loss, and sidestepping the unique characteristics of social organizations. The standards ignored the need to create accounting statements that shed light on how well social organizations are carrying out their mission and the effect they are having on the stakeholders that they are intended to serve.

An indication that the major accounting organizations were treating nonprofits the same as profit-oriented businesses is evident in regulations governing nonprofits, which increasingly refer to them as "not-for-profit," a point that Campbell (1998, 28) highlights:

> Once upon a time we were called nonprofit organizations to emphasize that the provision of service took precedence over the permanent amassing of funds. The breakeven philosophy was the dominant management ethic and adherence to that ethic demanded honest and diligent management, along with the timely disbursement of public funds. Now, universities are labeled not-for-profit to signify the acceptability of retaining surplus funds (i.e., profits) to make future expenditures and to offset/anticipate future funding uncertainties. Implicit in the new nomenclature is the abandonment of the nonprofit breakeven philosophy, which was both a financial and an ethical responsibility to maximize the benefits, returned to the public within the current year. If management is entirely relieved of the public obligation inherent in the breakeven philosophy, what alternative ethic will emerge to prevent undue hoarding of resources? With tacit approval for an "OK-to-profit" ethic, is the final and irrevocable "must-profit" phase far behind?

As suggested by Campbell's remarks, there are fundamental differences between social organizations and profit-oriented businesses that should be enshrined in the accounting practices that are applied to them. First, while the primary targets of a business's financial statements are the investors and creditors, the primary targets of a social organization's reporting are members, funders, clients, and the community (Richmond 1999). Second, the main objective of accountability for social organizations is not profit maximization but stewardship (or trusteeship), quality, and social impact. Social organizations should be evaluated on the extent to which they are achieving their social objectives and contributing to the community. If an organization's services are not transacted in the market, creative methods must be established for evaluating the services and including them in accounting statements. Third, social organizations in general rely heavily either on volunteer labor or on social labor in the form of the contributions of members (a point that will be developed in Chapter 2).

The limitations of conventional accounting are particularly problematic for the subset of nonprofits that rely heavily on either grants or donations from such external sources as government and from individuals, corporations, and foundations. For organizations of this sort, conventional accounting documents their costs without assessing their benefits (Anthony and Young 1988; Henke, 1989). These organizations are portrayed as users of resources rather than as creators of value through their services to society. Their financial accounts are one-sided and lack information upon which to base decisions affecting the organizations and the communities they serve. Additional information is required to assess the impact of individual nonprofits as well as the sector as a whole.

To redress the imbalance between the known costs and the unmeasured benefits of nonprofit organizations, new tools of analysis must be created. Current attempts at evaluation are hampered by several factors including a lack of standard definitions about the classes of social organizations (Quarter 1992); inconsistencies in methods of record-keeping and reporting (Cherny, Gordon, and Herson 1992); the absence of agreement about outcomes and their measurement (Henke 1989); and the need for social indicators that can assist in evaluating non-monetized contributions and outputs (Land 1996). The situation is complicated by a dearth of conceptual and theoretical frameworks for studying nonprofits (Hirshhorn 1997; Salamon 1995).

In addition, new methods of analyzing social organizations in their broader contexts must also be developed. Milofsky's (1987) argument for a contextual analysis of neighborhood-based organizations can be adapted to include social organizations in general. He notes that what is needed is to "see organizations in context—as parts of inter-organizational systems or ecologies whose members make strong demands on one another" (1987, 278). Nozick (1992, 74) calls for an ecological perspective for understanding communities: "Unity in diversity is the key ecological concept here where the smallest 'part' is understood to be an autonomous, living system in itself yet part of a greater whole."

Social organizations can be understood more fully if they are studied contextually as organisms that affect and are affected by their communities. Within that context, accountants are active participants in shaping reality, a point of view that runs counter to the widely held perception of accountants as passive recorders of information.

A CHANGING CONTEXT FOR ACCOUNTING

At this time, the accounting profession is struggling with a range of issues related to a shift to a knowledge-based economy (Canadian Institute of Chartered Accountants 2000; Financial Accounting Standards Board 2002; McLean 1995; Upton, Jr. 2001). The dominant approach in accounting is known as the "industrial paradigm" or "historical cost accounting." This approach refers to accounting procedures developed at the beginning of the twentieth century for production-oriented organizations. Although some of its fundamental premises and procedures have been challenged by accounting theorists (for example, issues surrounding the valuation of depreciation, inventory, and goodwill), this paradigm has persisted relatively intact since the 1930s (Skinner 1987).

With the growing internationalization of commerce, the accounting profession has relied on "generally accepted accounting principles," or GAAP, in order to create consistency and comparability in the way financial results are presented. These principles may vary from country to country, but theoretically they "express a collective judgment as to the best accounting theory and its practical application" (Skinner 1987, 665). Any departure from GAAP procedures must be explicitly disclosed in the notes to the financial statements.

The development of the GAAP is a double-edged sword. On the one hand, the GAAP provides guidance and a set of rules for the recording of financial transactions. On the other hand, these rules are based on an industrial paradigm that generally limits social and environmental considerations. Indeed, what is seldom recognized by adherents to GAAP and by conventional accounting texts is that "accountable events" are not neutral but socially determined. The formulation of GAAP and accounting standards involve choices as to when transactions should be first recognized and how they should be measured—choices that not only affect business decisions but also shape social reality (Gray, Owen, and Adams 1996; Hines 1988; Morgan 1988). For example, corporations are rewarded with increased stock value and market share for finding the cheapest way of producing a particular product or of supplying a particular service. This reward structure may cause corporations to attempt to push wages down and may result in shifting production to cheap-labor markets, where women and children are paid a pittance by Western standards. Some sports footwear and other major apparel manufacturers have adopted this strategy. The emphasis on profits may also lead corporations to ignore the environmental consequences of production and even to engage knowingly in environmental degradation.

Critical perspectives of the conventional accounting models challenge the notion that accounting is an objective, neutral, value-free, and technical enterprise that simply attempts to capture a picture of reality—much like a disinterested photographer snapping a picture of an event. Critical perspectives question what is included and what is left out in accounting and look for reasons and the consequences (Morgan 1988). Furthermore, critics of conventional accounting have prompted an interest in alternative forms that broaden the scope of the issues to be addressed and, by so doing, have sparked a variety of initiatives to assess the extent to which companies contribute to the achievement of social and environmental goals—hence, building a better society (Boyce 1998; Gray 1992). It has been argued that conventional accounting does not simply take its cues from the profit-oriented reward structure but actively contributes to it. By emphasizing profit based on historical-cost transactions, conventional accounting favors shareholders and company executives at the expense of workers and the environment (Greider 1997).

While not agreeing with critical accounting theorists, mainstream groups such as the Association of Chartered Accountants in the United States (ACAUS) give tacit consent to this argument by acknowledging that the accounting profession has actively contributed to economic development "since it was only through the use of more precise accounting methods that modern business was able to grow, flourish and respond to the needs of its owners and the public" (ACAUS 1999, 1). Gray and Bebbington (1998) take this argument further and suggest that, without accounting, transnational corporations that dominate international economies would not have evolved. Even recognizing that this claim is speculative, there is much evidence that the relationship between capitalist expansion and accounting is reciprocal—that is, accounting has contributed to the development of transnational corporations and transnational corporations have contributed to the development of accounting.

Moreover, it can be argued that accounting, by the very act of "counting" certain things and excluding others (deemed as irrelevant to the enterprise of doing business), shapes a particular interpretation of social reality, which in turn has policy implications (Hines 1988). By focusing on the measurement of socially constructed categories such as profit, accountants deal with complex realities in a restricted way, treating the economy, community, and environment not only as separate but also as mutually exclusive entities. From this perspective, accountants are not just technicians but also active participants who construct a particular reality (Morgan 1988).

The transition to a knowledge-based economy is leading to a rethinking of accounting practice and the search for a new paradigm. This search comes not only from critics but also from mainstream accounting organizations. With the increase of knowledge-based companies, the accounting profession has been under pressure to come up with ways to account for knowledge-based assets, or "intellectual capital." In recognition of the inadequacies of the current accounting model to reflect the importance of intellectual capital, the Canadian Institute of Chartered Accountants launched (in 1996) the Canadian Performance Reporting Initiative. This initiative subsequently has been expanded to address information and reporting needs in other areas such as environmental performance, social and ethical responsibilities, and employee well-being (CICA 2000). As opposed to past financial reporting, which is based on capital maintenance and income measurement, the Canadian Performance Reporting Initiative proposes that performance reporting should be based on the total value created by an enterprise. Assuming that this change occurs, a CICA report estimates that this new accounting paradigm would have to be developed in a period of

10 to 15 years in contrast to the 60 years it took to create the industrial paradigm (McLean 1995).

Another sign of the changing times in accounting is the Global Reporting Initiative, which, since its inception is 1997, has involved major accounting associations and other related groups in creating guidelines and a set of international indictors that organizations can use in reporting on economic, environmental, and social performance (Global Reporting Initiative 2000). Among the organizations represented are the Association of Chartered Certified Accountants (United Kingdom), the Canadian Institute of Chartered Accountants, and (from the United States) the Council on Economic Priorities, the Coalition for Environmentally Responsible Economies, and General Motors. The Global Reporting Initiative discusses both qualitative and quantitative measures and creates a model reporting format for organizations to follow.

Whereas there is some indication that the accounting profession is moving to assess the social impact (positive and negative) of profit-oriented businesses, most of this activity has bypassed nonprofits and cooperatives. Rather, as already noted, there is an increasing trend to draw such organizations into accounting formats that are applied to profit-oriented businesses. For nonprofits depending upon unearned revenues, there is increasing pressure for greater accountability (Cutt and Murray 2000; Hall and Banting 2000). These organizations depend on government funding, and the trend is toward project rather than core funding (Akingbola 2002; Smith and Lipsky 1993). Project funding tends to be for short-term contracts and requires onerous reporting of expenditures and results. As a consequence, nonprofits depending upon government are being forced into increased accountability to justify their outputs. Given that their major outputs may not involve market transactions; there is a need for an accounting paradigm that properly illustrates the value that they generate. This book and the models that are presented in Chapters 4 to 7 are designed to address that need.

BOOK OUTLINE

This book is organized as follows: Chapter 2 outlines the concept of the social economy and its underlying dimensions; it also groups organizations within the social economy. In Chapter 2, the common features of nonprofits and cooperatives are discussed, and social organizations are situated in relation to the private and public sectors. This chapter creates a foundation for the discussion that follows.

Chapter 3 discusses social accounting theory and practice over the past 30 years. It elaborates on the definition of social accounting presented in this first chapter and discusses the components of that definition. It looks at social accounting in relation to social auditing, social reporting, corporate responsibility, and accountability. The chapter also discusses earlier social accounting models, including those that utilize an integrated approach of building economic and social factors into an accounting statement.

Chapter 4 introduces several differing approaches to measuring social return on investment and focuses on the Community Social Return on Investment model. The Community Social Return on Investment model was developed originally by Betty

Jane Richmond (1999) as part of her award-winning doctoral thesis at the University of Toronto.[2] This model is applied to a nonprofit community-based training program for people with disabilities and accounts for the ratio of incoming to outgoing resources.

Chapter 5 presents a Socioeconomic Impact Statement and a Socioeconomic Resource Statement based on the Rochester (New York) Junior Achievement program. The Socioeconomic Impact Statement analyzes the social and economic impacts of this organization in relation to its stakeholder groups and the three sub-sectors of society: public, private, and the social economy. The Socioeconomic Resource Statement is a variation of a balance sheet that includes financial, physical, and intellectual capital. These statements are based on the work of Abt and Associates (1974), Belkaoui (1984), Estes (1976), Flamholtz (1985), Linowes (1972), and Seidler (1973). In addition, the Socioeconomic Impact Statement is used to look at the environmental impact resulting from the changes in commuting habits of employees in California who were offered a choice between free parking and an equivalent cash allowance.

Chapter 6 presents an Expanded Value Added Statement of a student-housing cooperative (WCRI). The model was originally created by Mook and applied by Richmond and Mook (2001) to a university residence complex that is run by students as a cooperative. This chapter takes the Value Added Statement, based on audited financial statements only, and expands it to include the value of social labor contributed by members of the cooperative. The Expanded Value Added Statement also accounts for indirect outputs of the organization such as skills training and personal development of its members and consultation services donated by the organization to other cooperatives.

Chapter 7 focuses on the value added by volunteers, which is significant for many nonprofits, and presents this information in Expanded Value Added Statements for five charitable nonprofits. It includes the impact of their volunteer contributions on the value added created by the organization and also shows the impact of volunteering on the volunteers themselves. Particular issues unique to each nonprofit are discussed.

Chapter 8 presents a social accounting toolkit that explains how to assess outputs and other social variables that either could be included in accounting statements or could be used separately by an organization. This chapter is oriented to managers of nonprofits and cooperatives and offers, among other things, detailed examples on how to assess volunteer functions, the number of hours that are contributed and how to assign a market value to them, and out-of-pocket expenses. The social accounting toolkit also illustrates how managers can identify an organization's outputs and place a value on them.

Chapter 9 compares the models presented in Chapters 4 to 7 to conventional accounting statements and discusses the advantages of models that integrate social and economic information. It suggests next steps to move this work forward, including building a supportive infrastructure to create standards that can guide a fuller form of social accounting for social organizations. It sets this issue in the context of the movement for greater public accountability as well as movements to redefine the gross domestic product and social or ethical investment.

QUESTIONS FOR DISCUSSION

1. What are the main differences between financial accounting and social accounting? Provide two examples to illustrate these differences.
2. "The main orientation of financial accounting is to the shareholders." Do you agree or disagree with this statement, and why?
3. Describe the main arguments advanced by critical accounting theorists against conventional accounting and explain whether you agree or not with them.
4. Why do the authors argue that social accounting is particularly relevant for nonprofits and cooperatives?
5. Is it appropriate to use the same accounting statements for nonprofits and cooperatives as for profit-oriented businesses?
6. What are the limitations of the 1993 ruling (No. 116) of the Financial Accounting Standards Board with respect to donated services? What are the implications of this for nonprofits and cooperatives?
7. To what extent should accounting reflect an organization's social impact? What are the potential difficulties and risks of doing so?
8. Do you feel that the so-called new economy justifies the creation of a new approach to accounting? Why or why not?
9. Why do you think that the field of social accounting is not as developed as the field of financial accounting?
10. What are the pros and cons of the supplemental and integrated approaches to social accounting?

NOTES

[1] For other examples, see Back Porch Radio Broadcasting, Inc., a non-commercial, listener-sponsored, member-controlled community radio station in Madison, Wisconsin: www.netphoria.com/wort/about/finances/FY99audit.pdf; the American Kidney Fund Inc: www.akfinc.org/AboutAKF/2000/AboutAKFFinancial8.htm; or the Canadian Parks and Wilderness Society: www.cpaws.org/aboutus/cpaws-statements-2001-0331.pdf. For an example on how volunteer contributions are treated if they meet FASB 116 requirements, see the U.S. Annual report of Médecins Sans Frontières/Doctors Without Borders: www.doctorswithoutborders.org/publications/ar/us2000.pdf.

[2] The thesis, *Counting on Each Other*, won the 1999 Gabriel G. Rudney award for the outstanding dissertation from ARNOVA, the Association for Research on Nonprofit Organizations and Voluntary Action.

Chapter 2

The Social Economy

Nonprofits and cooperatives are frequently acknowledged as organizations with a social purpose, but their economic impact is often ignored or trivialized. This is particularly true for nonprofits, especially for those with a substantial amount of income that is unearned in the market. For cooperatives, defined by the International Co-operative Alliance (the apex organization representing 760 million members in more than 100 countries) as "an autonomous association of persons united voluntarily to meet their common economic, social and cultural needs and aspirations through a jointly-owned and democratically-controlled enterprise" (International Co-operative Alliance 1998, Article 5), the economic role is more widely recognized. Nevertheless, when considering economic impact, the tendency is to think of the private sector rather than nonprofits and cooperatives.

The primary purpose of this chapter is to highlight the distinctiveness of nonprofits and cooperatives from both profit-oriented businesses and the public sector as the rationale for a different form of accounting. The distinctiveness will be dealt with in the context of three issues around which this chapter is organized:

> the economic impact of nonprofits and cooperatives;
> the social economy as mechanism for classifying these organizations; and
> the common features of organizations in the social economy.

This chapter serves as a background to Chapter 3 on social accounting and forms a basis for the development of appropriate accounting frameworks for nonprofits and cooperatives.

ECONOMIC IMPACT

To illustrate the economic impact of nonprofits and cooperatives, let us start with a simple example. In many countries, volunteers deliver meals to homes of people in need. One of these programs, called Meals on Wheels, was started in Britain during World War II as a service to people who, during the bombing known as the Blitz, lost their homes and their ability to cook for themselves. The original program was organized by the Women's Volunteer Service for Civil Defence, which not only delivered meals to their homeless neighbors but also brought refreshments to canteens used by people in the military. This service was the prototype of the Meals on Wheels program that has spread internationally.

The first Meals on Wheels program in the United States began in 1954 in Philadelphia for homebound seniors and other shut-ins (Meals on Wheels Association of America 2001). The meals were delivered primarily by high school students referred to as "Platter Angels" and were paid for in part by the beneficiaries and in part by a grant from the Henrietta Tower Wurtz Foundation. The Philadelphia prototype was followed by other cities throughout the United States. In 1972, the U.S. Congress enacted legislation, now called the Elderly Nutrition Program, which transfers funds to state and community programs for both congregate and home-delivered meals, with special attention to low-income minorities. By 1998, the funding for these programs amounted to $486 million, with additional contributions from other levels of government and from participants.

In Canada, the first Meals on Wheels program was introduced in Brantford, Ontario, in 1964, by the Independent Order of Daughters of the Empire and the Canadian Red Cross (Ontario Community Support Association 1993). A 1997 survey prepared for the Canadian Association for Community Care (Goodman 1997) presents an illuminating analysis of Meals on Wheels. The survey found that there were nearly 800 such programs in Canada serving about 1 million meals per month (nearly 12 million per year). Congregate Dining programs, where recipients share group meals in a center rather than in the privacy of their dwellings, made up 16 percent of the total meals served in 1997. In addition to seniors, the home-delivered meals were sent to disabled people, early-discharge patients from hospitals, people with HIV/AIDS, and prenatal and postnatal mothers at risk. The programs were almost exclusively nonprofit (99 percent), using a large cadre of volunteer labor (about 150 per program) in combination with a small staff (about 10 full-time and a similar number of part-time employees per program). Taken together, there were nearly 125,000 volunteers working alongside about 16,000 staff (full- and part-time).

Few would regard Meals on Wheels as an economic entity. These programs were set up for a social purpose—to serve people in need—and, therefore, they could be referred to as social organizations. Because these organizations are nonprofits (that is, corporations without shares), none of their income is distributed as dividends to shareholders. Instead, all of their income is used to maintain and expand their services. Yet, like businesses in general, Meals on Wheels programs purchase supplies on the market and also employ people who, in turn, pay taxes and participate in the economy through the expenditure of their earnings.

The cost of home-delivered meal programs in Canada is about $53 million (Goodman 1997), an estimate that includes the fee paid by the clients (averaging about $4 per meal) and the $1.50 per-meal subsidy from governments and charitable organizations to cover the remaining costs. The estimated cost, however, does not include the contribution of the 125,000 volunteers who deliver and help with preparing the meals and who also assist with the administration of the programs. The volunteers supplement the labor of the paid staff and thereby bring the service to a greater number of recipients and at a lower cost than would be possible by employees only. Clearly, with or without the volunteer labor, Meals on Wheels has a significant economic impact.

Nor is Meals on Wheels one of a kind. As noted in the Chapter 1, the Johns Hopkins Comparative Nonprofit Sector Project (Salamon et al. 1999), involving research in 22 countries, indicates that in 1995 nonprofits (excluding religious organizations) had $1.1 trillion in revenues or an average of 4.6 percent of the gross domestic product. Salamon et al. (1999, 9) graphically summarize the economic impact of nonprofits when they state: "If the nonprofit sector in these countries were a separate national economy, it would be the eighth largest economy in the world, ahead of Brazil, Russia, Canada and Spain." The value added by these nonprofits (their total income less external purchases) was $840 billion. This same study found that nonprofits employed nearly 19 million full-time-equivalent paid workers, or 5 percent of non-agricultural employment. If the full-time equivalents of volunteers are added on, the nonprofit labor force increases to 7 percent of the non-agricultural labor force.

In the United States alone in 1998, there were 1.6 million nonprofits (5.8 percent of the total number of organizations), whose expenditures represented 6.7 percent of the national income (about half a trillion dollars) and whose 10.9 million paid employees represented 7.1 percent of the workforce (Independent Sector 2002a). These figures from the Independent Sector, the apex advocacy group for nonprofits in the United States, are similar to those of Sokolowski and Salamon (1999), who estimate nonprofits (excluding religious organizations) at 6.9 percent of the gross domestic product and with a workforce representing 8.8 percent of non-agricultural employment and 18.5 percent of service employment. The full-time equivalent of volunteers adds another 5.7 million to the workforce.

Nonprofits in the United States employ 7.1 percent of the workforce, a relatively large percentage compared to other countries. The Netherlands has the largest at 12.6 percent, followed by Ireland (11.5%), Belgium (10.5%), and Israel (9.2%), with the Eastern European countries of Romania, Slovakia, Hungary, and the Czech Republic at the other end of the scale, between 0.6 and 1.7 percent (Salamon et al. 1999). Other Anglo countries—United Kingdom, Australia, and Canada—are similar to the United States. Nonprofits in the United Kingdom sharply increased their numbers during the first half of the 1990s, picking up services formerly provided by government such as education, health care, housing, and aid to an aged population. Increased state funding fueled most of the growth resulting in total revenues of $74.9 billion or 6.6 percent of the gross domestic product and a workforce of 1.47 million or 6.2 percent of national employment (Kendall and Almond 1999).

In Canada, which was not part of the Johns Hopkins Project, there were 80,000 nonprofits with a charitable status in the year 2004, a subset of a broader nonprofit sector estimated at 161,000 (Hall et al. 2005), but excluding organizations that are not incorporated. Nonprofits with charitable status have revenues of (Cdn.) $112 billion, employ 2 million people (54 percent full-time), and have a volunteer labor force estimated to be another 1 million full-time equivalent jobs (Hall et al. 2006).

Whereas the economic impact of nonprofits is often ignored, this is less so for cooperatives. Nevertheless, the stereotype of these organizations as small and economically insignificant is belied by the data. Canada, which keeps national records of cooperative economic performance, is illustrative. In 2003, about 9,200 cooperatives brought in $35.8 billion of revenues and employed around 155,000. Agriculture cooperatives, although having declined in importance due to the demutualization of some of the largest ones, were still marketing and processing a large share of farmers' production, notably in poultry, dairy and hogs. Two cooperatives are among the top 12 corporations in the food and beverage-manufacturing sector in Canada. Moreover, 8 non-financial cooperatives are among the top 500 corporations in Canada; two of these are among the top 100 corporations (Co-operatives Secretariat 2005). Le Mouvement des caisses Desjardins, the umbrella organization for credit unions/caisses populaires in francophone Canada, is the largest employer in Quebec with a workforce of more than 39,000, and is the sixth largest financial institution in Canada with assets of $118 billion in 2005.

These figures demonstrate that the many social organizations that are the backbone of our society also have an economic significance. This economic significance may be downplayed because, in some cases, a portion of the revenue is unearned—that is, in the form of grants or donations from either government or donors. However, the services that are made available through unearned monies are often so essential that if they were not supplied by social organizations, there would have to be an alternative mechanism. Ironically, if that mechanism were a profit-oriented business, then the value to the economy would not be questioned. But when the service comes from social organizations, and particularly from organizations depending upon unearned revenues, the tendency is to not recognize their economic significance. Therefore, when the Red Cross provides disaster relief, it is a social service; when a profit-oriented firm does the same, then it is business. Similarly, when health care services are made available through nonprofit hospitals, then it is a social service; but when the same service comes from profit-oriented firms, then it is business.

We proceed on the assumption that even though services are supplied by organizations set up for a social purpose (social organizations), their economic impact must still be considered both within the broader society and within the organization. Moreover, the accounting must not only be for paid labor but should also include the important volunteer contributions that add to the value of social organizations. Similarly, the accounting should illuminate the impact of such organizations, not simply categorize their expenditures.

THE SOCIAL ECONOMY

In this book, the label social economy is used in reference to nonprofits and cooperatives, signifying both their social and economic impacts. Social economy is a label widely used in such Francophone areas as France, Belgium, and Quebec (Defourny 1999; Defourny and Monzon Campos 1992; Jeantet 1991; Lévesque and Mendell 2004; Snaith 1991; Vaillancourt 2002) but in recent years has achieved greater currency among Anglophone scholars in Western Europe and North America (Policy Research Initiative 2005; Quarter 1992; Quarter et al. 2001a; Quarter et al, 2003; Shragge and Fontain 2000).

There are varying definitions of the social economy, but ours is broad and inclusive of the entire array of organizations that have a social mission: A bridging concept for organizations that have social objectives central to their mission and their practice, and either have explicit economic objectives or generate some economic value through the services they provide and purchases that they undertake. The term *social economy* puts up front the economic value of social organizations—that they produce and market services, employ people, may own valuable assets, and generate social value. Nevertheless, the dominant discourse equates the private sector and its outputs with "the economy." Government is either characterized as a support to the private sector or, more often, perceived as a drag upon it in that businesses pay taxes to government and thereby reduce their own net incomes. Moreover, as government's role in financing a social safety net has come under attack through the neoconservative agenda, the link in the public's mind between the private sector and the economy has been strengthened further. As for the many organizations that are not within the private or public sectors, they are either invisible or, more charitably, labeled as the "third sector."

The social economy sometimes is used as a catchall for organizations that are neither in the private nor public sectors although, as will be illustrated subsequently, such a conceptualization is inadequate because there is also an overlap between some social organizations and the private sector and between others and the public sector. Our research suggests at least three fundamental groupings for social organizations: public sector nonprofits, market-based social organizations, and civil society organizations.[1] We shall discuss each in turn.

Public Sector Nonprofits

Some may view the label *public sector nonprofits* as an oxymoron since the stereotype of a nonprofit is an organization that is separate from government. Nevertheless, there is a large group of nonprofits predominantly with a charitable status that, like government agencies, supply public services. Organizations of this sort depend heavily upon government funding—some in the form of grants that cover the cost of their core services and others in the form of billings to government programs for services rendered (for example, health care billings by hospitals). Organizations that bill for specific services are analogous to those that are market based in that their revenues are "earned." It is a judgment call as to whether such organizations should be classified as public sector nonprofits or as market based. Our inclination is the former because such organizations are also influenced to a degree by government policy. Even though they operate at arm's length from the state, public sector nonprofits might be viewed as either in a "partnership" with government (Salamon 1987, 1995) or even as an extension of it (Smith and Lipsky 1993). As shown in Figure 2.1, these organizations are in the nexus between the social economy and the public sector. Because of this overlap, there is a debate as to whether they are sufficiently independent to be viewed as separate from government. Nevertheless, they also raise money from other sources, as reflected by their charitable status that allows donors to receive an income tax deduction.

All public sector nonprofits serve a constituency external to the organization rather than a membership. Therefore, in addition to their dependence on government funding, their external orientation is a second characteristic. Within the external orientation, there are two sub-classifications: those that serve the public at large and those that serve specific groups (for example, people with low income, with various types of disabilities or some specialized need such as food or shelter). Those serving the public at large include heritage institutions, nature parks, museums, art galleries, historic sites, planetariums, zoos, botanical gardens, and archives. Although some such organizations are administered directly by a level of government, most are administered by nonprofits such as religious organizations, historical societies, and institutions of higher learning. Other examples of this classification of organization are hospitals, institutions of higher education, and research institutes.

In addition, there is a broad array of public sector nonprofits that serve publics who either have low income or have some specific set of difficulties that require assistance. Such organizations fit the classic definition of "charities," as distinct from simply charitable status, in that they assist people who are either indigent or find it difficult to cope without substantial external organizational support. Examples are the John Howard and Elizabeth Fry Societies (devoted to working with and advocating for men and women who come into conflict with the law); Big Brothers and Big Sisters (with volunteer members who form supporting relationships with children lacking a parent); Children's Aid societies; and the many adoption, counseling, and family service agencies (Catholic Family Services, Jewish Family Services, Chinese Family Services, et al).

Some such organizations are more recent—for example, food banks, hostels for transients, homes for single teenage mothers, and the many facilities for abused children or children whose families feel they would be better served in a special facility. There are thousands of homes for other kinds of needs—Aboriginal friendship centers, shelters for women who are being abused by their husbands or partners, homes for those with psychiatric and mental disabilities, drop-in centers for seniors, homes for the aged, et al.

There is also an elaborate infrastructure that supports such organizations—social planning and community councils, the community information centers that publish listings of the many services in their jurisdiction, and the volunteer bureaus and centers that recruit and refer volunteers to organizations in need. Like the organizations they assist, these are nonprofits attempting to meet a social need with some combination of government funding, charitable donations, and volunteers. The mix can vary, but the common characteristic of such organizations is that their revenues come predominantly from government, that volunteers supplement their staff, and that they serve people outside of the organization rather than its members.

In large part, these organizations form an institutional infrastructure that supports the family, particularly, those with low income that cannot afford to purchase all the services that they require. Public sector nonprofits have taken on greater significance in the modern world because the family is less self-sufficient than in the past and people are less engaged socially within their neighborhoods (Putnam 2000). As such, many nonprofits and government programs have evolved to compensate for the added pressure on the family, and particularly on families with low income or with minimal support—for example, a single parent with children. With decreased levels of spontaneous support within neighborhoods, formal organizations have attempted to fill the breach. Moreover, as part of the neoconservative agenda, governments have looked to nonprofits to deliver services rather than engaging in direct delivery.

Market-Based Associations

This grouping refers primarily to cooperatives and nonprofits that compete in the market for their revenues and, therefore, occupy the nexus between the social economy and the private sector. The market-based cluster consists primarily of cooperatives with share capital (for example, credit unions, farm marketing, and food retailing cooperatives). However, this cluster also includes some nonprofits that rely primarily on revenues earned from the market, and also can include social purpose businesses set up to provide employment for persons with special challenges such as a psychiatric handicap.

Self-sufficient social organizations run counter to the stereotype. However, among most forms of cooperatives and some types of nonprofits, there is a strong tradition of self-sufficiency (Craig 1993; MacPherson 1979). Generally, cooperatives are small organizations, but as noted, some in such endeavors as farm marketing, insurance, and finance are large corporations and found on *Fortune* magazine's list of the largest corporations (Co-operatives Secretariat 2005).

Commercial nonprofits are less usual, but there are some examples: Blue Cross, a large nonprofit franchise of an American-based corporation; Travel CUTS, a system of travel agencies across Canada set up by the Canadian Federation of Students to help students and others obtain discount air tickets; and the American Automobile Association and similar organizations found in many other countries. Nonprofits that are somewhat less commercial but still cover a substantial portion of their costs through the market include recreational organizations such as the YMCA, the Boy Scouts and Girl Guides, competitive sports organizations, and many types of performing arts groups (theater, music, dance, opera, and orchestras).

The organizations in the market-based group differ from the public sector nonprofits in the source of their revenues—these come primarily from the market as payments for service rather than from government—and they also may differ in their orientation. Whereas all public sector nonprofits serve a public external to the organization—either the public at large or people with particular needs—some market-based nonprofits serve the public and market-based cooperatives serve a membership.

Civil Society Organizations

Civil society organizations are the third major grouping and arguably the purest example of social organizations in that (unlike the previous two groupings) they neither overlap with the public sector nor with the market. In the latter part of the eighteenth century, scholars conceived of a social space distinct from the state that could serve as a means to counteract despotism (Keane 1998). Among political theorists of the nineteenth century, Alexis de Tocqueville is most often associated with this viewpoint. In his travels to the United States, he was impressed with the voluntary associations and their role in sustaining political democracy (Tocqueville 1969).

Two subgroupings of these organizations fall within the civil society category—first, nonprofit mutual associations, and second, volunteer organizations serving the public but supported in total by donors and volunteers.

Nonprofit Mutual Associations

Unlike public sector nonprofits, nonprofit mutual associations are oriented toward a membership who finance their services through their fees and may also choose to take part in decision making through voting at meetings and, perhaps, even serving in the governance. Although there is some debate as to whether member-based associations should be classified as nonprofits, in that legal definitions focus on the "public interest," the predominant tendency among theorists is toward inclusiveness (Salamon and Anheier 1997; Salamon et al. 1999). In our view, a membership—particularly if it adheres to basic human rights criteria of openness—is simply a subset of the public. A religious congregation, for example, is usually open to all those wishing to affiliate with the faith. In other words, "association" is central to nonprofits (Lohmann 1992) and social organizations more generally, and finds its purest expression among mutual associations.

Like market-based cooperatives, the members of nonprofit mutual associations pay for the cost of the service. However, in the case of cooperatives, the members generally pay for each service as it is purchased; for mutual associations, the general procedure is for the membership fee to cover the cost of the organization's services. The members of a union local, for example, pay dues, not a fee for each service. The practice of a blanket payment (either a membership fee or dues) is one followed by nonprofit mutual associations in general, though it may also be supplemented by payments for particular services. Whereas a charitable status is rare for market-based organizations, it is found among nonprofit mutual associations, though not as commonly as for public sector nonprofits.

The most common mutual association is a religious congregation in which people with a common faith come together to provide a service to themselves. Religious congregations have spin-off associations for education, recreation, and burial and also intersect with associations set up for other purposes—for example, ethno-cultural groupings. The same is true for the myriad of ethno-cultural associations; they too intersect with other associations for such purposes as youth education, recreation, and other social activities. Social clubs and self-help groups, including those on the Internet, are other prevalent types of mutual associations (Baym 1996; Cooper 2000; Ferguson 1997). While some are dismissive of Internet associations because of a lack of face-to-face interaction, this venue has become commonplace for self-help groups, for persons sharing a common hobby, or for those with a shared concern. Internet associations are a new and burgeoning form that tends to be overlooked in estimations of the size of the social economy, because even though they may have a formal structure they are normally unincorporated. Recent research indicates that there are almost 25,000 online support groups in the health and wellness section of Yahoo! Groups alone (Eysenbach 2004).

Many mutual associations are strictly social in their mission. Others relate their service to the economy. These include trade unions and their local affiliates; non-certified staff associations; and managerial, professional, consumer, and business associations. In modern societies, the average person will belong to several associations of this sort. These associations might also be viewed as interest groups in that they offer support for their members. Variations include tenant associations, neighborhood groups, ratepayers, and home and school societies.

Cooperatives are also a form of mutual association insofar as they serve a membership. We have classified them as market based because often they supply services that are in competition with the private sector. However, where cooperatives are not in competition with the private sector (non-market housing), then they could be classified as civil society organizations.

Volunteer Organizations

Of nonprofits serving the public, there is a small subgroup that is funded entirely by donors, membership fees, and fund-raising events and for whom volunteers contribute a substantial portion of their workforce. While these are not mutual associations in that their orientation is to the public rather than to their membership, they are also neither public sector nor market based. They most closely approximate civil society associations and are largely dependent upon volunteers. With the increasing role of government in funding nonprofits, these organizations are a dying breed. However, there are some striking examples in human rights such as Amnesty International, in basic service provision such as Habitat for Humanity, and in the many health care foundations that raise funds for medical research into, for example, breast cancer and heart disease.

Many advocacy groups fit into this category. Even though they are funded by members who may also serve as volunteers, their orientation is to the public and to changing public policy. Groups associated with the environment, feminist issues, human rights, and peace are common examples. Such groups might be better classified as sociopolitical, but unlike political parties that contest elections, they are typically associated with broader social movements that lobby for social change outside of the electoral process.

Classification Summary

Table 2.1 presents this three-group classification of the organizations in the social economy and summarizes each category's distinct features on two dimensions: primary source of funding and orientation toward either the public or members.

As can be seen from the table, for public sector nonprofits, the government is their primary source of funding and their orientation is to the public, either the public at large or specific publics in need. For market-based organizations, their revenues are earned either from service charges to members of cooperatives or from the public (in the case of nonprofits). For civil society organizations, either membership fees or donations are the primary source of funding. Within civil society organizations, mutual associations are oriented to their membership whereas volunteer organizations are oriented to the public.

Table 2.1 Classification by Funding Source and Orientation

Characteristics	Public Sector Organizations	Market-Based Organizations	Civil Society Organizations
Funding Source	• Primarily government • Secondarily donors	• Nonprofits: revenue from clients • Coops: service charges from members	• Mutual associations: members' fees • Volunteer organizations: donors primarily
Orientation	• Either public at large or particular publics in need	• Nonprofits: public at large • Cooperatives: members	• Mutual associations: members • Volunteer organizations: Public

While this classification system can be used to illuminate the different types of organizations within the social economy, there are some organizations that bridge the categories. Meals on Wheels, for example, the organization with which we started this chapter, receives much of its income from the users of the service, but the providers are not operating within a competitive market. Rather they are furnishing a service to people in need, with the cost defrayed in part by the enormous contribution from volunteers and a subsidy from government. Meals on Wheels does not lend itself to a simple classification, but using our system, it would fall primarily within the civil society category as a volunteer organization. Similarly, social cooperatives organized around employment for groups with special challenges are organizations that earn part of their revenues from the market, but they rely on subsidies either from government or from foundations, and therefore also do not lend themselves to a simple classification.

Relationship between the Social Economy and the Other Sectors

Figure 2.1 portrays the social economy in relation to the better-known private and public sectors. A Venn diagram is used to signify the dynamic interrelationship between the social economy and the private and public sectors.

As shown in the figure, the private sector interacts with the public sector in that government regulations and tax policies affect businesses; a significant part of commerce involves government contracts; and some public sector businesses compete in the market. The same type of interaction occurs with the various components of the social economy. As can be seen, public sector nonprofits overlap with the public sector. They receive much of their funding from government, are influenced to a degree by government policies, yet they have their own board of directors and shape relevant policy.

Market-based organizations overlap with the private sector; as noted, they compete in the market and derive their revenues from the consumers of their services. Again, there is a debate as to where the private sector ends and the social economy begins. Some market-based cooperatives and mutual insurance firms have such a strong commercial emphasis that it is a stretch to argue for their inclusion in the social economy. Then there are some profit-oriented businesses that emphasize their social mission. This point will be discussed further in the section on the defining characteristics of the social economy.

Civil society associations are the group of social-economy organizations that are least influenced by either the private or public sectors. Nevertheless, this group of organizations interacts with the private and public sectors and also derives some financial and volunteer support from those parts of the economy. Civil society, which will be discussed later in this chapter, is derived largely from mutual associations.

UNDERLYING CHARACTERISTICS

Organizations of the social economy share some common characteristics that will be discussed under four categories: social objectives, social ownership, volunteer/social participation, and civic engagement. We begin with a clarification: Our reference point is broader than formally incorporated organizations and includes unincorporated associations that are duly constituted (for example, union locals, home and schools, tenant groups, and Internet self-help and social groups). All of the organizations are self-governing (bearing in mind the constraints of external funding from such sources as government and donors), and all of the organizations have a measure of formality; therefore, their continuation does not depend upon the participation of particular individuals. Admittedly, for some organizations, the line between self-governance and external control is blurred, and for other organizations establishing precise criteria to meet a threshold for formal structure is problematic. These concerns are not dwelled upon but simply mentioned. Our framework is broad and is intended to be inclusive.

Figure 2.1 The Social Economy in Relation to the Private and Public Sectors

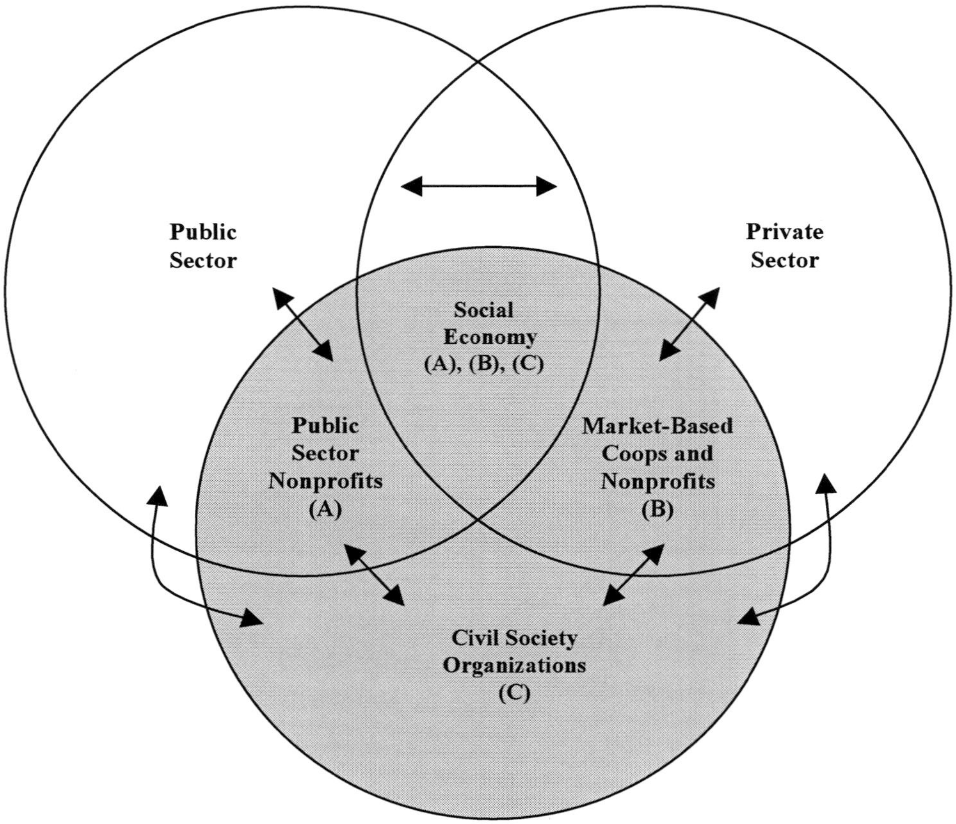

Social Objectives

As stated, organizations in the social economy are set up to meet social objectives that, as a rule, are written into the charter of the organization. Among social organizations, these social objectives take on different forms, depending upon whether the organization is serving a public in need (charitable objectives), meeting the needs of a membership (mutual aid), or competing in the market for its revenues.

Charitable Objectives

Since their religious origins in the Middle Ages in England, charitable organizations have had a lengthy tradition of social giving (Hopkins 1987). Members of religious organizations believed that they were furthering the purpose of their religion by assisting those in need. As charitable activities broadened from their narrow base through the church, English society attempted to spell out what was permissible, as reflected in the Statute of Charitable Uses (or Statute of Elizabeth) of 1601:

> Relief of aged, impotent and poor people; the maintenance of sick and maimed soldiers and mariners, schools of learning, free schools and scholars in universities; the repair of bridges, ports, havens, causeways, churches, sea banks and highways; the education and preferment of orphans; the relief, stock or maintenance of houses of correction; marriages of poor maids; supportation, aid and help of young tradesmen, handicraftsmen, and persons decayed; the relief or redemption of prisoners or captives; and the aid or ease of any poor inhabitants covering payments of fifteens, setting out of soldiers, and other taxes (cited in Monahan and Roth 2000, 28).

That statute reflects the beginnings of the secularization of charity from its religious roots and, to a degree, from a strict focus on the relief of poverty. The growth of the profession of social work may be seen as an outcome of this secularization of services with a charitable purpose.

The concept of charity has been broadened from its original notion of relieving poverty and now includes such social objectives as the advancement of education, the advancement of religion, and other purposes beneficial to the community. These objectives have permitted organizations with such functions as international aid, education, youth programs, health care, family services, culture and the arts, and heritage and environmental protection to be classified as having a charitable status. Therefore, a distinction can be made between charity as a community's response to those in dire need and organizations with broader charitable objectives (meeting the criteria required for charitable status under the taxation laws that permit donors to achieve a tax benefit). Although modern charities are of both types, organizations meeting the broader criteria are more commonplace. This change can be called the universalization of charity.

Mutual Aid

While charitable organizations often involve the delivery of assistance by the more fortunate to the less fortunate, nonprofits serving a membership (mutual associations) and cooperatives are based on the principle of self-help or mutual aid

(Craig 1993). The members of these organizations share a common bond of association (for example, a common heritage, occupation, or location) and a need that they attempt to meet through a service to themselves. The organizations have their roots among exploited groups in society (MacPherson 1979) but, unlike the recipients of charity, they have sufficient strength to help themselves. Some of the oldest associations in the New World were mutual benefit societies in which people, often of common religion, ethno-cultural heritage, or geographic origin (a city from which they emigrated), arranged services like insurance and burials for members. In rural areas, farmers formed mutual property-and-casualty insurance organizations because of difficulties in obtaining affordable services. Similarly, credit unions were started in the latter part of the nineteenth century in Germany and, at the beginning of the twentieth century, through Catholic parishes in Quebec, because of either the unavailability of consumer loans or usurious interest rates (Kenyon 1976). About the same time, farm-marketing cooperatives were started in order to enable their members to obtain a fair price for their products and to make the basic purchases that they required (MacPherson 1979).

Over the years, people with common bonds such as a place of work, profession, business, religion, or ethnic identity have formed a broad array of nonprofit mutual associations and cooperatives. While some of these adhere to the tradition of being organized around exploited groups (a union local or workplace association), others simply involve a common social interest (a historical society), a shared experience (the members of a Legion club who have fought in a war), a profession, or some other commonality, including a privileged status such as the members of a golf club or a business association. The bonds of association might differ, but such organizations are set up to meet social and cultural objectives.

Social Versus Commercial Objectives

It could be argued that by satisfying their customers, a profit-oriented business also meets social objectives. While this argument has some validity, particularly in the service sector, capital invested in profit-oriented businesses, and especially in mature companies (as opposed to small owner-operated firms), has a very weak social commitment. With the exception of small owner-operated enterprises that are tied to a particular neighborhood or some larger firms that depend upon a particular location for their products (for example, resource extraction), profit-oriented businesses remain loyal to a community only as long as they obtain a competitive rate of return. When a greater return is possible from other investments or from manufacturing products elsewhere, profit-oriented businesses will shift their loyalties. By comparison, social organizations not only regard the service as first but also have loyalties to either a defined community or a defined membership. An apparel manufacturer, for example, may move production to countries where labor rates are cheap, whereas social objectives and the location of the community will guide the decisions of a religious body (or any social organization for that matter). In that respect, social organizations differ from the rootless, impersonal structures of mature profit-oriented businesses.

There are profit-oriented businesses with social investment criteria that more closely resemble the practices of organizations in the social economy. For example, a handful of profit-oriented businesses mirror the ownership arrangements of nonprofits in that their shares are held in trust and, like nonprofits, are owned by no one (Quarter 2000). The German firm Zeiss operates in this manner, as do a handful of firms in the United Kingdom. (John Lewis Partnership, Scott Bader) and the Netherlands (Endenburg Electric). Similarly, there are other businesses that are created to carry out a social mission—Newman's Own, which donates to charitable causes all of its after-tax profits ($125 million in 20 years), is one such example (Newman's Own 2002), as is the British firm, Traidcraft, that assists cooperatives and small producers in poorer countries in gaining a fair price for their products (Evans 1997). Social purpose businesses for groups like the psychiatrically handicapped are another example (Trainor and Tremblay 1992). Such firms are similar to market-based social organizations, and in Figure 2.1, they could be located in the overlap between the private sector and the social economy. However, the norm for organizations in the social economy is the exception for profit-oriented businesses.

Nevertheless, even for social organizations, there is a tension between social and commercial objectives that has been heightened by the neoconservative agenda of cutbacks in public funding. For organizations earning their revenues in the market, it is necessary to be competitive, and this may involve matching the standards of profit-oriented businesses. For organizations relying on government funding, there is increasing pressure to compete for contracts and to earn a greater portion of their revenues from other sources (Akingbola 2002; Smith and Lipsky 1993). The term *entrepreneurship* has found its way into the nonprofit culture and has influenced how these organizations operate (Dees 1998).

For a social organization to achieve the spirit of its mission, commercial goals should be subsumed within its social objectives. But if these objectives are being sacrificed for commercial success, then the organization is moving away from the social economy. It is problematic to lay down a clear set of operational criteria that determine whether a social organization is achieving an appropriate balance. Those in the dubious category would be large market-based cooperatives and mutual insurers.

Social Ownership

Profit-oriented businesses are pieces of property that belong to their owners, normally shareholders, and therefore can be bought or sold for personal gain. The shareholders are the primary beneficiaries of profits paid out as dividends and also the beneficiaries of profits that are reinvested in the firm—because retained earnings are likely to enhance the value of the property. The context of private ownership is important for understanding the significance of the distinct ownership arrangements in the social economy. All forms of nonprofits, including those with a charitable status, are organizations without shareholders. It is common in the United States to refer to nonprofits as "private" (Independent Sector 1997; Salamon and Anheier 1997), signifying their independence from government. That descriptor can also be misleading because it implies that nonprofits are like private sector businesses. In this book, nonprofits are labeled as social to emphasize their distinctiveness from the private and public sectors. Although their assets are a form of property, they belong to no one unless the organization's dissolution clause specifies otherwise. For organizations with charitable status, in the event of dissolution, the usual practice is to pass the assets on to another charity with similar objectives. For example, if a religious congregation closes, the assets normally would go to the umbrella organization. For other nonprofits, including cooperatives without shares (for example, housing, child care, and health care), the normal practice is similar. Exceptions might be some social clubs that, upon closure, might divide their property among their members. Cooperatives with shares (for example, food retail and farm marketing organizations, credit unions) also might specify that, in the event of dissolution, the net assets would be divided among the members. When a cooperative or club can be demutualized, and the assets divided among the members, that organization loses its some of its distinctiveness from a profit-oriented business. Normally, a cooperative has an indivisible reserve that represents social property available for use by future members.

However, for social organizations, dissolution for reasons other than financial insolvency is highly unusual. Although such organizations have assets, they do not exist to enhance their members' personal wealth. Whereas personal gain is the hallmark of ownership in the private sector and share value is a primary consideration in its future disposition, social benefit is the defining characteristic for organizations in the social economy. The purpose of such organizations is to provide a service either to members or to the public, and organizational arrangements are undertaken with that objective in mind, not personal gain.

Even where social organizations have shares, as in most cooperatives, they do not serve the same purpose as in a profit-oriented business. Such shares do not reflect the value of the organization or what speculators are prepared to pay on the stock market; rather they have a relatively constant value and are comparable to a membership fee (Ellerman 1990). They can go down in value if the cooperative has financial difficulties, but in general they stay at a constant level (or at an initial value adjusted for inflation). When members leave, the reimbursement normally is the original contribution plus a modest interest rate agreed to by the organization.

Similarly, when a social organization has a year-end surplus, the use of that income is guided by its primary objective, improving and broadening the availability of the service. For cooperatives with shares, surplus earnings may result in a patronage dividend, not based on shareholdings as in the private sector but either on the use of the service by members or on an egalitarian basis. When organizations in the social economy lose money (that is, have a year-end deficit), unless the loss can be absorbed through reserves, their service is usually reduced or the cost to patrons is increased. If the losses become too great, the organization may have to close.

Therefore, the financial dynamics of a social organization differ from those of a profit-oriented business. Although some social organizations may hold valuable assets, the concept of ownership as in the private sector is not that applicable. Rather the assets of social organizations can be characterized as a social dividend passed from generation to generation. These social dividends are the building blocks of society—blocks that are the property neither of private individuals nor of the government. Private individuals may contribute to creating these building blocks through donations of their wealth. In some cases, such donations may involve vast amounts of money—for example, the fortunes of Andrew Carnegie, John D. Rockefeller, Henry Ford, Will Kellogg, George Soros, Robert Bosch, Bill and Melinda Gates, Warren Buffett, and the Pew and McArthur families. Such donations represent the conversion of private wealth to social wealth, or to the building blocks of the social economy. However, the primary creators of social wealth are the public-at-large through lesser donations, through volunteer participation, and through taxes, which create the basis for government grants to social organizations.

Whereas the ownership arrangements for social organizations are distinct from those of profit-oriented businesses, the difference from the public sector is not as clear-cut. Government assets are also a form of social property intended to serve the public good. These assets may be part of government departments per se (that is, the civil service) or they may be held at arm's length through government corporations. These corporations are set up to supply a service to the public for such reasons as the government wants some influence over policy or because it is difficult for the private sector to earn a profit. In such corporations, a level of government holds the shares and has the same rights as shareholders in a profit-oriented business. But a government corporation differs from a profit-oriented business in an important way—its primary purpose, like government departments in general, is to serve the public and not to meet the shareholders' needs for a return on investment. The beneficiary of any profit or any increase in the value of the assets is the government representing the public-at-large. When a government corporation is privatized, the public interest and not personal gain ought to be the primary motivation. Therefore, ownership in the public sector has qualities similar to that in the social economy.

Arguably, the view that no one owns the organizations of the social economy is based on a narrow definition that equates ownership with property rights. As Dahl (1970) suggests, ownership can be conceived as a bundle of rights, and the rights for members of social organizations differ from those of shareholders in the private sector. In the social economy, members do have the right to control the organizations to which they belong. But unlike owners in the private sector, they are unlikely to benefit financially from the sale of their assets. Members of social organizations, through their representatives on the board of directors, are analogous to trustees or stewards, with the responsibility to see that the assets are being utilized in a manner consistent with the organization's objectives. In other words, social organizations are trust arrangements that are passed through generations so that they may continue to serve members of a society.

Volunteer/Social Participation

The label *voluntary* is often applied to organizations in the social economy because most rely on the contributions of volunteers for their services. For nonprofit mutual associations and cooperatives, the volunteer component is oriented to enhancing the services of the organization for its membership; for that reason, we refer to this form of uncompensated service as social labor. It has the same character as volunteer service, but rather than being oriented to the public or groups external to the organization, it is intra-organizational. This distinction between volunteer service and social labor is used in the Expanded Value Added Statement presented in Chapter 6 and will be referred to in other places in the book. The distinction is not usually made in national surveys, which tend to lump together all forms of volunteer service.

According to the National Survey of Nonprofit and Voluntary Organizations conducted by Statistics Canada in 2003: "Virtually all nonprofit and voluntary organizations rely on volunteers to some degree, and more than half rely solely on volunteers to fulfill their mission" (Hall et al. 2005, 32). For tasks other than serving on the board of directors, Sharpe (1994) found that about 70 percent of nonprofits with charitable status used volunteers (about 63 per organization). In other words, while all charitable organizations have a volunteer board of directors, most also have volunteers in other types of services, and some rely heavily on volunteers. Nor, as noted earlier, is volunteering limited to nonprofits with charitable status; volunteering occurs in all sectors of the economy, and within the social economy among organizations with and without charitable status. The supply of services using a combination of paid labor and volunteers is referred to as coproduction (Brudney 1990). Among organizations engaging in coproduction, social organizations with a charitable status are its heaviest beneficiaries.

U.S. data for the year 2000 indicate that 44 percent of adults over the age of 21 (83.9 million) volunteered with formal organizations contributing a total of 15.5 billion hours. That amount of service was equivalent to over 9 million full-time positions (Independent Sector 2001a). In the United Kingdom there were 16.3 million volunteers for nonprofits in 1995 with full-time equivalence of 1.47 million positions or 6.3 percent of the paid labor force (Kendall and Almond 1999). In Canada, a survey for the year 2003-2004 estimated that there were 12 million volunteers (45 percent of the population aged 15 and over) who contributed 2 billion hours with a full-time job equivalence of 1 million (Hall et al. 2006). These patterns are similar to those discerned by Salamon et al. (1999) in their study of 22 countries, where 28 percent of the population, or 10.6 million full-time equivalents, volunteered. In those countries, volunteers represented 56 percent of the paid workforce of nonprofits—that is, for every two hours of work by paid employees in nonprofits, volunteers contributed more than one hour. These surveys indicate that volunteer contributions are important to religion, education, social services, recreation, sports and social clubs, and health organizations. Informal volunteering (outside a formal organizational framework) is also a major form of service.

In spite of the large amounts of volunteer service, it is misleading to refer to organizations that use volunteers as voluntary because the term implies grassroots groupings without either a permanent administrative structure or paid staff. Such an impression is quite erroneous. Rather, most volunteers fit into bureaucratized, mature social organizations often crossing many locales, and these organizations reserve for their volunteers specific positions with expectations that exist apart from the individuals who fill them. In other words, these positions are not voluntary in the sense that they are created by volunteers but rather are predefined by staff for the volunteers. The volunteers might give these roles their own personal touch, and some might perform better than others; but in general the expectations associated with each position exist apart from particular volunteers. Moreover, the organizations with which volunteers are associated are sufficiently stable that they do not depend upon particular individuals. Volunteers are needed for the organization to execute a full complement of services, but the turnover among individuals who execute these tasks does not necessarily change the organization's character.

Volunteers can also be differentiated according to their degree of involvement, some having tasks that involve substantial time and a strong organizational identification (for example, a Scout troop leader) and others having a passive affiliation such as a token membership. Putnam (1995) refers to such a passive role as "tertiary" in that it involves only a weak link to an organization—for example, a financial donation (often characterized as a membership fee). Nevertheless, these nominal forms of involvement are of importance to organizations because they assist with financing and may be used to enhance their influence. For social movement organizations (advocating on behalf of particular issues or groups), having a large membership may influence the public's perception of their initiatives. For example, Amnesty International has been amazingly successful in mobilizing supporters, who number nearly 2 million in more than 160 countries around the world (Amnesty International 2001). Using the standard of Amnesty International (Canada), about 10 percent of supporters are active members and have a regular role in organizing Amnesty's campaigns for human rights.[2] Moreover, passive members of an organization can be mobilized for specific campaigns such as letter writing, petitions, and demonstrations. With the advent of the Internet and other forms of modern communication, such mobilizations have become easier (Brunsting and Postmes 2002; Deibert 2000).

Even for those social organizations that have a relatively apolitical role, having large cadres of volunteers—whether they are active or passive—is status enhancing. In its annual report, the American Red Cross can claim with justification that "With more than 35,000 paid employees and nearly 825,000 volunteers, we are prepared to respond at a moment's notice" (American Red Cross 2005, 6).

Volunteer Participation and Voluntary Associations

The Red Cross and Amnesty International are examples of mature social organizations operated by a permanent staff that also mobilizes large cadres of volunteers. In addition to mature social organizations, there are also voluntary associations. Smith (1997, 115) describes voluntary associations as "grassroots" and defines them as "locally based, significantly autonomous, volunteer-run, formal, nonprofit groups that have an official membership of volunteers and that manifest significant voluntary altruism." Smith's emphasis on grassroots groups would be limited to a subset of nonprofit mutual associations and cooperatives that lack the administrative and bureaucratic arrangements of mature social organizations (for example, neighborhood groups, tenant associations, home and schools, and social clubs). Voluntary associations rely upon volunteers both for their activities and for maintaining a relatively simple organizational framework.

Milofsky (1987, 278) refers to voluntary associations as "neighborhood-based organizations" and argues that they should be "treated as subordinate parts of a larger social system, the community." With the modernization of society, there has been a profound change in the nature of community from that of people situated in a place with of comprehensive interpersonal ties to that of social networks, some relatively impersonal, based on a specific shared interest and possibly unrelated to a specific geographic location (Christenson 1994; Wilkinson, 1994). One aspect of the changing nature of community is the increased role of government in support of the organizations of the social economy, particularly public sector nonprofits (Hall and Banting 2000; Martin 1985; Salamon 1995; Salamon and Anheier 1997; Salamon et al. 1999; Sharpe 1994; Smith and Lipsky 1993). Indeed, many of the largest nonprofits (hospitals, universities), which in their origins might have been supported by donors such as a religious organization, have become highly dependent upon government financing and, therefore, influenced by government policy. Such organizations can hardly claim to be voluntary, but as with most nonprofits, they normally involve volunteers. In other words, modern community revolves less around the local neighborhood in which individuals form voluntary associations and more around a broader society that includes government agencies that serve the public and that also support social organizations that operate at arm's length from government (Salamon 1995).

Therefore, the weakening of local, geographically based communities in modern society has shifted volunteer participation from voluntary associations to mature social organizations. But modernization has also stimulated a contrary trend. Modern forms of communication have increased the opportunities for people to form voluntary associations through the Internet, albeit associations based on very weak interpersonal connections. These include discussion groups and online self-help groups for concerns related to physical and mental health and social problems such as addiction (Baym 1996; Cooper 2000; Eysenbach et al. 2004; Ferguson 1997). The Internet, therefore, may be transforming the notion of voluntary association from its original roots in stable neighborhoods to a non-geographic cyberspace. Whether these interactions satisfy the meaning of community is open to question. However, they do represent a form of voluntary association that is on the rise at a time when geographically based voluntary associations are in decline and volunteering is occurring primarily in mature social organizations. These mature social organizations have become the social infrastructure of a reconstructed community, based less on local neighborhoods and more on a space that lacks clear boundaries.

Civic Engagement

In his critique of American society, Robert Putnam (1993, 1995, 1996, 2000) argues that social or civic engagement is a key component of social capital that is on the decline. While his primary focus is analyzing the reasons for the decline, he also describes the important role of mutual associations in engaging people with each other. Putnam (2000, 384–85), who traces the role of mutual associations historically, writes:

> During the years from 1879 to 1920 civic inventiveness reached a crescendo unmatched in American history, not merely in terms of numbers of clubs, but in the range and durability of the newly founded organizations. From the Red Cross to the NAACP, from the Knights of Columbus to Hadassah, from Boy Scouts to the Rotary club, from the PTA to the Sierra Club, from the Gideon Society to the Audubon Society, from the American Bar Association to the Farm Bureau Federation, from Big Brothers to the League of Women Voters, from the Teamsters Union to the Campfire Girls, it is hard to name a major mainline civic institution in American life today that was not invented in these few decades.

Putnam notes that for the last three decades of the twentieth century there has been a decline in civic engagement—newer associations (for example, business associations or other interest groups) are more narrowly defined, are less likely to involve their members in an active manner, and are more transient. The emergence of the Internet during the 1990s represents the epitome of this pattern. In spite of changing patterns of social interaction, the decline in direct forms of participation, and the increased dependence on government to support public sector nonprofits, the organizations of the social economy remain a social infrastructure for civic engagement. It is through organizations of this sort that members of a community connect with each other, even if the patterns of association have become far less personal and spontaneous than in the past.

The proponents of civil society also emphasize the value of association, though much of the current interest in civil society has been spurred by the collapse of communism in Eastern Europe and by the powerful role of citizens' movements such as Solidarity in Poland. As such, the current theories of civil society are anti-government or, to borrow the critique of Hall (1995, 2), can be characterized as "societal self-organizing in opposition to the state." While that view may be valid in societies with a tyrannical government and where social organizations receive minimal support from the state, it seems unbalanced where state social programs have an important role in some minimal redistribution of wealth and in sustaining social organizations that are necessary supports for members of society. Some of the anti-state perspectives of civil society are unmistakably conservative in their orientation—for example, Green (1993), who argues for a "civic capitalism" that is reminiscent of Thatcherite conservatism in the United Kingdom.

Primarily, the civil society proponents are searching for a space—distinct from both the state and the market—that offers focal points for constructive forms of civic engagement. In a world in which vast power resides with transnational corporations and, to a lesser extent, with state institutions, dynamic social organizations are reflective of a pluralism that is characteristic of a democratic society. Having a variety of viewpoints and a culture that encourages people to organize around their viewpoints are important features of civil society and reflective of vibrant civic engagement. In addition, by creating a framework through which the members of a society can relate to each other, social organizations present opportunities for reconstructing the ties that occur more spontaneously in a society with strong local communities. This role is vital in a democracy and is an essential aspect of civic engagement. Even though social organizations are capable of being destructive (Barber 1998; Seligman 1998), the vast majority are engaged in humanistic services (to borrow Samuel Martin's [1985] label) to improve the quality of social life. These services include education, culture, religion, recreation, labor rights, health care, political association, to name but a few—services that are basic to humanity.

There are differing expressions of civic engagement within social organizations. In some—particularly those with an active membership—civic engagement is central to the organizational culture. Such organizations include some forms of cooperatives (in particular, worker, housing, and farm marketing cooperatives) and many types of mutual associations, neighborhood groups, and social clubs. Such organizations become a sub-community within a broader society in which the members engage with each other around shared services and may participate in the governance to make policy and planning decisions. Members sit on planning committees, and if there is a board of directors, the members elect it from among their group according to the principle of one member/one vote. These organizations might be described as a social democracy, not in the sectarian political sense but quite literally democracy within a social institution. Voting rights in such organizations are accorded on the basis of one member/one vote rather than on the basis of property holdings as in profit-oriented businesses (Ellerman 1990).

Where mutual associations are small and highly personal grassroots associations (often referred to as collectives), civic engagement can become quite intense. Such organizations are usually not incorporated: Rather than a board as its legal representative, there is a less formal arrangement involving broader participation in decision making (Rothschild-Whitt 1982). This small size often leads to a "face-to-face" direct form of democracy, as in feminist collectives. Social relations are highly personal, roles are flexible and interchangeable, decisions are arrived at through consensus, and management (to the extent that it exists) is often a shared responsibility. Because decision making can be emotionally charged and conflicted (Mansbridge 1982), such arrangements are not necessarily a recipe for harmony, but they do reflect a direct form of civic engagement with a high level of member participation.

Similar forms of intense civic engagement can occur in public sector nonprofits with a closed membership (for example, rape crisis centers, and food banks) in which the employees, volunteers, and for some matters the board members, attempt to achieve consensus on issues. These organizations think of themselves as collectives, and even though membership is closed, they endeavor to practice democracy internally.

At the opposite extreme, there are many civil society organizations (mutual associations and volunteer organizations) with members that are uninvolved or passive. One reason is that the service of the organization is not especially important to the members or—in the terms of Kurt Lewin (1935)—is a small part of their life space. A passive membership is typical of such member-based organizations as credit unions, retail food cooperatives, and professional, labor, and business associations. Essentially, a small group (such as the director or the chairperson of the board of directors) runs the organization with the tacit consent or tolerance of the larger group. On occasion, the leaders may resort to proxy voting because they require member participation to satisfy the constitution. This is most likely where the membership is widely dispersed. This pattern of a passive membership, referred to earlier as tertiary membership (Putnam 1995), is reflective of the decline of civic engagement in the modern world. Nevertheless, while far from the ideal, these organizations still represent a social location with which members can identify. Moreover, even in this type of arrangement, members may on occasion choose to become involved—for example, because they have more time available, when they are upset with a particular decision, if they suspect financial mismanagement, or if there is some external threat to the organization. In some respects, there are parallels between these arrangements and a political democracy where the electorate is uninvolved but still cherishes the opportunity to participate when it sees fit.

Even among public sector nonprofits such as hospitals and social service agencies with a closed membership consisting of the board of directors only, volunteer board members can make enormous time commitments and engage with each other to achieve consensus in deliberations. Moreover, through such organizations, volunteers participating in service roles connect with each other and become associated with a broader purpose.

These variations from the ideal type notwithstanding, it appears that organizations in the social economy do afford their members the opportunity for civic engagement. They not only contribute to the pluralism that is a hallmark of a democratic society but also engage in the practice of democracy, acculturating their members with decision-making skills and with knowledge about organizations that can be generalized to the political domain. Of most importance, in a world in which civic engagement is in decline, the organizations of the social economy are locations through which ordinary citizens can engage with each other in constructive activities.

CONCLUSION

The term *social economy* is based on the premise that social organizations (organizations established to meet social objectives) also have economic value. Although these organizations are not the mainstream of the economy, they employ people, purchase goods and services in the market, and have valuable assets. Moreover, they mobilize large cadres of volunteers who contribute to these organizations but whose contribution is excluded from conventional accounting statements.

In this chapter, we have discussed four defining characteristics of social organizations. First, these organizations start from a social purpose that ideally takes precedence over any commercial objectives. Second, their physical assets are social property that is owned by no one; either they have no shareholders or they have shares (as in a cooperative) that are tantamount to a loan to the organization. Third, the organizations of the social economy generally have a high level of volunteer participation—not simply on the board of directors but also for other services. Within nonprofit mutual associations and cooperatives, volunteer participation is referred to as social labor—that is, an intra-organizational contribution rather than a contribution to the broader community. Fourth, social organizations are venues for civic engagement. Moreover, these organizations tend to exhibit a high level of democratic decision making, either through member participation or through shared responsibility by the staff, volunteers, and board.

Earlier in this chapter, social organizations were classified into three primary groups: public sector nonprofits, market-based organizations, and civil society organizations (mutual associations and volunteer organizations). Of these three groups, civil society organizations reflect the defining characteristics most strongly. They have strong social objectives, are under social ownership, rely heavily on volunteers (not only for their governance but also for their services), and are primary locations for civic engagement, including democratic decision making.

Market-based organizations probably reflect the defining characteristics most poorly in that they may emphasize commercial objectives to a greater extent than their social objectives, and some can be demutualized and, therefore, may not represent social ownership ideally. Although they do not rely as heavily on volunteers as civil society organizations, social labor as reflected in service on committees is an important feature of cooperatives. Also, most organizations of this sort practice representative democracy in selecting their governance, though not always with a high level of member participation.

Public sector organizations fall between the civil society and the market-based group in that also have strong social objectives (often associated with a charitable status), represent social ownership strongly, use volunteer labor as an important supplement to their workforce, and support civic engagement through the mobilization of volunteers in humanitarian services and also on their board of directors. However, their boards of directors tend to be closed and are not reflective of a democratic ideal.

The unique features of social organizations serve as part of the rationale for creating distinct social accounting models, as presented in Chapters 4 to 7. It is important that accounting practices move beyond a narrow range of financial considerations, such as net income, and deal with broader considerations, including social inputs and social outputs that generally are excluded. For civil society and public sector organizations in particular, it is essential that accounting frameworks recognize that volunteers are an important part of their workforce and that many of their outputs are not transacted through the market.

This chapter serves as a background to the subsequent chapters that focus on social accounting, initially the theory and then through working models that can be applied. Through understanding the uniqueness of social organizations, we come to appreciate that different accounting frameworks are needed.

QUESTIONS FOR DISCUSSION

1. Why are organizations like Meals on Wheels often not perceived as economic entities, even though they have a clear economic impact and undertake economic activities?
2. What factors would you consider in order to assess the economic contribution of nonprofits, and why?
3. The social economy attempts to group nonprofits and cooperatives under a common umbrella that labels them as social organizations. Given what you know about these organizations, is this an adequate label? Why or why not?
4. What are the three main types of social organizations identified by the authors, and what are the main differences between them?
5. Some argue that public sector nonprofits should be considered as part of the social economy. Others argue that this is inappropriate because they are simply part of the public sector. What are the strengths and weaknesses of each argument?
6. Similarly, some argue that nonprofits and cooperatives that earn their revenues from the market should be considered as part of market-based social organizations. Others argue that they should be viewed as part of the private sector. What are the strengths and weaknesses of each argument?
7. What are the main characteristics of social organizations presented in this chapter? What other characteristics would you consider?
8. "Social objectives take on different forms, depending upon whether the organization is serving a public in need, meeting the needs of a membership, or competing in the market for its revenues." Discuss.
9. It can be argued that social ownership is an oxymoron, because if property is social, it is not owned by anyone. Is it reasonable to suggest that social organizations are social property that belongs to no one? Why or why not?
10. In your view, is civic engagement useful as a defining characteristic of the social economy? Is the definition of civic engagement presented in this chapter satisfactory? If not, how would you modify it?

NOTES

[1] Variations of this categorization were used by Quarter (1992), Quarter et al. (2001a), and Quarter et al. (2001b).

[2] This information was obtained through a phone interview with the head office of Amnesty International in Ottawa, Canada, on July 19, 2006.

Chapter 3

Social Accounting: Theory and Practical Applications

In this chapter, we define social accounting and discuss its relationship to other related concepts such as accountability, social auditing, social reporting, and social responsibility. There is already a sizable literature about social accounting but primarily related to profit-oriented businesses. Our focus is on social organizations—primarily nonprofits and cooperatives—and on working models. This requires addressing the challenging problem of measuring social phenomena that lack a market value. Nevertheless, the existing literature on social accounting is quite useful—both its critique of conventional accounting and some earlier social accounting models developed for profit-oriented businesses. Therefore, the existing literature forms a building block for our conceptualization of social accounting presented in this chapter and the models presented in Chapters 4 to 7.

After defining social accounting, the chapter discusses in detail the key components of the definition. As part of that discussion, the predominant model of social accounting, also known as a social audit, is presented for discussion, including its tendency to separate the social from the economic. The concluding part of the chapter presents an integrated approach to social accounting that seeks to broaden financial statements by including items related to social value.

DEFINING SOCIAL ACCOUNTING

Although accounting as a professional field has a lengthy history, dating back to at least the mid-nineteenth century (Tinker 1985), social accounting is more recent and burgeoned during the early 1970s (Mathews 1997). Earlier proponents of broadening the domain of corporate accounting—for instance, Blum (1958), Bowen (1953), and Goyder (1961)—created a foundation for the field to move forward. All were struggling with the same issue of corporate accountability and putting in place mechanisms through which corporations would be more socially responsible.

Goyder's (1961) book, *The Responsible Company*, was forthright in its call for a social audit: "In an economy of big business, there is clearly as much need for a social as for a financial audit" (1961, 109). In a similar vein, Bowen (1953, 48–49) stated that:

The directors of a corporation are trustees, not alone for stockholders and owners, but also for workers, suppliers, consumers, the immediate community, and the general public. According to this view, the board of directors should serve as a mediator, equitably balancing the legitimate interests of the several principal beneficiaries of corporate activity.

These early proponents were concerned about the growing power of the modern corporation and its lack of accountability to anyone other than its shareholders, and they visualized the need for broader accounting and accountability frameworks that would address this concern.

While social accounting involves a diverse set of themes and practices that have evolved since that period, the underlying ethos that Bowen, Blum, and Goyder enunciated has remained intact. Nevertheless, social accounting, although moving ahead, remains marginalized within the accounting profession and has focused on academic critiques of the limitations of accounting rather than providing models that can be applied.

The term *social accounting* implies that there is a form of accounting that is not social. Yet, as others have argued, the terminology of financial accounting and "profit" itself are social constructs. Accounting primarily reflects the needs of owners and managers of profit-oriented businesses (Hines 1988; Morgan 1988; Tinker 1985). However, there is nothing inherent in accounting that necessitates its limitation to this set of interests. Social accounting has attempted to reorient accounting to a broader set of social variables and social interests. It is upon this tradition that the current manuscript is built and uses the term *social accounting*—but with the acknowledgment that, as Tinker (1985) and others have pointed out, all accounting can be construed as social.

The field is also referred to as social and environmental accounting because, in its formative period, the environmental movement influenced it. At times, environmental issues have dominated the field, but at present the issues are broader (Bebbington, Gray, and Owen 1999). By opting for the term *social accounting*, we are not attempting to diminish the importance of environmental concerns.

There are varying definitions of social accounting. All share the common features of expanding the range of criteria that are taken into consideration when measuring performance and looking at the organization in relation to its surrounding environment, both social and natural. Additionally, all emphasize that the audience for social accounting is broader and may differ from that for other forms of accounting. Here are some definitions that others have used:

Ramanathan (1976, 519):
The process of selecting firm-level social performance variables, measures, and measurement procedures; systematically developing information useful for evaluating the firm's social performance; and communicating such information to concerned social groups, both within and outside the firm.

Estes (1976, 3):
The measurement and reporting, internal or external, of information concerning the impact of an entity and its activities on society.

Gray, Owen, and Maunders (1987, ix) and **Gray, Owen, and Adams** (1996, 3):
The process of communicating the social and environmental effects of organizations' economic actions to particular interest groups within society and to society at large. As such it involves extending the accountability to organizations (particularly companies), beyond the traditional role of providing a financial account to the owners of capital, in particular, shareholders. Such an extension is predicated upon the assumption that companies do have wider responsibilities than simply to make money for shareholders.

Mathews and Perera (1995, 364):
At the very least, social accounting means an extension of disclosure into non-traditional areas such as providing information about employees, products, community-service and the prevention or reduction of pollution. However, the term "social accounting" is also used to describe a comprehensive form of accounting which takes into account externalities.

Traidcraft (2000, 1):
Social accounting is a systematic means of accounting for the social impact of an organisation. It can be compared to the way that financial accounting provides the means to account for an organisation's financial performance.

Institute of Social and Ethical AccountAbility (2000, 1):
Social and ethical accounting is concerned with learning about the effect an organisation has on society and about its relationship with an entire range of stakeholders—all those groups who affect and/or are affected by the organisation and its activities.

As can be seen, these definitions share the common feature of broadening the domain of accounting, attempting to deliver accountability to a broader array of stakeholders, and in so doing influencing the creation of a more socially responsible corporation. As with Blum, Bowen, and Goyder, the more current proponents of social accounting have focused primarily on profit-oriented businesses rather than social organizations, though as will be shown, there is some work with nonprofits and credit unions (Brown 2001; Zadek, Pruzan, and Evans 1997). Although the focus of this manuscript is social organizations, our definition is intended to have a more general application.

The definition that we propose is **a systematic analysis of the effects of an organization on its communities of interest or stakeholders, with stakeholder input as part of the data that are analyzed for the accounting statement.** This definition has four components that we will discuss in turn:

1. a systematic analysis;
2. the effects of an organization;
3. on its stakeholders; and
4. stakeholder input.

A SYSTEMATIC ANALYSIS

Many of the definitions of accounting in texts and from professional associations emphasize its information-producing role. For example, the Accounting Principles Board of the American Institute of Certified Public Accountants (AICPA) has maintained the following definition since the 1970s:

> Accounting is a service activity. Its function is to provide quantitative information, primarily financial in nature, about economic entities that is intended to be useful in making economic decisions—in making reasoned choices among alternative courses of action (1970, Section 1023).

In a similar vein, one of the major accounting texts (Larson et al. 1999, 10) emphasizes "useful information." Some other major texts have a similar emphasis but go beyond the focus on "providing information" and stress interpretation. For example, Pyle, Larson, and Zin (1984, 26) propose "the art of recording, classifying, reporting, and interpreting the financial data of an organization." Similarly, Meigs, Meigs, and Lam (1988, 4) refer to "interpreting economic activity," and Kaplan and Atkinson (1989, 1) use the verbs "classifying, processing, and analyzing" in relation to information. Our definition shares the view that accounting is more than simply reporting information; rather it involves a systematic analysis of information about the organization.

At the organization level, accounting tends to follow a system of rules that is generally accepted (Generally Accepted Accounting Principles or GAAP) and is understood throughout the profession (though not necessarily by nonprofessionals). Therefore, when accountants create an income statement, they are not only engaged in the analysis of data but are also following a system with rules that others utilize.

That is not to say that the only legitimate forms of accounting are those that follow the formats and agreed-upon standards of professional governing bodies. As Meigs et al. (1988, 4) point out in their text, "nearly everyone practices accounting in one form or another on an almost daily basis. Whether you are preparing a household budget, balancing your check book, preparing your income tax return, or running a large business, you are working with accounting concepts and accounting information." Their point is relevant to social accounting because it emphasizes that accounting is much broader than the systems approved by professional organizations and can apply to personal and household tasks as well as to business and community organizations. Moreover, their statement also implies that although all forms of accounting share rules of logic, the practice can take on many forms. Without approved procedures by a professional association, it is necessary to innovate, as has been done in social accounting.

Many refer to social reporting or social auditing and oddly avoid the term *accounting*. Perhaps this tendency reflects a concern about avoiding criticism from the profession; perhaps it is done because social accounting remains new and experimental and, therefore, using a name other than accounting seems less threatening. Nevertheless, it is necessary for social accounting to have a beginning point. Even if the systems of analyses lack the approval of professional bodies, this does not mean that they are not accounting.

Arguably, there is a difference between social reporting and accounting. The latter does more than report information or even engage in obvious interpretations; rather it analyzes. Therefore, a section in a corporate report that refers to minority representation over time as a percentage of the workforce involves analysis but perhaps with less complexity than would be needed to meet the standard of accounting. Moreover, because such reporting does not conform to a standardized format (as does a financial accounting statement) but rather utilizes *ad hoc* presentations that seem logical under the circumstances, there is a reluctance to label it as accounting. Therefore, we return to our earlier point that social accounting involves not only an analysis but also a systematic analysis. In the absence of the accounting profession's participation in creating forms that fit with social accounting, the participants in this process have to be innovators and convince their audiences that the information yielded from these analyses are logical and meaningful. As will be suggested later in this chapter, there are already precedents that meet the standard, and as will be suggested in the final chapter, the task of generating generally agreed-upon systems is largely shaped by the politics of accounting.

THE EFFECTS OF AN ORGANIZATION

Organizations, whether they are profit-oriented businesses or social organizations, have an impact upon various stakeholders, both internal and external. For a profit-oriented business, its services are measured by the market, as reflected by sales figures. Other impacts such as the well-being of purchasers or the firm's effect on the natural environment generally are ignored in formal accounting statements, though these additional effects may result in bad publicity and have a negative impact on sales. For example, a tobacco-product corporation may be very successful at marketing but may also cause immense health problems with huge costs that society and consumers must absorb. The accounting statement will include its sales and the return to its shareholders but will not deal with the health costs resulting from this corporation's products.

This pattern is prevalent for profit-oriented businesses in general, including those with broader social impacts that are positive. For example, by reducing pain, a drug manufacturer's products may make it possible for people who would otherwise be unable to engage in gainful employment to be relatively self-sufficient. To a degree, sales figures for this firm would reflect the impact of the product. However, there are also broader effects than the sales figures such as the ability of the drug's users to earn a living, reduced health costs, and the tax benefits to government, to name but a few. Typically, accounting does not address the broader effects; it is limited to the firm's market transactions and the related expenditures. The analysis of broader social effects might be included in an annual report or in supplementary reports as a form of corporate social reporting, but it normally would be segregated from the conventional financial accounts.

For a social organization, the limitations of market transactions are accentuated, especially for organizations with "unearned revenues," that is, monies from grants and donations rather than from market transactions. In traditional accounting terms, such organizations lack a market measure of the impact of their services—not only the direct impact of sales for a market-oriented organization but also the broader social impacts that the field of social accounting attempts to address.

Assessing the social effects of nonprofits and cooperatives is of particular importance because such organizations are based on a social mission. As noted in Chapter 2, their raison d'être is to supply a service to communities, either defined as beneficiaries of the organization's services or as members. The clients of human service organizations with a charitable status are most often people who are unable to manage without special assistance, for example, people on low incomes or with health problems. Normally, there would be no market transaction associated with the service, and as such there would be no record of the service's market value that would be entered into an accounting statement.

There are other distinct features of social organizations, discussed in Chapter 2, that suggest different forms of accounting are required. To make available their services, many social organizations rely on volunteers or unpaid labor. Because no market transaction is involved, this component of the organization's labor force does not normally appear on the accounting statements. Yet for organizations in which the bulk of the labor force is volunteer, this is a major oversight. Without their involvement, the level of service would be drastically curtailed; in some cases, the organization might not function at all.

For all of these reasons, new accounting frameworks are needed for social organizations. Some reasons overlap with those presented by the critics of conventional corporate accounting and some relate specifically to the distinctness of social organizations.

A critical issue in addressing this matter is assessing the value of non-market or non-monetized services, a point that is underlined by Estes (1976, 108): "The greatest objection to social accounting is an apparent lack of valid and reliable measurement techniques. Accountants and businessmen [sic] may express an acceptance of the general concept of corporate social accounting, but lack confidence in their ability to assign suitable numbers to social effects." This issue will also be addressed in Chapters 4 to 7, where actual accounting models are presented. At this point, the discussion will be more general.

Estimating a Market Value for Volunteer Service

For social organizations, a social accounting framework should estimate a market value for volunteer services. There are two general schools of thought. The first is based on what economists refer to as "opportunity costs." This label is derived from the assumption that "the cost of volunteering is time that could have been spent in other ways, including earning money that could, after taxes, be spent on desired goods and services" (Brown 1999, 10). Because time might have been spent generating income, the opportunity cost is tied to the hourly compensation that volunteers normally receive from paid jobs that they hold. However, this procedure could be problematic because the skills associated with a volunteer service may differ substantially from those for which a salary is being received (Brown 1999). The rate of pay that Bill Gates received from Microsoft for his services would not be an appropriate standard if he were to spend a day volunteering at a local food bank. An opposite problem might arise if the food bank volunteer were unemployed and, therefore, without an hourly wage. It would be incorrect to suggest that the service is worth nothing. After considering the complexities of estimating opportunity costs, including the portion of a paid worker's hourly wage that goes to taxes, and after adjusting for any fringe benefits, Brown (1999, 11) suggests that volunteer time "be valued at roughly one half to six sevenths of the average hourly wage." In her view, higher values should be applied when volunteers have increased responsibilities relative to their paid work and that lower values should be applied in the opposite circumstance.

Variations of Brown's (1999) procedure to estimate opportunity costs of volunteers were undertaken by Wolfe, Weisbrod, and Bird (1993) and Handy and Srinivasan (2002). Wolfe et al. estimated the marginal opportunity costs by asking volunteers what they would have received if they had worked additional hours for pay. Volunteers not in the labor market (retired, students, unemployed) "were asked what they believed they could earn if they decided to seek paid employment" (1993, 31). Handy and Srinivasan (2002) also asked volunteers to estimate how much their tasks were worth, thereby arriving at a lower figure than the marginal opportunity cost.

These procedures vary, but they share the common feature of looking at the value of volunteering from the perspective of the volunteer and what an hour is worth to that person. They differ from the approaches that use "replacement costs" and thereby evaluate the cost of volunteers from the perspective of the organization, as if it had to pay the market rate for such a service. Most of the research that estimates the value of volunteers, including our own work, utilizes replacement costs. There is a debate as to whether volunteers substitute for paid labor by doing jobs that would otherwise require compensation or they supplement paid labor (Brudney 1990; Ferris 1984). However, the replacement-cost framework sidesteps the issue and assumes that volunteer functions should be calculated at the value for similar services in the labor market.

Replacement costs are calculated using differing methods. Many organizations estimating the value of volunteers simply calculate a gross average based on the average hourly wage in a jurisdiction. For example, the Independent Sector—an advocacy organization for nonprofits in the United States—utilizes the average hourly wage for non-agricultural workers published in the Economic Report of the President plus 12 percent for fringe benefits (Independent Sector 2001, 2002b). For Canada, Ross (1994) suggested a weighted average of hourly and salaried wages based on Statistics Canada data for employment earnings. He calculated both national and provincial averages.

However, the predominant trend for applying replacement cost estimates to volunteers is to base the calculation on the type of service (Brudney 1990; Community Literacy Ontario 1998; Gaskin 1999; Gaskin and Dobson 1997; Karn 1983). For example, Community Literacy Ontario uses an hourly rate for volunteer literacy workers based on a survey of the average annual salary of full-time support staff of 94 community organizations that supply training. The Volunteer Investment and Value Audit (VIVA), developed in the United Kingdom, uses market comparisons based on both the job titles and the component parts of the jobs (Gaskin 1999; Gaskin and Dobson 1997).

One criticism of using replacement costs is that volunteers are less productive than paid labor and, therefore, replacement costs could overestimate their value (Brown 1999). Another critique is that organizations that use volunteers are often under financial constraints, and if volunteers are unavailable, they simply reduce the level of service (Handy and Srinivasan 2002). Also, market rates for similar jobs might not evaluate properly the contribution of volunteers, as they might bring higher levels of skill than the volunteer task requires (Brown 1999). Moreover, although organizations that use volunteers obtain a valuable service, they also absorb costs of training and supervision. This point is emphasized in the Volunteer Investment and Value Audit (VIVA), which is a cost-benefit analysis based on a ratio of the comparative market value of volunteer functions (using replacement costs) divided by the organization's expenditures on volunteers (Gaskin 1999; Gaskin and Dobson 1997).

As seen in Chapters 4 to 7, our applications utilize replacement costs in estimating the value of volunteers. However, our comparisons are organization specific, and we attempt to take into account some of the aforementioned criticisms in our estimates.

Estimating a Market Value for Other Non-monetized Outputs

Although establishing an appropriate value for volunteer labor is a major factor in creating a social accounting framework for social organizations, there are also other outputs that do not involve market transactions and, therefore, creative approaches are required in order to evaluate them. In one of the earlier works in social accounting, Estes (1976) struggled with this issue and proposed a number of creative techniques. His examples are largely in relation to profit-oriented businesses, but they are also relevant to social organizations.

Surrogate Valuation: "When a desired value cannot be directly determined, we may estimate instead the value of a surrogate—some item or phenomenon that is logically expected to involve approximately the same utility or sacrifice as the item in which we are interested" (Estes 1976, 110). He gives the example of estimating the value of building facilities loaned to civic groups and suggests as a surrogate the rent that would be paid for commercial facilities of a similar quality. Another example, which we use in our case studies, is establishing a surrogate value for the personal growth and development of volunteers from participating in a nonprofit organization. As a surrogate, we use the cost of a community college course in personal development.

Survey Techniques: This procedure involves asking participants what a service is worth to them. To assist in establishing an accurate estimate, Estes (1976) suggests using, as a prompt, a list of either prices or consumer items and asking the respondents to situate the service in relation to others on the list.

Restoration or Avoidance Cost: "Certain social costs may be valued by estimating the monetary outlay necessary to undo or prevent the damage" (Estes 1976, 115). Road salt corrodes automobiles, but frequent washings can prevent the damage, something that can be easily priced. Similarly, it is possible to estimate the cost of restoring environmentally damaged land to either industrial or residential use. In the event of a plant closure, many governments require a cleanup of the work site to residential standards, a liability that can be determined.

This type of cost estimate is commonly done in relation to environmental damage. For example, the Carnegie-Mellon University estimated that the cost associated with pollution in Pittsburgh in 1963 was $2 billion; the estimate included the hospital and doctors' costs associated with increased respiratory diseases from pollution (Rose 1970). A similar study estimated the effect of air pollution on property values and found that a decrease in air quality negatively impacted on the sale prices of houses. It estimated that in 1965, the property-value losses in 85 U.S. cities totaled $615 million (Estes 1972). The loss of or damage to outdoor recreational facilities that are publicly available has been costed by such standards as the fees needed to replace the facilities (Crutchfield 1962).

Analysis: Government agencies often have elaborate data banks and statistical analyses that can be used to estimate the value of social outputs. For example, from such data it is possible to estimate the increased earnings associated with volunteering (Day and Devlin 1996, 1998; Devlin 2000, 2001). These studies estimate that volunteers earn about 6 to 11 percent more as a result of their volunteer experience.

As is recognized by persons engaged in social accounting, establishing market values for non-monetized items requires creativity and flexibility. Often there is reluctance to undertake such procedures because professional accounting bodies do not sanction them. One reason for this is uncertainty among professional accountants as to what amount is appropriate. Professional accounting organizations have studied issues related to the environment and a broader array of social matters (American Accounting Association 1972a, 1972b, 1973, 1989; American Institute of Certified Public Accountants 1977; Canadian Institute of Chartered Accountants 1993a; Institute of Chartered Accountants in England and Wales 1992),[1] but the change in practice has been slow.

Nevertheless, there are cases where accountants do make estimates. Human resource accounting does assign values to non-monetized items (Flamholtz 1985), and within financial accounting, estimates, which arguably lack precision, are made for inventories and the depreciation of assets. However, in general, conventional accounting has shunned assigning market values to non-monetized items. The concerns notwithstanding, ignoring obvious areas of organizational value or apparent liabilities because of tradition seems inappropriate. This type of work would be made easier if there were established benchmarks or indicators that were generally accepted. In order to facilitate this goal, the Institute of Social and Ethical AccountAbility was set up in the United Kingdom to help develop international codes and standards by which organizations could be evaluated (Institute of Ethical and Social Accountability 2000; Zadek et al. 1997).

In Chapters 4 to 7, where non-monetized social outputs are given a market value, the surrogate approach is adopted.

Attribution

Another issue in assessing organizational impact is attribution—assigning a weight to various factors that influence results. Comparison groups and longitudinal studies—traditional methods of determining attribution—require resources beyond those of most social organizations. For example, a nutrition program to improve seniors' diets may be associated with positive improvements in clients' health, but it would be difficult to control for other contributing factors such as medical interventions that occurred at the same time and, therefore, unequivocally determine whether the program causes better health. Mayne (1999, 5) observes that it is not possible to determine definitively the extent to which a government program contributes to a particular result, noting that "measurement in the public sector is less about precision and more about increasing understanding and knowledge." This analysis can also be applied to social programs. Mayne proposes the following steps for establishing the contribution of a program to a result:

➢ presenting the logic of the program;
➢ identifying and documenting behavioral changes;
➢ using clear indicators;
➢ tracking performance over time;
➢ discussing, and where possible, testing alternative explanations; and
➢ gathering multiple lines of evidence (Mayne 1999).

According to Mayne (1999), a reasonable case can be made for a program's impact, but it requires more data than are currently gathered by government programs and, by extension, many of the social organizations that they fund.

The Need for Social Indicators

Olson (1969) highlighted the need for social indicators in a report that the U.S. Secretary of Health, Education and Welfare prepared for the president. Olson's (1969, xi) introduction stresses that there is an unmet need: "The Nation has no comprehensive set of statistics reflecting social progress or retrogression. There is no Government procedure for periodic stocktaking of the social health of the Nation. The Government makes no Social Report." He goes on to lament the domination of economic indicators but points out that the equation relating national income to national well-being doesn't stand: "It seems paradoxical that the economic indictors are generally registering continued progress—rising income, low unemployment—while the streets and the newspapers are full of evidence of growing discontent" (1969, xi).

Olson produced a creative list of social indicators for such issues as health and illness, social mobility, the physical environment, income and poverty, and public order and safety. Indicators for such issues could be of value to social accounting, even though Olson's unit of analysis was national rather than the organization. In both cases, data are analyzed that allow for a judgment or interpretation of a social condition. Although social indicator research is an important aspect of effective social accounting, in general these related fields have proceeded in parallel to each other.

Social indicator research is of two types: first, studies demonstrating that the social costs associated with phenomena are often ignored; and second, research that creates national and international standards for social progress—for example, the Human Development Index and other UN reports (United Nations Human Development Report 2002) or the Oregon Department of Human Services benchmarks that attempt to assess whether there is progress toward a better quality of life (Oregon Department of Human Services 2002; Stein 1996). Of particular interest for this chapter are the studies demonstrating that accounting frameworks pay no attention to relevant social costs. In effect, these studies present a cost-benefit analysis with a broadened frame of reference, but they also create social indicators that social accounting frameworks could utilize. There are many such studies, so our examples are necessarily selective.

The classic example of such a study was undertaken in 1976 for the Joint Economic Committee of the U.S. Congress, chaired by Senator Hubert Humphrey. This path breaking study by Harvey Brenner, a professor at Johns Hopkins University, and often referred to as the Brenner Report (Brenner 1976), attempted to estimate the social costs of increased unemployment by examining stress indicators—suicide, state mental hospital admissions, state prison admissions, homicide, mortality from cirrhosis of the liver and cardiovascular-renal disease, and total mortality—during a time frame from about 1935 to 1974 (the time frame varied to a degree for each criterion). While this research cannot claim cause-and-effect relationships between unemployment increase and the stress indicators, it presents evidence of a relationship between these variables—that is, an increase in unemployment is associated with a worsening of the stress indicators. For example, Brenner estimated that a 1 percent increase in unemployment resulted in a:

➢   4.1 percent increase in suicide;
➢   3.4 percent increase in state mental hospital admissions;
➢   4 percent increase in state prison admissions;
➢   5.7 percent increase in homicide;

➤ 1.9 percent increase in mortality due to cirrhosis of the liver, and, cardiovascular-renal disease; and
➤ 1.9 percent increase in total mortality.

In summarizing the findings of the study, Senator Humphrey stated:

The 1.4 percent rise in unemployment during 1970 has cost our society nearly $7 billion in lost income due to illness, mortality, and in added state prison and mental hospital outlays. To this must be added public outlays of some $2.8 billion annually over the 1970-1975 period for jobless and welfare payments associated with the sustained 1.4 percent rise in unemployment. Additional outlays not included here are the costs of care in federal institutions. Even excluding these latter outlays, the cost of the sustained 1.4 percent rise in unemployment during 1970 is at least $21 billion. And as noted earlier, this entirely excludes the impact of the further increase in unemployment since 1970 as well (1976, ix).

The Brenner Report was not simply a cost-benefit analysis of unemployment increases but also created a standard that accounting frameworks could apply. When a corporation downsizes, resulting in layoffs and unemployment, there are costs to society that do not enter into the firm's accounts because they are perceived as being someone else's problem. However, such costs could be included, and Brenner's report provides a social indicator of the cost.

Other studies have followed this same pattern but for different social problems—for example, the economic cost of affective disorders (Rice and Miller 1995); the economic costs of depression (Jonsson and Rosenbaum 1993); the economic benefits of investing in child care (Cleveland and Krashinsky 1998; Cohen and Fraser 1991; Townson 1986; Verry 1990); and the hidden costs of plant closings, particularly in the mid-1980s in the United Kingdom (Gray, Owen, and Adams 1996; Harte and Owen 1987).

These studies demonstrate that by broadening the social criteria for evaluation, a different picture emerges. For example, the classical view of child care expenditures is as a cost to society; however, the research indicates that they are also a benefit in that women are able to enter the labor force in greater numbers, and their children function better in school and eventually become more productive members of society. The Cleveland and Krashinsky (1998) study, for example, estimates that for every public dollar invested in child care, the incremental benefits are double that amount.

Summary of the Effects of an Organization

If social accounting frameworks are going to assess properly the effects of an organization, it is necessary to measure variables such as volunteer labor and outputs that normally would not be monetized. In the absence of established benchmarks or indicators for evaluating these outputs, innovation is required. The research on social indicators creates procedures on how non-monetized variables can be assessed and also suggests standards that might be applied. Nevertheless, there are social factors that are not easily quantifiable. For such factors, a descriptive or qualitative presentation is possible, a point emphasized by Blake, Frederick, and Myers (1976, 41): "Many social factors simply cannot be stated or measured in quantitative terms. One way out of this dilemma is to design meaningful non-quantitative measures that will allow comparisons to be made." Although "counting" is the root of the word "accounting" and accounting statements normally use quantitative presentations of economic data, accounting texts also emphasize that accounting involves communicating information (Garrison, Chesley, and Carroll 1993; Kaplan and Atkinson 1989; Larson et al. 1999). Information presentations need not be numerical. In the models that we present in Chapters 4 to 7, market comparisons are made for social factors and then analyzed within financial statements. However, it is not our intention to suggest that this is the only approach to dealing with social accounting.

COMMUNITIES OF INTEREST OR STAKEHOLDERS

For a social accounting framework to analyze the effects of an organization, there must be an object—that is, the effects on what? In a general sense, the object is society, and in a simple society, that might be sufficient. However, in the modern world, society is complex and amorphous, and the outreach of an organization can be extensive. Therefore, it is more logical to characterize society in terms of groups or communities of interest that are affected directly by an organization. The same argument can be made with respect to the organization per se, and particularly if it is large and complex. Ramanathan (1976, 523) refers to these communities of interest as "social constituents" and defines them as "the different distinct social groups with whom a firm is presumed to have a social contract." He is not explicit about how he uses the term *social contract*, but presumably he means an ongoing social relationship. In the organizational literature, these communities of interest are viewed as stakeholders, implying that they have a stake in the results of the organization.

Freeman (1984, 46) presents the most widely used definition of a stakeholder: "any group or individual who can affect or is affected by the achievement of the organization's objectives." This definition casts a wide net and is refined by Clarkson (1995) who subdivides stakeholders into primary and secondary. In his words, "A primary stakeholder group is one without whose continuing participation the corporation cannot survive as a going concern" (Clarkson 1995, 106). He identifies primary stakeholders as: employees, customers, suppliers, investors, and government and communities that supply laws, regulations, infrastructure, and markets. Clarkson's list is directed to profit-oriented businesses and would have to be adapted for social organizations. For example, for social organizations, there may be sources of financing but not investors in the same sense as for profit-oriented businesses. Similarly, volunteers and members would usually play a more important role.

Clarkson defines secondary stakeholders as "those who influence or affect, or are influenced and affected by, the corporation, but they are not engaged in transactions with the corporation and are not essential for its survival" (1995, 107). As an example of secondary stakeholders, Clarkson refers to the media and environmental groups. Clarkson does not refer to the natural environment per se as a stakeholder, but presumably he includes it with environmental groups. Conceptually, the natural environment should be classified as a primary stakeholder to signify its importance both to the organization and to a social accounting framework.

Clarkson argues that satisfying the needs of all of the primary stakeholders is vital to the survival of the organization. This claim is disputed by Jawahar and McLaughlin (2001, 402) who suggest that among the primary stakeholders, "at any given point in time, some will be more important than others." With respect to profit-oriented businesses, they argue that "shareholders and creditors are likely to be the primary suppliers of critical start-up funds" (Jawahar and McLaughlin 2001, 406) and are, therefore, the most important stakeholder in the formative stage. For social organizations, the dominant stakeholder may not be as evident. With the exception of nonprofit mutual associations and cooperatives, which generally are oriented to one dominant membership group, social organizations will often have different stakeholder groups represented in their governance.

However, the issue of whether a stakeholder has defined rights in the governance of an organization is different from whether it is affected by it. With respect to their governance, profit-oriented businesses normally limit the rights of stakeholders other than shareholders and executives (Gray, Owen, and Adams 1997; Jordan 1989). However, the business affects other groups such as users of the service, employees and the surrounding community, and the natural environment. If an industrial plant produces large amounts of toxins, the affected groups can be quite distant.

Therefore, in arguing that social accounting must look at the effects of an organization in relation to its stakeholders, the issue of legal rights for stakeholders in governance is not necessarily relevant. For example, employees may have limited rights within a business, but they depend upon the business for their livelihood, and their role is vital to the quality of services. As a result, the accounting statement ought to address the business's impact on the employees. For a nonprofit, volunteers are often an important component of their labor force and affect the organizational outputs. The natural environment is both affected by the organization in the energy it uses and the toxins it emits, and it affects the organization in that the quality of the air and water affect the ability of the employees to perform their duties.

There is a practical reason for looking at the effects of an organization in relation to stakeholders rather than society more generally. Stakeholders are defined groups who can make available a perspective on how an organization affects them. For the natural environment, there are groups that can speak on its behalf. Also, from our preceding definition, social accounting includes stakeholder input as data from which the accounting statement is prepared and ideally engages stakeholders in a process of ongoing organizational change (Gray, Owen, and Adams 1997; Henriques 2001). In other words, the stakeholders become active participants in the process. Having defined groups simplifies this task.

STAKEHOLDER INPUT AS PART OF THE DATA

The predominant model for social accounting is a stakeholder- one that solicits feedback from the representatives of an organization's primary constituents and may involve them in verification. The origins of this model came from Blum (1958), Bowen (1953), and Goyder (1961), who began articulating the need for a broader accounting framework as part of a critique about the need for corporate social responsibility and greater accountability. Elaborations of the framework were presented—a Process Audit (Bauer and Fenn 1973) and a Social Process Audit (Blake et al. 1976). All of these analyses were confined to specific programs rather than extending to the organization as a whole.

A variation of this model was developed in the United Kingdom by the New Economics Foundation (see Zadek et al. 1997) and other variations have been created elsewhere. Its original applications were to profit-oriented businesses, but it has also been applied to social organizations (Brown 2000, 2001; Heritage Credit Union 1998; Metro Credit Union 1996, 1997, 2000; VanCity 1998, 2000; Zadek et al. 1997).

This model is most often referred to as a social or ethical audit. The New Economics Foundation states that a social audit "assesses the social impact and ethical behavior of an organization in relation to its aims and those of its stakeholders" (Pearce, Raynard, and Zadek 1995, 1). This approach attempts to organize the input from stakeholders into a report about the organization's social performance, often using qualitative feedback and descriptive data from surveys of the extent to which the organization is meeting stakeholder expectations. An excellent example is the evaluation undertaken by The Body Shop International, the parent company for a private sector multinational franchise, which has promoted such issues as animal rights, protection of the environment, human rights, and fair trade practices (Sillanpää 1997, 1998; Quarter 2000; Wheeler and Sillanpää 2000). The Body Shop refers to its social account as an "ethical audit" and maintains a unit by that name to conduct that endeavor. Undertaking a careful evaluation of its social impact is important to The Body Shop because a key element in its marketing strategy is to reach socially conscious consumers. Through its public affairs department, The Body Shop organizes campaigns on social issues, often in conjunction with nonprofit agencies. These campaigns are not add-ons but part of The Body Shop's persona and, therefore, central to its business operation.

What is impressive about The Body Shop's process is that in spite of its size, it systematically solicits the views of key stakeholders in a comprehensive manner, using open meetings, interviews, confidential focus groups, and surveys. The Body Shop's ethical reviews are extensive. The initial review, undertaken in 1995, was 134 pages (The Body Shop 1996); the 1997 report (called a Values Report) was 218 pages (The Body Shop 1998). Although the methodology was similar, the 1997 report also addressed issues raised in the 1995 document.

The stakeholder groups that participated in the consultative process included employees, franchisees, customers, suppliers, representatives of communities in the company's Trade Not Aid partnerships, representatives of local communities, and shareholders. They were consulted about aspects of the company's mission, goals that were related to their specific stakeholder group, and about the company's success in meeting them. As well, respondents suggested further steps to advance the company's social goals.

By obtaining feedback from representatives of Littlehampton, England (site of the headquarters of The Body Shop International), local community satisfaction with social performance was assessed. Nearly half of all directly employed staff were based there (The Body Shop, 1996). A special town meeting was convened, with the presence of 10 representatives of The Body Shop, 50 community leaders, other interested individuals, and the verifying organization (The New Economics Foundation). The town meeting analyzed several aspects of the company's relationships in the community. The resulting report commented on the company's role as one of the largest employers in the area, on its volunteering in local communities, and on its need to communicate better about local planning issues. As well, the report set out the company's next steps, which included launching a new approach to volunteering and offering a wider range of possibilities for participation (The Body Shop 1996). An important feature of social accounting is to change organizational behavior (Brown 2001). In that regard, it can be viewed as a feedback mechanism to the organization from its constituents.

Social Auditing Versus Social Accounting

The Body Shop's social statement is prepared internally and verified or audited by the New Economics Foundation, an external organization. Based upon our preceding definition, the initial preparation of the social accounts represents social accounting in that an internal unit undertakes an analysis of the firm's social performance with input from its key stakeholders as part of the data. Therefore, we differentiate this approach from an "audit," which, according to accounting texts, is defined as attestation or "an independent examination of the accounting records" (Meigs et al. 1988, 31). Similarly, Power (1997, 17) writes: "Over time, this general definition has been filled out and adjusted in various ways, but the core idea of an independent examination remains." As will be seen in the examples that follow, many of the organizations using this model do not differentiate clearly between the accounting and auditing function. In some cases, the term *social audit* seems appropriate; in other cases, the organization evaluation is either social accounting or a hybrid of social accounting and auditing.

Another example is Ben & Jerry's Homemade Inc., the Vermont-based ice cream producer. In 1989, this company was a pioneer in creating a model that assessed the social performance of the corporation as a whole, not simply one program (Lager 1994; Parker 1997). To undertake the assessment, Ben & Jerry's hired John Tepper Marlin of the Council on Economic Priorities, a U.S. organization that evaluated companies on their social performance (not necessarily with their cooperation). Technically, Marlin would have been an auditor. The report evaluated the effects of the company on five stakeholder groups—communities, employees, customers, suppliers and investors.

The 1989 report of Ben & Jerry's, although generally positive, was frank about criticizing the company for the lack of minorities in its labor force. Following that, Ben & Jerry's had the report prepared by a volunteer committee of employees with William Norris of Control Data Corporation serving as the auditor. From that point, Ben & Jerry's returned to having an external auditor lead the process (Parker 1997). Ben & Jerry's has continued these social assessments annually, quite remarkably publishing the unedited conclusions, criticisms and all, and has attempted to rectify shortcomings (Parker 1997). These social performance evaluations were distinct from Ben & Jerry's financial accounts in that they focused on social issues rather than on the economic matters normally addressed in financial statements.

The Body Shop's social evaluation is primarily internal social accounting with an external audit; and Ben & Jerry's has vacillated but in the main involves external social accounting and auditing. Other examples of a social audit have been those conducted by external groups doing their own independent examination of the company's record on social matters (such as a plant closing or a company's impact on the environment), often without the agreement of the organization (for example, the work of the Public Interest Research Centre in the United Kingdom; see Medawar 1976). In these cases, the relationship between the evaluators and the organization may be antagonistic.

Traidcraft, a U.K. firm, has undertaken a process that buys the products of small businesses and farmers' cooperatives from the South at a fair price. This indicates that there is a growing recognition of the distinction between accounting and auditing (Evans 1997). After its first social account, undertaken in 1993 by Simon Zadek of the New Economics Foundation, the organization used its own in-house accountants to prepare its social accounts. From that point, the New Economics Foundation served as the auditor of the internally prepared account and was assisted by an audit review group consisting of independent experts and practitioners in the field. The auditor's report, which is included in the publication of the social account, is not uncritical and typically notes areas where improvements are needed. This separation between the accounting function and the auditing function represents a departure from the earlier social audits (Gray 1998).

Objective Versus Subjective

About the same time that Ben & Jerry's initiated its social evaluation, the Sbn Bank of Denmark undertook a similar process, which led to an "Ethical Accounting Statement" (Pruzan 1997). Like Ben & Jerry's, the Sbn's approach was stakeholder based, but its focus was highly subjective: "An Ethical Accounting Statement provides measures of how well an organization lives up to the shared values to which it has committed itself. [It] is not objective. It does not prove anything, but it draws a rich and informative picture of how the stakeholders perceive their relationships with the organization" (Pruzan 1997, 69).

The philosophy underlying this approach may be labeled as postmodern and tends to deny an objective reality (Guba and Lincoln 1989). From this perspective, the organization is nothing more than the shared perceptions of its stakeholders. An obvious limitation of this approach is that, without some form of benchmarking or external comparisons, the social statement will only supply subjective information from a variety of viewpoints. This may be helpful, but it does not seem sufficient for an accountability framework or for an organization to effect change.

The social accounting statement of Traidcraft also struggles with finding a balance between the subjective perceptions of stakeholders and objective benchmarks or indicators, but unlike Sbn, it acknowledges that objective standards are needed. Essentially, Traidcraft was attempting "to improve the market deal for small producers in the Third World while ensuring, somehow, that everyone involved in Traidcraft was fairly rewarded for the contribution they made" (Evans 1997, 85). The major issue that the assessors of Traidcraft have struggled with is determining what is a "fair price." Standards are set by the fair-trade organizations but commercial traders perceive these as unrealistically high. The assessors of Traidcraft attempted to use a standard based on asking the suppliers and also making comparisons with those of other buyers.

Although social accounting has struggled with creating a balance between the objective and the subjective, this work goes beyond simply subjective reporting. The Body Shop, for example, has had to defend its fair-trade and animal rights policies against critics by providing hard data that support its view that it is living up to its social mission (Quarter 2000).

Other Issues

To standardize social accounting, the Institute of Social and Ethical AccountAbility (2001) (and its related AA1000 Standards Guide) has attempted to create a set of guidelines. These guidelines suggest seven key elements of social and ethical accounting:

➢ planning (understanding the mission and values);
➢ stakeholder engagement and dialogue;
➢ measurement;
➢ reporting and disclosure;
➢ auditing and verification;
➢ commitment to improve performance; and
➢ embedding the process within the organization.

A growing number of organizations are creating social accounts as part of their ongoing operations, thereby satisfying the demand for "embedding," one of the principles of AA1000, which calls for building social and ethical accounting into mainstream operations, systems, and policy making. In other words, within the last decade, the professionalization and standardization of the process of creating social accounts have occurred to a much greater extent than previously. AA1000 guidelines also emphasize the importance of a separate audit of the accounts (Institute of Ethical and Social Accountability 2000).

Another framework and set of sustainability reporting guidelines were developed by the Global Reporting Initiative using a consensus-seeking process involving many stakeholders (GRI 2005). The guidelines' aim is to ensure a balanced representation of an organization's sustainability performance, while facilitating comparability.

The creation of social accounting processes such as those described above is putting pressure on corporations to become involved. For example, the magazine *Business Ethics* issues a Corporate Social Responsibility Report that ranks the 100 best corporate citizens according to eight stakeholder-service categories—total return to stockholders, community, governance, diversity, employees, environment, human rights and product—as taken from shareholder returns and ratings by the KLD Research and Analytics of Boston (Business Ethics 2006). KLD (Kinder, Lydenberg, Domini) normally screens companies for ethical or social investment funds with criteria that are similar to those used by *Business Ethics* (Kinder and Domini 1997).

Although the Corporate Social Responsibility Report is externally directed social accounting, it involves the cooperation of the participating organizations that complete a survey for KLD. The firms that receive a high ranking in this report typically advertise the results. The headline on Intel's Web site reads: "Intel ranked #11 in *Business Ethics* 2002 List of the 100 Best Corporate Citizens" (Intel 2002). IBM issued a special press release announcing that it "Takes Top Spot Among 650 Leading U.S. Public Companies" (IBM 2002). Arguably, these comparisons are normative and, therefore, only reflect the performance relative to other competitors rather than an ideal. Nevertheless, these practices do indicate a growing tendency to create a form of social accounting and social accountability.

AN INTEGRATED APPROACH TO SOCIAL ACCOUNTING

A distinct characteristic of the predominant tradition in social accounting has been its separation from financial statements, which focus on economic issues. For most organizations, the social account is presented as an addition to financial accounting and generally is treated as a less important piece of the picture. Ironically, this is true not only of profit-oriented businesses but also of social organizations. However, as suggested in Chapter 2, it is artificial to segregate the social from the economic. The social economy framework is predicated on the assumption that the social and economic are inextricably linked, a point also emphasized in the field of alternative economics (Daly and Cobb 1994; Ekins 1986; Mies 1986; Schumacher 1973; Waring 1996, 1999).

Within the predominant tradition in social accounting, segregation between the social and economic is accepted. Indeed, as mentioned at the beginning of this chapter, the label *social accounting* gives tacit approval to this segregation because it implies that there is a field of accounting reserved for social phenomena. Arguably, it would have been more appropriate to refer to our approach as socioeconomic accounting.

However, we opted to build on a tradition and to try and influence it, and that requires some acceptance of that tradition's language. Moreover, within social accounting there are models that attempt to synthesize the social and economic. In one of the earlier conceptual pieces, Grojer and Stark (1977, 350) state: "We decline [sic] financial accounting as a subset of social accounting because we think it is neither possible nor desirable to separate economic from social factors." That philosophy, which we enthusiastically endorse, will underline the models that are presented in Chapters 4 to 7. However, before that point, we present some of the attempts at creating social accounting statements that integrate the economic with the social. The following discussion considers five models:

➢   a Socio-Economic Operating Statement (SEOS);
➢   Social Impact Statements and Assessments;
➢   an Elaborated Social Impact Statement;
➢   a Cooperative Social Balance; and
➢   an Integrated Social and Financial Balance Sheet and Income Statement.

A Socio-Economic Operating Statement (SEOS)

Linowes (1972, 1973) proposed a Socio-Economic Operating Statement (SEOS) that could be added to the profit and loss statement and balance sheet. The statement was to include "expenditures made voluntarily by a business aimed at the improvement of the welfare of the employees and public, safety of the product, and/or conditions of the environment" (1973, 40). Voluntary expenditures were emphasized because those required by either law or contract were perceived as "necessary costs of doing business" (1973, 40).

The Socio-Economic Operating Statement differentiated between "improvements" and "detriments"; the latter was defined as inaction by management to matters that are brought to its attention and to which it should be responding favorably. Linowes (1972, 1973) admitted that the definition was open to interpretation. Examples that Linowes gave of "improvements" were the early implementation of a socially beneficial action required by law (for example, pollution abatement equipment); tangible benefits for employees that are not specified in collective agreements; and donations either in cash or in kind for the organization or the employees. Examples of "detriments" are neglecting to install safety devices or pollution reduction devices.

To arrive at the "total socio-economic contribution or deficit for the year," the estimated market value of the "detriments" is subtracted from the "improvements," leading to either a positive or negative balance. The Socio-Economic Operating Statement looks at the "improvements" and "detriments" in relation to three categories: people, environment, and product. These categories lack the distinctiveness of stakeholders.

Linowes visualized his statement as being prepared by an interdisciplinary team headed by an accountant and audited by another team. At the time that Linowes developed this framework, he was a partner in an international firm of certified public accountants and past president of the District of Columbia Certified Public Accountants. Therefore, he was aware of the practical challenges faced by professional accountants. In spite of his impressive credentials within the profession, there was not much take-up of the Socio-Economic Operating Statement.

Social Impact Statements and Assessments

A variation of the Socio-Economic Operating Statement was undertaken by Estes (1976) and referred to as a Social Impact Statement. For the organization, he totaled the "social benefits" and the "social costs" and subtracted one from the other to arrive at either a "social surplus" or "deficit." Both Estes's and Linowes's approaches are elaborate cost-benefit analyses, but rather than being used to evaluate one specific program or event, as cost-benefit analyses often do, these analyses were envisaged as regular statements that organizations would prepare in conjunction with other financial statements.

Another study—Davidson, Cole, and Pogorlec (1997)—follows from this same tradition. The researchers extend understanding of the indirect economic impacts of nonprofits by using standard multiplier coefficients (most often applied to the economic impacts of profit-oriented businesses) to calculate the ripple effects of the Catholic Church's expenditures in Tippicanoe County, Indiana. They observed that monies from salaries paid by the diocese along with purchases of goods and services are recycled several times. For example, local businesses and banks, which are the recipients of these expenditures, use them to purchase other goods and services; merchants, who receive these payments, use them to purchase more goods and to pay salaries, which in turn are used to purchase other goods, and so on.

The researchers matched this observation with the U.S. Department of Commerce and the U.S. Economics and Statistics Administration's use of multiplier coefficients to estimate the impact by geographic area of recycling private and public sector monies within the economy. Davidson et al. (1997) accounted for the direct effects of the diocese's expenditures and used the coefficients developed for the Tippicanoe area to estimate the indirect economic impact on the community. They concluded that the Catholic Church was the county's fourth largest employer, managing 2 percent of the workforce. Its direct contribution to the economy was worth over $82 million, and using the multiplier coefficient for the area, the church's total economic impact was estimated to be over $191 million—a ratio of about 3 to 1 of indirect to direct effects of spending. Comparing the Catholic Church with other enterprises, the researchers concluded that the diocese's impact was one fourth the size of Purdue University's and six times the benefit of the local airport (Davidson et al. 1997).

Like Linowes and Estes, the Davidson et al. study demonstrates how social impact can be assessed, in this case with social organizations. While the appropriateness of multipliers in terms of projecting social impact is open to debate (Gunderson 2001), this study demonstrates that resources entering into the organization as revenues go on to enrich the community as expenditures. It lists revenues as incoming resources and expenditures as resources returning to the community. It also demonstrates that the impact of spending continues through several cycles. However, the study stops short of calculating the social-economic effects of the diocese's programs. Ideally, an accounting framework would not only register the economic impact of expenditures on the community but also account for the direct and indirect effects of its programmatic output.

An Elaborated Social Impact Statement

A variation of the foregoing social impact statement was developed by Land (1996), who distinguishes between three components: output; outcome; and side-effect indicators. Using the example of a Meals on Wheels program, he notes that output indicators could include the numbers of meals delivered and people served; outcome indicators could focus on the characteristics of the program's clients as well as on client satisfaction; and side-effect indicators could examine the impact of the delivery of meals on the clients' nutritional or health status as well as the clients' assessments of their overall well-being.

Land (1996) suggests that client information should be collected and interpreted within the context of the specific organization. He (1996, 17) states: "Although difficult to carry out in practice, all of the foregoing impacts can be measured," even though he acknowledges that there is little systematic collection of this type of data on a national level. He points out that if data were available for selected output, for outcome and for some side-effect indicators for a sample of Meals on Wheels programs, it would be possible to estimate the corresponding national levels of such indicators. However, aggregating data about generalized characteristics may obscure key specific information about a particular organization. Nevertheless, Land is making an important point that without the creation of benchmarks or indicators for social products, it is difficult to move forward with social accounting frameworks. The approach to social return on investment described in Chapter 4 is based on the framework that Land (1996) recommends. In that respect, Land (1996) has helped to create an important foundation for social accounting.

Cooperative Social Balance

In Italy, which has a powerful cooperative sector, those associated with the National League of Cooperatives publish a Social Balance or Cooperative Social Balance (Vaccari 1997).[2] This statement is intended to indicate the extent to which Italian cooperatives fulfill their social mission, a practice specified by law. The paper by Vaccari (1997) is based upon the presentation of a second-tier association of 320 consumer cooperatives with nearly 3 million members and 1994 sales of 4.5 billion pounds sterling. The process leading to the Social Balance has many of the same features as the New Economics Foundation model for social accounting. Each of the key stakeholders participates, and benchmark indicators are established, but using both qualitative and quantitative presentations of data.

The Social Balance statement itself utilizes items that can be both costed and organized by five stakeholders—members, consumers, employees, civil society, and the cooperative movement. The figures are presented for the current year and the year previous, allowing for points of comparison. Some of the items would not differ from those of a profit-oriented business—for example, the items associated with support for civil society are simply corporate donations, and the costs associated with "training and maintenance of a high-quality work environment" might be viewed as staff training. However, other features are unique. Costs associated with the stakeholder cooperative movement are the cooperative's indivisible reserve—that is, the portion of its net assets that is social property and belongs to no one. Similarly, the cooperative's investment in member participation at meetings and in member representation on the board of directors and committees is another unique feature of the social balance.

An Integrated Social and Financial Balance Sheet and Income Statement

The Abt Model, produced by Clark Abt of Abt and Associates, was another early attempt at social accounting (Abt and Associates 1974). Abt produced a balance sheet that tried to estimate an organization's impact on the following stakeholders—staff, clients, owners, the neighboring community, and the general public. As with the Socio-Economic Operating Statement, the impacts are expressed in dollars, and there is a balance carried from year to year. Unlike the models referred to earlier, this balance sheet does not attempt to create a financial statement that is additional to those that are normally done. Rather, it seeks to modify existing statements by adding items that broaden the issues regularly addressed and by breaking down the balance sheet by stakeholders. For example, for the stakeholder, the general public and community, the assets include "public services paid for through taxes," whereas the liabilities include a costing of the "environmental resources used" (paper, electricity, and transportation).

Abt also produced a Social and Financial Income Statement, using the same principles as for the balance sheet—a broader array of variables, including those for which market values have to be estimated, and a breakdown by stakeholder groups. For the stakeholder community, the benefits are "local taxes paid by the company," "local tax worth of net jobs created," "environmental improvements," and "reduced parking space"—viewed as a benefit to the local community because fewer employees take vehicles to work and, therefore, the company contributes to reducing pollution. Some other social items that Abt built into the statement were:

➢ "inequality of opportunity"—treated as a cost to the stakeholder staff and calculated by the difference of earnings between a minority or female member and a non-minority or male;

➢ "layoffs and involuntary terminations"—treated as a social cost to the stakeholder staff. This item is valued at one month's salary for those who found employment within 60 days and two months' salary for those who found employment after 60 days;

> ➤ "staff overtime worked but not paid"—a subsidy of the staff to the stakeholders society and clients; and
> ➤ "environmental resources used through pollution"—treated as a social cost to the stakeholder society because these are effects of production for which the company does not pay.

Aside from creative approaches to estimating the financial value of social variables that normally are not included in financial statements, an impressive feature of Abt's approach is that it takes existing financial statements and modifies them. Although Abt's work gets referred to in the research literature on social accounting, it appears that relatively few organizations have made use of it. Ironically, Abt's model was directed largely at the business sector when, perhaps, it might have had greater appeal to social organizations—because understanding social impacts should be central to a proper evaluation of their activities and a stakeholder approach fits the logic of their structure.

Belkaoui (1984) presented a model of an income statement for a university, adapted from Lee Seidler of the accounting firm Peat, Marwick, Mitchell, & Co., that integrates social benefits and costs with those that are generally found in conventional income statements. On the social benefits side are the "value of instruction to society" and the "value of research to society." On the social cost side are "tuition paid to the university" and "cost of research and state aid." However, among the earlier attempts, a social accounting statement oriented to a social organization appears to be exceptional.

CONCLUSION

In general, social accounting statements tend to be non-financial and qualitative rather than an integration of the economic and the social. Some descriptive statistics are used to assess attitudes on particular matters, but usually financial calculations are not included in these statements. Even where financial data are used to create social statements, these statements tend to be segregated from the items that typically appear in financial statements. These social accounts are usually supplements to the financial statements that deal with economic variables.

In Chapters 4 to 7, models are presented of financial statements that integrate social and economic effects of an organization. In our view, the integrative approach has the advantage of placing the social account on the same level as the account of economic matters. It raises the question as to whether a profit is really a profit if only some of the costs are included. As shown in the following chapters, through integration a different picture emerges of the accounts.

Many of the examples given previously are from profit-oriented businesses, albeit a peculiar breed in that their social mission is an important part of their business. It is important to learn from these examples, but the models that follow in Chapters 4 to 7 are based on social organizations—primarily nonprofits, including a student housing cooperative.

QUESTIONS FOR DISCUSSION

1. Which definition of social accounting do you prefer, and why?
2. "Accounting should limit itself to financial information." Discuss.
3. Should the social costs associated with smoking cigarettes be included in the financial statements of a tobacco manufacturer? If no, why? If yes, what type of information would be needed in order to include them?
4. What are the differences between social reporting, social auditing, and social accounting?
5. For estimating a value for volunteer contributions, do you prefer opportunity costs or replacement costs? What do you see as the strengths and weaknesses of each procedure?
6. Social accounting is based upon stakeholder involvement in providing input and feedback. What are the benefits and potential risks of stakeholder involvement?
7. The typical approach to social accounting is qualitative and does not use financial statements. What are the pros and cons of translating into quantitative estimates such qualitative organizational effects as the impact on the environment, health, personal and community well-being, and learning?
8. In your view, why were the attempts of the 1970s at broadening financial statements to include social accounting items not picked up by the accounting profession?
9. What changes would be needed today for the accounting profession to include more social accounting items on financial statements?
10. What do you think of the seven-point guideline to standardize social accounting suggested by the Institute of Social and Ethical AccountAbility? What indicators would you use to gauge how well an organization is meeting this guideline?

NOTES

[1] For a discussion of this issue internationally, see Ahmed Belkaoui, *Socio-economic accounting*, Westport, CT.: Quorum, 178–182 [1984].

[2] Since 1977, France has required organizations employing over 750 persons to create a social balance sheet [*bilan social*] that discloses information on such themes as health and safety, remuneration and fringe benefits, and industrial relations. In 1982, this law was extended to organizations employing more than 300 (Belkaoui 1984).

Chapter 4

A Social Return on Investment Approach

In this chapter, we present a social return on investment approach to looking at nonprofit value. Different variations of this approach are shown, and one—the Community Social Return on Investment model—is applied in a case study of the Computer Training Center,[1] a nonprofit organization that provided training in Toronto for people on social assistance because of various forms of disability. The Community Social Return on Investment model represents an early effort to uncover how nonprofits create value in their communities. It developed methods for identifying and calculating nonprofit outputs and for assigning a comparative economic value to them, and it was a catalyst for the creation of the value added models described in Chapters 6 and 7. The rationale and procedures for the Community Social Return on Investment model are presented here to add to the discussion of how nonprofit value is calculated from a social accounting perspective. The chapter is divided into the following sections:

➢ an introduction to two other social return on investment models;
➢ the Community Social Return on Investment model;
➢ creating a report for a Community Social Return on Investment model; and
➢ a discussion of the differing approaches to social return on investment.

SOCIAL RETURN ON INVESTMENT: THE ROBERTS AND BENSON APPROACHES

Social return on investment (often referred to by the acronym SROI) is a form of social accounting for nonprofit organizations that was developed in the 1990s as a response to the increased emphasis on accountability and on philanthropy as a social investment. Like other approaches to social accounting, social return on investment has attempted to broaden the concept of return to include social impacts.

There have been several variations of a social return on investment model. Perhaps the best known is the model developed by the Roberts Enterprise Development Fund. This fund was established in 1997 from an earlier initiative—the Homeless Economic Development Fund, founded in 1990 in the San Francisco Bay area (Roberts Enterprise

Development Fund 2001). In 1999 and 2000, the Roberts Enterprise Development Fund invested $3.3 million in nonprofits that employed people who were homeless, in recovery from drug addiction, or had suffered mental illness.

In 1997, the Roberts Enterprise Development Fund began to track the impact of its investment in seven nonprofit organizations in the San Francisco Bay area from among the 23 social purpose enterprises which they ran. As of 2000, the foundation had invested over $1.35 million to develop its social return on investment framework.[2] The Roberts Enterprise Development Fund changed its name to REDF and has shifted its emphasis from furthering the SROI model to the development of social impact measurement that meets the specific needs of participating organizations (REDF 2006). This move follows a 2002 report (revised in 2005) that identifies issues raised by the SROI approach such as the difficulty of capturing the full array of social benefits from employment programs, attributing client outcomes to programs, and the complexity and costs of SROI analysis—all factors that make this approach unfeasible for most nonprofits (REDF 2005). In spite of its challenges, the relevance of the Roberts SROI model is in its ability to factor a range of social outcomes into a blended social and economic return on investment report thus creating a more detailed picture of an organization's impact.

The SROI model generates three measures of value and three measures of return. The measures of value are:

➢ **Enterprise Value**—the economic value the organization creates based on excess cash it is expected to generate over its lifetime adjusted for government subsidies for the training programs and social operating costs (additional staffing and lower productivity associated with running a business as a rehabilitative training center);

➢ **Social Purpose Value**—refers to the social value that the organization creates and is made up of two items—savings to the taxpayer (reduced welfare payments, lower criminal justice system costs, and reduced use of food stamps) and new tax revenues that are generated when trainees in the business get jobs. The social costs of running the business as a rehabilitative center are then subtracted;

➢ **Blended Value**—the total of the organization's economic and social value, less the total of long-term debt.

From these three measures of value, three measures of return are calculated:

➢ **Enterprise Index of Return**—the amount of enterprise value divided by the financial investment in the organization to date;

➢ **Social Purpose Index of Return**—the amount of social purpose value divided by the financial investment in the organization to date; and

➢ **Blended Index of Return**—the amount of Enterprise Value plus Social Purpose Value less the total of long-term debt, divided by the financial investment in the organization to date.

In addition to the Roberts model, another social return on investment model using three measures has been created by Dennis K. Benson, the author of a book on this topic (Benson 1999). This model was initially used to calculate returns on employment training programs but has been broadened to calculate the return on investment for health and human services. The Benson model looks at returns from three different perspectives:

➢ **Return on Investment to Taxpayers**—a measure of the payback to taxpayers for their investment in employment training programs. It includes calculations for increased taxes paid by program graduates, increased earnings by the graduates, and costs saved through the diminished need for welfare and food stamps.

➢ **Return on Investment from New Disposable Income Added to the Local Economy**—a measure of how much new money is added to the local economy through increased earnings, which are then reduced by money going to taxes and from the reduced payments to welfare and food stamps.

➢ **Return on Investment from the Economic Impact of Social Programs**—a measure that adds together the economic benefits from social programs and calculates their ripple effects on the economy. Economic benefits include taxes paid, social security payments by employer and employee, new disposable money added to the local economy from wages of employed program graduates, and program costs. Program costs (primarily salaries) are the monies spent by the agency to run its programs. In this model, program costs are seen as a benefit because wages (spent by agency staff) circulate in the local economy. This is similar to the way in which Davidson, Cole, and Pogorlec (1997), referred to in Chapter 3, treated monies spent by Catholic services in Tippicanoe County. Like Davidson et al., Benson uses U.S. Department of Commerce figures for multiplier effects to assess the ripple effects of this spending on the local economy.

The Roberts and Benson models both depart from conventional accounting by attributing to the activities of nonprofits economic benefits such as taxes paid when clients become employed and social costs saved when clients reduce their need for income supplements and food stamps. Unlike the social accounting models presented in this book which use a one-year time frame, both Roberts and Benson use projections over time to establish the return on investment.

The main contributions of both models is their shared emphasis on expanding the number of stakeholders for whom they are reporting and their careful documentation of areas in which nonprofits contribute economically—areas that are not included in conventional accounting for nonprofits. However, they stop short of including volunteer contributions and other non-monetized inputs and outputs that should be an important part of accounting for social organizations.

COMMUNITY SOCIAL RETURN ON INVESTMENT MODEL

Another approach to measuring social return on investment is the Community Social Return on Investment model. This approach was developed to examine how social organizations create value from the perspective of the community. It involves fewer calculations than the Roberts or the Benson models, but like them it measures social variables, assigns a proxy value to them, and merges financial and social information, including the social costs saved by clients using the program. As with the Roberts and Benson models, the Community Social Return on Investment model has been used to assess the social return on investment of agencies working with clients facing severe barriers to employment (Richmond 1998). However, the Community Social Return on Investment model differs from the Roberts and Benson models in three ways:

➢ It looks at one year in the life of the organization and does not project economic benefits;
➢ It develops a comparative economic value for social outputs;
➢ It includes a value for volunteer contributions.

The Community Social Return on Investment model is directed to the community rather than a philanthropist as an investor, as is the Roberts model. Like the Benson (1999) model to measure the Return on Investment from the Economic Impact of Social Programs, the Community Social Return on Investment model focuses on how the community benefits economically and socially from the services furnished by a nonprofit agency.

Social organizations are created to provide a service to a community—either the public at large or a subset of the public that chooses to become members. Therefore, the Community Social Return on Investment model focuses on the intersection of the social organization and the community. Designing a tool that is acceptable to both management and communities and will be used by them requires focusing on their common interests—the sustainability of effective social organizations. For these reasons, the Community Social Return on Investment model views social organizations as stewards of common resources, and it assesses their effectiveness in that role. If a social organization does not utilize resources effectively, it is not likely to survive (Milofsky 1987).

In the Community Social Return on Investment model, an organization's financial statements are restructured to represent an inflow and outflow of resources for a period of one year. This conceptualization is also compatible with the systems model for understanding how human service programs operate (Henke 1989; Martin and Kettner 1996). Figure 4.1 depicts a one-year cycle, showing the forward flow of incoming resources (or inputs) into a training program to the outgoing resources (or outputs).

Figure 4.1 Template for a One-Year Community Social Return on Investment

Incoming Resources		Outgoing Resources
Revenues		Expenditures
Value of Volunteer Activities		Value of Volunteer Activities
	➡	Value of Outcomes:
		Primary
		Secondary
		Tertiary
Total		
Return on Investment: Ratio of Incoming Resources to Outgoing Resources		

Utilizing the classical definition of productivity—the ratio of outputs to inputs (Brinkirhoff and Dressler 1990)—the model provides feedback to the organization on its productivity and stewardship of resources, as reflected by its social return on investment ratio (see Figure 4.1). This information can be used to enhance the organization's next productivity cycle.

As shown in Figure 4.1, the Community Social Return on Investment model utilizes the social as well as the economic features of an organization, creating a comparative economic value for the social outputs. It also attributes value to the social contributions of voluntary activity (see Hodgkinson and Weitzman 1988; Ross and Shillington 1989, 1990) and to social labor in the case of nonprofit mutual associations and cooperatives[3] (see Richmond and Mook 2001).

METHODOLOGY

As with conventional accounting statements, the first step is to obtain knowledge of the organization's field of activity, the corporate environment in which the organization operates, and knowledge of the organization itself. Thus, information was obtained on the programs and services made available by the Computer Training Center as well as the social and economic environment in which it functions.

At the time the study was done, the Computer Training Center was part of a network of similar community-based training agencies in Canada. The mandate of community-based training agencies is to provide participant-focussed employment-related training to the "severely employment disadvantaged"—that is, people facing complex systemic and personal barriers to employment (ONESTEP 2006; Rans 1989). Clients of these agencies include recent immigrants, older workers who have been laid off, mothers with little work experience who are receiving income supports, people with disabilities, youth who have not completed high school, women seeking entry into restricted trades, people in recovery from alcohol and drug dependency, and former offenders.

In 2006, member agencies of ONESTEP, an umbrella organization for community-based training agencies, provided programs to over 100,000 clients. Umbrella organizations such as ONESTEP are members of the Canadian Coalition of Community-Based Employability Training that was formed in 1992 (ONESTEP 2006). On average, community-based training agencies within the ONESTEP network have budgets of approximately $1.3 million and a median of 17 full-time staff equivalents, most of whom serve clients directly (ONESTEP 2006). ONESTEP'S data also show funding from the federal government's employment department (Human Resources and Social Development) accounts for almost half of a typical organization's revenues. Provincial ministries, other federal departments, charitable foundations, and individual donors are other funders.

The Community Social Return on Investment model was applied to the Computer Training Center's fiscal year 1994–1995. In line with the approach to evaluation proposed by Guba and Lincoln (1989), the information collected had the following features:

➢ A cooperative relationship was established with the organization;
➢ Negotiations were conducted with all of the participants to ensure informed consent and assure them of the confidentiality of their responses; management approval was sought for each stage of the process; interview questions were submitted to the executive director for approval;
➢ Prior to beginning the fieldwork, meetings were conducted with staff and clients in order to familiarize them with the research project;
➢ Draft results were provided to the organization;
➢ Feedback was incorporated into the final report.

Information was collected in the following stages:

➢ The agency's key internal and external documents for the fiscal year, as well as those for the years preceding and following, were examined. These documents included audited financial statements, mission statement, annual reports, program descriptions, reports to funders, evaluations completed within the five years prior to the fiscal year, client exit and follow-up reports (with the client's consent);
➢ Semi-structured interviews were conducted with 14 stakeholders: the executive director; one staff person; two members of the board of directors and volunteer committees; four fiscal-year graduates; four post-fiscal-year graduates; and two employers who hired fiscal-year graduates;
➢ Observations were taken of a two-hour breakfast meeting attended by approximately 20 referring agencies at which staff, volunteers, executive director, and graduates of the program presented information and answered questions. As well, clients were observed and engaged while participating in a computer training session.

CREATING A COMMUNITY SOCIAL RETURN ON INVESTMENT REPORT

From the information collected, the Community Social Return on Investment report was put together. This report consists of five sections, each of which will be discussed in turn:

1. background issues that give the reader knowledge about the context in which the agency operates;
2. an analysis of the incoming resources;
3. a discussion of the agency's outgoing resources and how these were given a market value;
4. a format for presenting the Community Social Return on Investment data; and
5. additional disclosure.

Background Issues

Context

This section describes the context in which the organization functions. For the Computer Training Center, the report indicates that it is located in Metropolitan Toronto, a city of approximately 2.5 million people. Employment patterns in the city shifted significantly when an economic recession in the early 1990s resulted in a significant loss of manufacturing jobs; growth in the service sector was not able to compensate. The overall unemployment rate rose to 10 percent and was even higher for particular subgroups of the population. Young people became especially disadvantaged—in 1992, the unemployment rate for men and women under 25 years of age was 24 and 15 percent, respectively (City of Toronto 1993; Committee of Planning and Co-ordinating Organizations 1992; Government of Ontario 1996).

At the time the study was completed, people with disabilities faced additional obstacles to employment. According to a national study, almost one half of working-age Canadians with disabilities were out of the labor force in the early 1990s (Roeher Institute 1992) and their rate of unemployment was about twice as high as for the rest of the population. As well, people with disabilities were almost twice as likely as the general population to have persistent histories of non-participation in the labor force. Discrimination appeared to be a problem. Nearly 74,000 employed adults with disabilities believed they had previously been excluded from paid positions (a situation that has not improved considerably today—see Crawford 2004). Within this context, the Computer Training Center made available employment-related training to those facing severe barriers because of a disability, often in addition to other barriers associated with being recent immigrants or youths.

Mission Statement

Another background section of the report was the description of the organization's mission. A mission statement need not be lengthy and can simply refer to the central focus of the organization. For the Computer Training Center, the mission was to enable adults with physical disabilities to acquire and enhance the skills necessary to obtain and retain employment involving the application of computer knowledge and skills (Computer Training Center 1995). The Computer Training Center aimed for high-quality equipment, instruction, and support for students in spite of the many barriers they faced. One of the key elements of the strategy was to recruit committed board members from the business and public sectors who would go beyond regular duties to mentor and make available contacts for students in the program. Another strategy was to set up a business advisory committee of 10 volunteers who would review the curriculum, coach and mentor, and seek out work placements for students.

Programs

Similarly, the report should briefly refer to the programs of the agency. The Computer Training Center provided skills training through three programs: computer programming, local area networking for microcomputers, and computerized office support. The center's curriculum also included employment-related skills such as job search and interview techniques, life skills, and business communications training.

Organization

Some details of the agency's basic structure and history were included as part of the background section of the report. The Computer Training Center was incorporated as a nonprofit with charitable status and was governed by a board of directors that met approximately 10 times each year and held an annual general meeting of the organization's membership. The members of the board of directors were also the organization's members and were self-electing; but as is the case with many nonprofits, management of the organization invited community members to its annual meeting and turned it into an opportunity to network and report back to the community. In 1994–1995, there were eight board members and 10 members on the business advisory committee. The Computer Training Center had 6.5 paid staff—an executive director, administrative assistant, three instructors, a service coordinator, and a part-time placement consultant.

Volunteers

Since volunteers are a vital component of the service, it is important to refer to them and their role in the background section of the report. The Computer Training Center's volunteers were members of the board and the business advisory committee.

These volunteers also assisted with interview preparation and job guidance, obtaining placements and jobs for clients, and in developing and evaluating curricula to reflect the needs of the job market.

Networks

Nonprofit agencies typically function as part of the social networks that they support, which, in turn, support them in providing their services. Therefore, related information should be noted in the background section of the report. During the 1994–1995 fiscal year, the executive director sat on the board of governors of a local community college, was the president of a cultural association, and served on the board of directors of a network organization for community-based training agencies. As well, the executive director was a board member of a professional association for rehabilitation programs. One other staff member also attended regular meetings of this association.

Financial Resources

Although the financial resources are part of the statement that is presented in Table 4.1, the total revenues and expenditures as well as the primary funding sources can be mentioned as part of the background section of the report. For the period February 1, 1994, to January 31, 1995, total revenues were $837,614 and total expenditures were $842,051. The primary funder was the federal government agency, Human Resources Development Canada (HRDC) (now called Human Resources and Social Development or HRSD).

Accountability

As a social organization, and particularly one dependent upon an external funder, it was important to report the Computer Training Center's accountability arrangements. For the period of the fiscal year 1994–1995, the agency:

➤ reported to its members (its board of directors) at its annual general meeting and submitted for approval a financial audit;
➤ reported its revenues, expenditures, and program results monthly to the federal funding agency, Human Resources Development Canada; and
➤ participated in six- and nine-month reviews conducted by Human Resources Development Canada.

In addition, the agency's program and financial files were subject to audit at any time by a Human Resources Development Canada project officer.

Incoming Resources

The second section of the report is the incoming resources. As indicated in Figure 4.1, incoming resources consist of revenues (documented in the audited financial statements) and volunteer contributions. The revenues reflect both the personnel and other expenditures of the organization. As shown in Table 4.1, the Computer Training Center's revenues for the fiscal year were $837,614. Estimating the value of the volunteer contribution was less straightforward and requires greater explanation.

Volunteer Contributions

Prior research with nonprofits used an average social service wage of $12.00 per hour to estimate the value of volunteer contributions (Ross and Shillington 1990). However, this estimate appeared low in the case of the Computer Training Center volunteers, who applied their extensive private sector management skills and contacts to augment the program. Therefore, a method was developed that attempted more accurately to reflect the value of the volunteer contribution for the 1994–1995 fiscal year. The organization did not track the hours spent by its volunteers so estimates were needed. The executive director of the organization estimated that 10 volunteers on the business advisory committee and eight board volunteers spent 2,896 hours serving on five committees: placement (614 hours); evaluation (216 hours); job guidance (1,600 hours); curriculum review (18 hours); and board of directors (448 hours). These estimates were corroborated in interviews with board volunteers. The executive director estimated the board members' average yearly salary to be $72,500, or $37.18 per hour (based on a standard measure of 1,950 hours of work in a year).

The executive director then estimated the percentage of executive skill capacity that volunteers utilized to complete their tasks with the center—20 percent of their professional capacity for each of the committees (for 2,448 hours) and 35 percent of their professional capacity for the board of directors (for 448 hours). Using these figures, the value of the committee work was calculated at $37.18 × 2,448 hours = $9,106 × .20 = $18,203. For the board of directors, the value was calculated at $37.18 × 448 = $16,656 × .35 = $5,830. Using the executive director's estimates, the total value of the volunteer contribution was $24,033.

These estimates by the executive director used a combination of opportunity costs (how much the volunteer received for an hour's work in the workforce) and replacement costs (assessment of what the task was worth to the organization). However, these estimates appeared low for four reasons:

➢   the researcher's prior experience with volunteers in similar capacities;
➢   observation of some of the center's volunteers applying their skills;
➢   descriptions of the Computer Training Center's volunteer tasks; and
➢   volunteer descriptions of their activities.

Because of the discrepancy between these points of view, the value of the volunteer contribution was assessed as the average of the following two procedures:

1. an estimate based on the assumption that the members of the board of directors and committees were using their full professional skills in their volunteer activities at the Computer Training Center; and
2. the executive director's estimate that the members of the board of directors and committees were using only 35 percent and 20 percent, respectively, of their professional skills in their volunteer activities at the Computer Training Center.

For the first estimate, working at 100 percent of professional capacity, the value of these activities was calculated as 2,896 hours × $37.18 per hour × 1.00, or $107,673. For the second estimate, working at a reduced level of professional skill, the calculations were 2,448 hours × $37.18 per hour × .20, or $18,203; plus 448 hours × $37.18 per hour × .35, or $5,830. Therefore, for the second estimate, the total was $24,033 ($18,203 plus $5,830). The average of these two estimates becomes $107,673 plus $24,033 divided by 2, or $65,853. This amount was entered into Table 4.1 as an incoming resource.

Outgoing Resources

Part 3 of the report, outgoing resources, is critical because it reflects the services that the agency is delivering to the community. Because of the nature of the Computer Training Center's clientele, there was no market transaction involved with its services. Therefore, as indicated later, it was necessary to create surrogates for their value (see Chapter 3). As shown in Table 4.1, the outgoing resources consisted of:

➢ the agency's expenditures;
➢ the value of its volunteer contributions;
➢ the estimated value of the clients' employment acquisition and enhancement; and
➢ the estimated savings from income benefits and related services.

Each of these outgoing resources and the procedure for assigning a value is discussed next.

Agency's Expenditures

The agency's expenditures of $842,051 were viewed as an outgoing resource because salaries and external purchases are returned to the community (Benson, 1999). The agency's staff used their salaries to make purchases, pay mortgages or rent, and sustain themselves and their families. Non-personnel items represented purchases of supplies and equipment that the agency required for its service. For the Computer Training Center, its expenditures were similar to its revenues—that is, its grants that it received from government were transferred through to the community. This is true of most public sector nonprofits.

Value of Volunteer Activities

As presented in Table 4.1, volunteers were both an incoming and outgoing resource. Like revenues, they represented a contribution from the community that permitted the agency to undertake its service; like expenditures, this contribution was returned to the community. Arguably, the value of volunteers that was returned to the community was enhanced as a result of the experience with the agency. As will be discussed in Chapter 7, volunteers develop skills through their volunteering experience that should be treated as value added. However, there are also costs associated with volunteer management. For the purposes of this statement, it was assumed that costs and benefits offset each other and that volunteer contributions that returned to the community at the end of the fiscal year were equal in value to the incoming value of this resource. Therefore, in the Community Social Return on Investment statement, the value of volunteers as incoming and outgoing resources was the same. The method for arriving at $65,853 was discussed earlier under incoming resources.

Employment Acquisition and Employment Enhancement

As mentioned previously, according to the organization's stated mandate and the terms of its contracts (verified through interviews with graduates), the two key primary outputs (direct effects of the program on the clients) were employment acquisition (skills training that led to jobs) and employment enhancement (successful completion of training that increased the chances of getting jobs). Three months after graduating, 23 out of 30 clients (77 percent) had found employment. Of the four graduates of the previous year who were interviewed, all had found work within three months of graduation, but one was unemployed at the time of the interview in 1996. The other three graduates had worked for the same employer since graduation, and two had received promotions. Given that all of them had been outside of the workforce for at least two years (a condition for entry to the program), it is assumed that the training intervention led to employment for these clients—in other words, the value created through employment could be attributed to the agency. This point might be subject to debate since there was no measure of what portion of those in similar circumstances would have found work without participating in the Computer Training Center's program. In other words, there was no control group against which the results of the Computer Training Center could be compared. However, given that the clients of the agency were without work for two previous years, our assumption about the agency's role in their employment seems reasonable. The graduates supported this interpretation when they were interviewed.

As shown in Table 4.1, the value of employment for the 23 clients who found work was $599,320 (rounded up), estimated by aggregating graduates' wages (see James 1987). This figure was arrived at by taking the average salary of the graduates ($26,057.39), as recorded by the agency, and multiplying by 23. As a check on the agency's figures, the four graduates who were interviewed reported average salaries of $28,850.

The figure of $599,320 that the agency reported as the 23 graduates' total salaries was used as a comparative market value for the employment acquisition output of the Computer Training Center and entered in the outgoing resources column of Table 4.1. The total of the employment acquisition category is understated because it does not include the value of employee benefit packages received by graduates. Two of the four graduates who were interviewed reported receiving benefit packages but were unable to ascribe a value to them.

In addition to employment acquisition, another primary output of the Computer Training Center was employment enhancement, which, as shown in Table 4.1, was also assigned a comparative market value. According to reports to Human Resources Development Canada, the government department that was the primary funder of the center, seven of the 30 graduates who successfully completed training had not found employment three months after graduation. However, the training enhanced these graduates' potential for employment, a result specified by the funder as being indicative of success. In spite of not achieving a paying job at the end of their training, the graduates of the program had developed new skills. If these skills were acquired from a profit-oriented business, the clients would pay for them, and the payment would be seen as a measure of their value. Because the clients did not pay for the service at the Computer Training Center, a surrogate procedure was applied to estimate its value to the seven graduates who did not become employed. First, an effort was made to find a similar private sector training program. However, none could be located that offered specialized computer and employment skills training for persons with a broad range of disabilities. Because no private sector equivalent could be found, the employment enhancement output was estimated using the amount per client that the funder granted to the center to deliver the specialized training. In 1995–1996, the per-client grant was $16,284. This figure was used as the comparative market value per unit of training. For the seven graduates, who did not find employment but whose employment chances were enhanced by training, the value was estimated to be $7 \times \$16,284 = \$113,988$.

As shown in Table 4.1, the primary outputs of the Computer Training Center—employment acquisition and employment enhancement—were valued at $599,320 and $113,988, respectively, or a total of $713,308. This value was a key component of the Computer Training Center's contribution to the community.

Savings from Income Benefits and Related Services

In addition to its primary outputs of employment acquisition and enhancement, the agency also had an effect on groups other than the clients—namely, tertiary outputs. For the Computer Training Center, the tertiary outputs were identified as the costs saved by the community when graduates who became employed and earned a salary no longer required income benefits and other related benefits.

To place a financial value on these savings, case files for the graduates were examined and the information from them was cross-checked with the interview data. In the year prior to training, income assistance for clients came from the following sources: Canada Pension Plan, Family Benefits Assistance, Workers' Compensation, private insurance, and welfare benefits. The case files did not record amounts being received; therefore, information from the interviews with graduates and clients was used to estimate the value of this by-product of training.

Because actual amounts were not available, the total income assistance in the year before entering the program was based on reported amounts received by eight program clients (four 1994–1995 graduates and four post-fiscal-year graduates). Their average was $588 in the year before entering the program. If this group is representative of the 23 clients who became employed as a result of training, the costs saved in their income benefits were $13,524 ($588 × 23).

In addition to income assistance, the four 1994–1995 graduates who were interviewed also reported receiving other benefits: vocational counseling (100%), prescription drugs (25%), and dental care (25%). Some also reported receiving accommodation devices—a special chair (25%) and a Braille reader (25%)—and one client reported receiving clothing supplements to assist in purchasing a professional wardrobe. However, graduates were frequently either unsure or not forthcoming about the types, amounts, or value of these goods and services. Based on the interviews, a modest value of $100 was assessed for additional benefits per client. For the 23 graduates who became employed, this amounted to $2,300 ($100 × 23) in further cost savings. Both this amount and the $13,524 of savings from income benefits are included as outgoing resources in the statement in Table 4.1.

Table 4.1 Community Social Return on Investment for Computer Training Center: 1994–1995

Incoming Resources		Outgoing Resources	
Revenues	$837,614	Expenditures (operating costs)	$842,051
Value of volunteer activities	65,853	Value of volunteer activities	65,853
		Outcomes:	
		Primary	
		Employment acquisition	599,320
		Employment enhancement	113,988
		Secondary	
		No equivalent market value could be found	
		Tertiary	
		Social savings from income benefits	13,524
		Social savings from related services	2,300
Total	$903,467		$1,637,036
Ratio of Incoming Resources to Outgoing Resources			1:1.81

Creating the Community Social Return on Investment Statement

Table 4.1 summarizes the resource flow for the Computer Training Center. The incoming resources consisted of:

➤ the revenues of $837,614 that the organization received from grants and other sources; and
➤ the estimated value for volunteers of $65,853—adding up to a total of $903,467.

The outgoing resources consisted of:

➤ the total expenditures, which served as proxy for the value of the financial return to the community from wages paid as well as products and services purchased;
➤ the volunteer contribution of $65,853;
➤ the estimated value of $599,320 for employment acquisition;
➤ $113,988 from employment enhancement;
➤ $13,524 in savings to society from benefits that would otherwise have been paid to the graduates of the program; and
➤ $2,300 of additional social savings for graduates who became employed.

In total, the outgoing resources amounted to $1,637,036, or $733,569 more than the incoming resources. In other words, for every dollar's worth of economic and social resources that entered the organization, $1.81 in economic and social value returned to the community. This ratio means that the Computer Training Center's expenditures for technology, individual instruction, specialized equipment, and employment assistance for graduates as well as the volunteer support required to help with training and job opportunities were offset by the center's positive impact on the community. This positive impact includes the value of employment acquisition and enhancement, the costs saved in income and other benefits, and the enhanced quality of life for clients (and, to some extent, their families).

Additional Disclosure

In addition to the outgoing resources of the agency that could be quantified, there were others for which it was not possible to assign a market value. These were classified as secondary outputs because even though they were related to the clients of the agency, they were not the primary goals. The following secondary effects on the clients were assessed through interviews with four of the graduates:

➤ increased self-esteem;
➤ reduced stress from employment;
➤ increased purchasing power;
➤ improved lifestyle;
➤ improved health; and
➤ improved family relations.

Table 4.2 shows the percentage of graduates for 1994–1995 and 1995–1996 who responded favorably to each of these possible indirect effects.

One 1994–1995 graduate and one 1995–1996 graduate reported greater stress and health problems during their training, but both indicated that there were improvements by the end.

Table 4.2 Secondary Outputs of the Computer Training Center

Areas of Enhancement for Graduates	1994–1995	1995–1996
Increased self-esteem	50%	75%
Less stress from unemployment	25%	75%
Increased purchasing power	50%	25%
Improved lifestyle	75%	75%
Improved health	25%	25%
Improved family relations	50%	25%

One graduate of the 1994–1995 program stated: "Without the preparation and connections that the Computer Training Center provided, I would never have gotten a job in this recession, and certainly not at a large, prestigious company.

A 1995–1996 graduate summed up his experience: "I'm six-and-one-half feet tall, and I feel it. I look forward to going to work. I feel wonderful about my job. I'm very glad I got directed to the course. I've opened up a door that I didn't think was possible, not just professionally but personally. My self-esteem has been boosted tenfold.

We did not assign a surrogate market value to these secondary outputs. However, the evidence from the surveys that there were secondary benefits was further supported by interviews with the clients.

John,[4] a male in his twenties and diagnosed with multiple sclerosis, lost feeling in his hands and feet, and then lost his job as a mechanic. After some time, his condition improved, and he went into remission. However, he realized that he needed to retrain:

It was scary at first. I am a fit person. I lift weights. When I walked into the Computer Training Center, I really felt bad because I was considered disabled, and it took me a long time to accept that. The Computer Training Center taught me to accept that you are not disabled, you are just as good as everybody else; everybody has a disability of some kind.

John became employed as a networker linking together computer systems in a large company and had received a promotion at the time of the interview in 1996. He expressed pride at his new status and referred to the enjoyment of company perks. As a result of his enhanced status, John stated that his relationship with his brother had improved; he felt that they had more in common.

Maria, a woman in her forties with a severe visual impairment, was a recent immigrant to Canada. She reported:

> The staff at the Computer Training Center gave me confidence in an area I thought I could never do. They offered a tremendous sense of professionalism, with high standards. The experience gave me something to talk to my husband about. It helped me to integrate into Canadian life.

Maria became an employment assistant with another agency that helps people with disabilities to train and find work. She noted that the staff at the Computer Training Center had helped her to work with her visual impairment: "They were generally accepting of my disability, giving it acknowledgment and dignity. In my country, we never discussed disability and what I had to do to cope. It was like suddenly being able to discuss the unspeakable."

Having had a difficult time in getting access to training when she first immigrated, Maria reported her pleasure at being able to help others. In her new position, she encountered some of the people with whom she had dealt as a client now relating to her as a colleague.

Summary of the Report

The Computer Training Center assisted persons with disabilities either in obtaining employment or in enhancing their chances of becoming employed. High unemployment in general and higher unemployment rates for persons with disabilities necessitated special programs to overcome the barriers to employment. Therefore, in order to be successful, the Computer Training Center required a high staff-to-student ratio, specialized volunteer assistance, and greater support from board members. In order to offer up-to-date computer training, the Computer Training Center acquired expensive equipment as well as highly specialized staff. However, the agency's placement rate of 77 percent indicates that its targeted training strategy was effective, particularly with a population experiencing such stringent barriers to employment.

Although some of the secondary and tertiary outputs of the training program could not be given a comparative market value due to a lack of appropriate measurements, the existing data yielded a social rate of return of $1.81 for each dollar invested. In spite of lacking complete data for all the areas of impact, this figure indicates that the Computer Training Center generated a positive rate of social return by investing community resources in a high-need group.

DISCUSSION

In applying a social return on investment approach there are two types of issues—practical and conceptual. At a practical level, social return on investment models radically undervalue the organization's outputs because not all of these can be counted or appraised. The methodology and resources do not yet exist that can capture all of the relevant data and estimate accurately the value of outputs. As well, the application of social return on investment models has been limited to employment-related and revenue-generating programs where the financial outputs are clearer than they are for social organizations that have unearned revenues (government grants, donations) and that do not receive a payment from their clients. This is a limitation that social return on investment models are trying to address; but without outputs that are sold in the market, they have to rely on surrogate measures for the impact of their programs. Therefore, the initial application of social return on investment has been limited to training and employment programs for which outputs are more easily quantified; however, the next steps are to apply the approach to a variety of programs across the nonprofit sector.

Of equal importance are the conceptual issues related to accounting for social return on investment. Each of the models described in this chapter differs to a degree in how social return on investment is conceptualized and what factors are included in its measures. As mentioned previously, the Roberts model creates an enterprise value and social purpose value and then blends them to arrive at a social return on investment (Roberts Enterprise Development Fund 2000). Benson's (1999) model analyzes social returns on investment from the perspective of the taxpayer and the community. The Community Social Return on Investment model compares incoming resources to outgoing resources and focuses on the community.

As well, outputs are defined differently in these models. The Roberts model includes only items that can be monetized such as earned revenues, program results (costs saved to the taxpayer), and income taxes paid by the employees (Roberts Enterprise Development Fund 2000). However, many nonprofits do not sell their services in the market and, therefore, need a surrogate value for their outputs. Otherwise there will be little to show as outgoing resources that can be used to calculate the social return on investment.

The Benson (1999) model includes as outputs the program costs and their ripple effects, which are added into the calculation of economic impact on the local economy. However, neither the Roberts nor the Benson model calculates a value for the volunteer time that is invested in the organization. Also, neither of them quantifies or puts a value on any of the non-monetized outputs of the agency which, for most nonprofits, are likely to be the largest category.

By comparison, to calculate the ratio of incoming to outgoing resources, the Community Social Return on Investment model uses one year only, a more practical but limited arrangement for most nonprofits. In calculating incoming resources, the Community Social Return on Investment model differs from the other two approaches by limiting financial inputs to revenues and including a value for volunteer activities. It also includes the value for volunteer activities as an outgoing resource that is released back into the community at the end of the year. The Community Social Return on Investment model uses the expenditures as a proxy value for the economic benefit that is received by the community from the agency's wages and purchases in the local economy. This is similar to Benson's approach, which includes the organization's expenditures and their ripple effects when calculating the overall social impact.

From the perspective of nonprofits and the community, it can be argued that expenditures (unless they are simply wasteful) represent benefits to the community, not costs to be lowered to increase profits—as for profit-oriented businesses. These differing interpretations of expenditures reflect the different interests of stakeholders—private sector investors who hope to make a financial gain by minimizing costs and a community that hopes to make a social gain for a reasonable cost. Private sector investors benefit when costs are kept low in relation to revenues. However, communities benefit when nonprofit expenditures are kept on a par with revenues. Even though their attitude to expenses differs, when profit-oriented businesses spend money, this also has a community and a tax benefit. In other words, from the perspective of the community, expenditures represent a benefit independent of the type of organization. From the perspective of the organization, however, a profit-oriented business has an attitude to expenditures that differs from a nonprofit. Therefore, the Community Social Return on Investment model classifies the expenditure of nonprofit revenues as an outgoing resource or an asset to the community (see Table 4.1). The agency's expenditures, representing wages and purchases in the local community, are used as the value of the community's benefit.

The community benefits when a nonprofit organization spends all (or almost all) of its monies in order to produce social goods or services. Monies not spent are at risk of being appropriated by funders at year-end or of leading to reductions in future allocations because the funders may perceive that the agency can manage with less. Reduced amounts of funding can be regarded as a loss to the community because service is likely to decline. From the perspective of the community, it can be argued that a reduced expenditure-to-income ratio results in a lower community social return on investment. This argument is also based on the observation that the trend is toward reducing government funding to nonprofits rather than redirecting the funds to other services (Eakin 2001; Hall and Reed 1995). If funds were simply redirected from one agency to another, the impact on the community would not change.

In attempting to highlight how value is created, the Community Social Return on Investment model reports impacts without adjusting for the costs of producing them. This limitation of the model led to the development of the Expanded Value Added Statement that follows in Chapters 6 and 7. The Expanded Value Added Statement builds upon an existing accounting format to include social items and to focus on additional stakeholders.

Social accounting attempts to transpose financial concepts to social organizations in order to place a proper value on their outputs. This is difficult to do and requires experimentation. There are also risks that market values or other metrics not suited to their purposes will be used to judge social organizations. For example, by emphasizing the savings of employment programs to society (such as reductions in income benefits and social service costs), there is a danger that these programs will be evaluated not by their mission and mandate to serve their clients well, but by how much public money they save, perhaps motivating programs to take additional clients on public benefits or clients who are "easier" to serve (REDF 2005). However, in the long term, developing appropriate accounting procedures can serve to counter the trend of extending to social organizations private sector values, language, and notions of success (Zimmerman and Dart 1998). The measures of efficiency of production and return on investment that are central to profit-oriented businesses transfer clumsily to the production of social goods. It is important to understand the uniqueness of social organizations and to create appropriate procedures for understanding their contributions. Such evaluations should be grounded in the communities to which the organizations relate as well as in the context of the specific organization. Assessments should take into account environmental and alternative economic perspectives and should use tools that are appropriate for examining the role of social organizations as major producers of social value. The Community Social Return on Investment model and the Roberts and Benson approaches to social return on investment are unique approaches that recognize the social value of social organizations.

QUESTIONS FOR DISCUSSION

1. What are the main differences between the social return on investment models proposed by Roberts and Benson?
2. If only financial reports are provided, what aspects of a nonprofit's performance are excluded? Why is it important to capture them?
3. In the case study examined in this chapter, financial accounting would present a ratio of revenues to expenditures of approximately 1:1. Social accounting presented a rate of return of 1:1.81. Discuss.
4. In the absence of clear records of volunteer contributions, how were volunteer hours estimated and valued for the Computer Training Center? What are the limitations to this approach? Can you think of an alternative?
5. In the Community Social Return on Investment model, why is volunteer value treated as both an incoming and outgoing resource? Do you agree with this approach?
6. What was the rationale for including the Computer Training Center's outgoing expenses as a benefit to the community? Do you agree with this approach?
7. How were the primary outputs calculated for the Computer Training Center? Do you agree or disagree with this method of calculation? Can you suggest improvements?

8. For social programs, how would you calculate indirect effects such as increased self-esteem, reduced stress from employment, increased purchasing power, improved lifestyle, or improved health?
9. What are the contributions and limitations of the Community Return on Investment model?
10. What are the risks and benefits of using a social return on investment approach with nonprofits? In your view, can the risks be overcome?

NOTES

[1] Computer Training Center is a pseudonym.

[2] The resulting reports are available through the Roberts Foundation's Web site (see www.redf.org).

[3] Social labor refers to the unpaid contributions of members to either a nonprofit mutual association or a cooperative.

[4] John and all subsequent names in this section are pseudonyms.

Chapter 5

Socioeconomic Impact and Resource Statements: Junior Achievement of Rochester

This chapter presents two new accounting statements—the Socioeconomic Impact Statement and the Socioeconomic Resource Statement. The first is analogous to an income statement and the second to a balance sheet. However, they differ from their conventional counterparts because not only do they use economic data typically found in such statements but also they include social information—hence, the name "socioeconomic." The Socioeconomic Impact Statement and the Socioeconomic Resource Statement can be used by different types of organizations including nonprofits, cooperatives, public sector agencies, and profit-oriented businesses.

The Socioeconomic Impact Statement and Socioeconomic Resource Statement were developed as part of a study of a nonprofit organization, Junior Achievement of Rochester, New York Area, Inc. Building on this research, a second case study is presented that considers environmental impacts using the Socioeconomic Impact Statement. This case study adapts the results of research undertaken by Shoup (1997), which looked at the benefits resulting from the changes in commuting habits of employees in California who were offered a choice between free parking and an equivalent cash allowance.

The statements in this chapter present a more complete story of an organization's performance than do conventional financial statements and embrace a much wider group of stakeholders. For example, they show the impact of volunteer contributions and, thus, reflect more accurately the value of the organization's goods and services as well as the resources owned by the organization to produce future value. The interconnections between all sectors of society—namely, the social economy, the private sector, and the public sector—are also demonstrated in these statements.

JUNIOR ACHIEVEMENT OF ROCHESTER

Junior Achievement is the oldest and largest economic education organization in the world. It was started in 1919 as small, after-school business clubs focusing on workforce preparation and entrepreneurship. Today, Junior Achievement operates in more than 100 countries, with over 213,000 volunteers and 2,700 paid staff. Through its 34 different programs, it reaches 7 million students per year from kindergarten to grade 12 (Junior Achievement 2006). Junior Achievement of Rochester has been in existence since 1968. It operates as a franchise of Junior Achievement, Inc. and runs 640 programs yearly in 65 elementary, middle, and high schools. Volunteer hours reported by the organization for the fiscal year ending June 30, 2001, amounted to just over 12,000 for over 900 volunteer placements. The full-time equivalent (FTE) of these hours is 5.77, or a bit more than the 5.5 paid staff. These contributions of volunteer services are not recorded in the conventional accounting statements because they do not meet the very specific requirements of the Financial Accounting Standards Board (FASB), Statement of Financial Accounting Standards No. 116 (Financial Accounting Standards Board 1993)—see Chapter 1. However, as will be seen, when included in the statements presented in this chapter, these contributions are significant.

Many of Junior Achievement of Rochester's volunteers can be considered "corporate volunteers"—that is, their employer encourages them to volunteer, even during their work hours. This raises an interesting issue as to whether persons who are encouraged by their employers and who provide the service during their normal hours of work satisfy the criteria for volunteering. In an important conceptual paper on this issue, Cnaan, Handy, and Wadsworth (1996) suggest that four dimensions determine the public's perception of a volunteer—free choice, a lack of remuneration, whether the contribution is to a formal organization, and whether the beneficiaries are strangers. Cnaan et al. propose further that the "net cost" to the volunteer is a critical factor in the public's perception, a point that was confirmed in a follow-up study (Handy et al. 2000). However, both of these studies emphasize that rather than perceiving volunteering as an either/or phenomenon, it would be best to conceptualize it on a "continuum ranging from pure to broad volunteering" (Cnaan et al. 1996, 381). While corporate volunteering might not fit the purest end of the continuum, it nevertheless fits many of the criteria. Employees may feel pressured to participate in corporate volunteering programs, but for any form of volunteering there is probably some form of benefit to the participants. This has led some economists to be skeptical as to whether there is a pure form of volunteering (Andreoni 1990; Bilodeau and Slivinski 1996; Freeman 1997; Thompson and Bono 1993; Vaillancourt 1994).

For most of the volunteers of Junior Achievement of Rochester who were participating in a corporate program while volunteering for the organization, their employer paid their wages. However, over 92 percent of the respondents to our survey indicated that they were still responsible for their work duties and did not get paid extra for completing them. In other words, these Junior Achievement volunteers were making an important contribution to a formal organization and to beneficiaries who were neither friends nor family, and technically speaking, they were not being remunerated for their service. Thus, we believe that the corporate volunteers for Junior Achievement of Rochester satisfy the criteria for volunteering and, in fact, make an important contribution to that organization and the schools that it serves.

In order to include volunteer contributions on social accounting statements, a comparative market value is assigned to them. Although differing techniques are used to estimate the comparative market value of volunteer contributions (see Chapter 3), in this case we have estimated the value according to the skills associated with the task. To that end, we have applied the U.S. Department of Labor, Bureau of Labor Statistics hourly wage rates for July 2000, from the National Compensation Survey.[1] Then 12 percent was added for fringe benefits, as suggested by the Independent Sector (2006) as appropriate for volunteer contributions in the United States.[2] Using U.S. Department of Labor, Bureau of Labor Statistics, the rates assigned to volunteer tasks at Junior Achievement were:

➢ board of directors—the $31.30 hourly wage rate for "executives, administrators and managers";
➢ company coordinators—the $26.85 hourly wage rate for "managers in service organizations, not elsewhere classified";
➢ teachers of the Junior Achievement curricula—the $25.86 hourly rate for "teachers, not elsewhere classified"; and
➢ special event volunteers—the $12.22 hourly rate for "administrative support occupations," not elsewhere classified.

Table 5.1 presents a task breakdown for volunteers in Junior Achievement of Rochester, the hours contributed by volunteers for each task, and the equivalent dollar values. Using these rates, the total value of volunteer hours was estimated to be $345,606.

Table 5.1 Volunteer Hours Contributed for the Year Ended June 30, 2001
Junior Achievement of Rochester, New York Area, Inc.

	Number of Volunteer Placements	Number of Hours	Average Hours per Volunteer	FTE	Rate	Value
Elementary school consultants	736	8,832	12	4.25	$25.86	$228,396
Middle school consultants	33	726	22	0.35	25.86	18,774
High school consultants	4	140	35	0.07	25.86	3,620
Company coordinators	45	990	22	0.48	26.85	26,582
Special events	75	525	7	0.25	12.22	6,416
Governance	36	792	22	0.38	31.30	24,790
Subtotal	929	12,005	12.92	5.77	$25.70	308,577
Fringe benefits (12%)						37,029
Total						$345,606

Sources: Number of volunteers and hours: staff.
Rates: U.S. Department of Labor, Bureau of Labor Statistics.[3]

In addition, for the fiscal year, volunteers absorbed $12,530 in out-of-pocket expenses (not reimbursed) that were related to these tasks at Junior Achievement. These contributions were for items such as travel, parking, and supplies. This amount was calculated from survey responses, which indicated that, during the year, 60 percent of Junior Achievement of Rochester board of director volunteers paid $76.66 on average from their own pockets without asking for reimbursement. In addition, 56 percent of the remaining volunteers paid $32.22 from their own pockets. Based on a total of 636 volunteers (not including special-event volunteers), this amounted to $12,530 (Table 5.2).

Table 5.2 Volunteer Out-of-Pocket Expenses Contributed
Junior Achievement of Rochester, New York Area, Inc.

	Number of Volunteers	% with Expenses	Per Volunteer Expenses	Totals
Board of directors	36	60	$76.66	$1,656
Other volunteers	600	56	32.22	10,874
Total	**636**			**$12,530**

Sources: Number of volunteers: staff estimate. Percentage of volunteers with expenses and amount per volunteer: OISE/UT 2002 Volunteer Value Added Survey.

THE SOCIOECONOMIC IMPACT STATEMENT

Much like an income statement or Statement of Operations, the Socioeconomic Impact Statement looks at the operating results of the organization for the fiscal year. However, instead of focusing on the bottom line (the net income that the organization realizes after expenses are subtracted from revenues), the Socioeconomic Impact Statement highlights the flow of monetary and social resources to and from stakeholders. The inclusion of social resources differentiates this statement from a conventional income statement.

The Socioeconomic Impact Statement builds on models proposed in the 1970s, including Linowes (1972) Socio-Economic Operating Statement and Estes (1976) Social Impact Statement. Other influences were the Social Income Statements proposed by Seidler (1973) and slightly modified for a university by Belkaoui (1984). Abt and Associates (1974) produced a Social and Financial Income Statement that broke down benefits and costs by stakeholders—company/stockholders, staff, clients/general public, and community. Focusing more specifically on human resources, Flamholtz (1974, 1985, 1999) proposed models for human resource accounting.

As shown in Table 5.3, the Socioeconomic Impact Statement is presented around stakeholders that are organized within three sub-sectors of society—social economy, private sector, and public sector (see Chapter 2). These sub-sectors can be viewed as organizers for presenting information—for each sub-sector, the flow of resources to and from related stakeholders is shown. The breakdown of stakeholders by sub-sector is:

➢ social economy—employees, volunteers, donors, other nonprofit and cooperative organizations;
➢ private sector—suppliers, banks, and other profit-oriented businesses; and
➢ public sector—public school system, public health care organizations, and the different levels of government.

The flow of resources to and from stakeholders is organized within three categories:

➢ inflows—resources flowing to a particular stakeholder;
➢ outflows—resources flowing from a particular stakeholder; and
➢ net inflow/outflow—the difference between the amount that flows in and the amount that flows out.

In order to put together a Socioeconomic Impact Statement, two sources of information are needed. First, and most straightforward, is the information from the organization's audited financial accounts.[4] Second, non-monetary items must be determined—for example, volunteer hours and personal benefits received by volunteers as a result of volunteering (see Chapter 8 for more detail on how to gather this information). From the non-monetary information, a comparative market value is created, as illustrated in Table 5.1. As a market equivalent for many services and goods furnished by nonprofits is difficult to establish, the alternative is to use the cost to the organization of those services and goods—in other words, the total of financial expenses and social inputs.

Socioeconomic Impact Statement: Junior Achievement of Rochester

Table 5.3 presents the Socioeconomic Impact Statement for Junior Achievement of Rochester for the fiscal year ending June 30, 2001. The table presentation breaks down the inflows, outflows, and net amounts by items associated with each stakeholder. The inflows and outflows are presented from the perspective of the stakeholder. To take an example, the estimated market value of volunteers is treated as an outflow from the volunteers and an inflow to the public school system. The amounts are the same, but volunteers make available this service through Junior Achievement to the public schools. It flows from the stakeholder volunteer to the stakeholder public schools.

Impact on the Social Economy

Under the social economy, the following stakeholders are considered: employees, other nonprofits, volunteers, and donors.

Employees

Inflows to employees consisted of the payments for salaries ($245,537) and benefits ($59,339) totaling $304,876. In exchange, employees furnished labor to Junior Achievement of Rochester valued at the same rate. Therefore, $304,876 appears as both an inflow and outflow, with a net of zero. Employees also paid federal and state taxes (estimated at $26,518 and $12,277, respectively) and received benefits of public services. A complete analysis of the use of public goods by the employees of Junior Achievement of Rochester was beyond the scope of this study—for illustration purposes, the assumption is made that the employees received the same value of services from paying taxes (an inflow to the social economy) as the amount of the taxes paid (an outflow).

Other Nonprofits and Cooperatives

The national office of Junior Achievement, of which Junior Achievement of Rochester is a franchise, was paid $32,576 as a fee for use of the name and $41,411 for materials used in programming. These amounts are represented as an inflow to the national office and also an outflow to the franchise, as shown by the $73,987 total. The net of the amounts is also zero.

Volunteers

Volunteers contributed both labor and out-of-pocket expenses to Junior Achievement of Rochester. The value of their labor was estimated to be $345,606 (see Table 5.1), while their non-reimbursed out-of-pocket expenses totaled $12,530 (see Table 5.2). These volunteer contributions, totaling $358,136, are treated as an outflow from volunteers and as inflow to the public school system.

Donors

For Junior Achievement of Rochester, various donors contributed cash and non-monetary items (such as office equipment, services, and materials) totaling $627,223. These amounts are treated as an outflow from the donors and also appear as a net outflow because the donors do not receive anything in return. As with volunteer labor, these donations flow into the public school system.

Table 5.3 Socioeconomic Impact Statement for the Year Ended June 30, 2001
Junior Achievement of Rochester, New York Area, Inc.

	Inflows	Outflows	Net Inflows (Outflows)
I. IMPACT ON THE SOCIAL ECONOMY			
EMPLOYEES			
Salaries and benefits	$304,876		
Labor provided		$304,876	
Federal taxes	32,927	32,927	
State taxes	15,244	15,244	0
OTHER NONPROFITS (JA, INC)			
Payment for franchise fees	32,576		
Payment for materials	41,411		
Materials and expertise provided		73,987	0
VOLUNTEERS			
Labor provided		345,606	
Out-of-pocket expenses provided		12,530	(358,136)
DONORS			
Individuals: cash		425,390	
Individuals: nonmonetary donations		61,058	
Foundations		42,012	
Other		98,763	(627,223)
	427,033	1,412,392	(985,359)
II. IMPACT ON THE PRIVATE SECTOR			
SUPPLIES PROVIDED			
Payments received	$232,376		
Supplies provided		$232,376	0
BANKS			
Interest paid	180		
Interest received		6,202	
Benefit from deposits		180	
Risk from monies lent	6,202		0
	238,758	238,758	0
III. IMPACT ON THE PUBLIC SECTOR			
PUBLIC SCHOOL SYSTEM			
Programs delivered in schools	988,469	0	988,469
FEDERAL GOVERNMENT			
Payroll taxes	32,927		
Services provided		32,927	
STATE GOVERNMENT			
Payroll taxes	15,244		
Services provided		15,244	
	1,036,639	48,170	988,469
Totals-Net inflows (outflows) from organization	$1,654,260	$1,651,150	$3,110

Impact on the Private Sector

Under the private sector, the stakeholders are suppliers and banks.

Suppliers

For the fiscal year, private sector suppliers provided Junior Achievement of Rochester with $232,376 of goods and services, for which they received payments for the same amount. Therefore, these amounts are both inflows (goods and services) and outflows (cash)—with a net of zero since the goods and services and cash payments are equivalent.

Banks

The bank earned $6,202 of interest on loans (an inflow) and paid out $180 of interest on deposits kept by Junior Achievement of Rochester (an outflow). In exchange, the bank supplied services equal to the same amounts. Therefore, for the stakeholder banks, both of these amounts appear as inflows and outflows and the net is zero.

Impact on the Public Sector

As public sector stakeholders, the statement includes the public school system and federal and state governments.

Public School System

The public school system received programming inflows made available to its students by Junior Achievement of Rochester. Over 780 programs, estimated to have a value of $988,469 (shown as an inflow), served almost 17,000 students. Since these programs were supplied without charge, their market value was estimated from the amounts that Junior Achievement of Rochester spent on them. Therefore, $988,469 value was derived from the monetary and social contributions to Junior Achievement of Rochester in order to run the programs—$627,223 from donors; $358,136 as the estimated market value of volunteer contributions; and an additional $3,110 increase in the organization's net liabilities. The total of these three items, $988,469, also appears as a net outflow from Junior Achievement.

State and Federal Governments

For tax year 2001, New York had a graduated income tax, with rates ranging between 4 and 6.85 percent of taxable income, while federal income tax ranged from 15 to 39.1 percent (Internal Revenue Service 2001; New York State Office of Tax Policy Analysis 2002). As noted earlier, the amounts paid by employees for both these taxes (estimated to be $26,518 federally and $12,277 state) are shown as an outflow from the stakeholder employees and an inflow to the state and federal governments. Likewise, the public sector services funded by tax payments are considered an outflow from that stakeholder. As mentioned, it is assumed that the value of services for the taxpayer is equivalent to the amount of the taxes paid.

Surplus (Deficit)

Overall, the net effect of this resource exchange was a net inflow into society of $3,110 from Junior Achievement of Rochester, resulting in an organizational deficit of $3,110. This amount increased Junior Achievement of Rochester's accumulated net liabilities to $90,669.

Discussion

The Socioeconomic Impact Statement arrives at the same deficit of $3,110 as the more conventional Statement of Activities done for Junior Achievement of Rochester. However, the Socioeconomic Impact Statement presents a much different picture of the organization. As shown in Table 5.4, the Statement of Activities illustrates that the organization's expenses for the year outnumbered its revenues by $3,110, and it also gives a breakdown of revenues and expenditures. However, this statement gives no idea of the value that Junior Achievement of Rochester created during the fiscal year, including the value that its many volunteers added to delivering its programs, raising funds, and participating in its governance.

Table 5.4 Statement of Activities and Changes in Net Liabilities
Junior Achievement of Rochester, New York Area, Inc.

For the Year Ended June 30, 2001	2001	2000
Unrestricted net liabilities		
Public Support and Revenue		
Contributions–Operating and project business	$377,658	$345,771
Contributions–Property and equipment	1,000	30,637
Interest	180	330
Special events (net of related expenses,	78,510	49,395
2001– $170,057, 2000– $168,484)	457,348	426,133
Expenses		
Program	388,451	400,574
Fund raising	30,439	39,935
Administrative	41,567	52,672
Contributions Operating and project business	460,457	493,181
Change in unrestricted net (liabilities)	(3,109)	(67,048)
Net (liabilities), beginning	(87,560)	(20,512)
Net (liabilities), ending	($90,669)	($87,560)

Source: Audited financial statements, 2001, p. 3.

By comparison, the Socioeconomic Impact Statement illustrates the impact of the organization on its key stakeholders and also indicates how the organization interacts economically and socially with all sub-sectors of society (Figure 5.1). It includes monetary and non-monetary items to end up with a more complete performance story.

As the figure indicates, there is a large inflow from Junior Achievement of Rochester to the public schools, and this inflow is achieved primarily because of the outflow from donors and volunteers. The Socioeconomic Impact Statement graphically illustrates this transfer whereas the Statement of Activities, or any conventional income statement, would not. For a nonprofit like Junior Achievement, not including the pattern of inflows and outflows misses the essence of the organization's contribution to society. This same point is illustrated next in the Socioeconomic Impact Statement of California commuters, which highlights the impact upon the environment.

Figure 5.1 Socioeconomic Impact Statement: Inflows and Outflows by Key Stakeholder Groups
Junior Achievement of Rochester, New York Area, Inc.

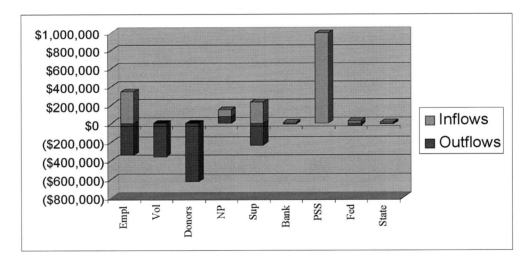

Legend: Empl=Employees; Vol=Volunteers; NP=Nonprofit organizations; Sup=Suppliers; PSS=Public school system; Fed=Federal government; State=State government

CALIFORNIA COMMUTERS

The Socioeconomic Impact Statement presented in Table 5.3 focused on community involvement, the use of human resources, and economic performance. To illustrate an organization's impact on the environment, data are adapted from research by Shoup (1997) on an innovative California program designed to reduce pollution. In California, since 1992, the law requires that employers of 50 or more persons in regions that do not meet the state's clean-air standards must offer commuters a choice between free parking or its equivalent cash value (referred to as "cashing out"). In order to study the impact of this policy, Shoup (1997) researched eight firms in the Los Angeles area that offered this employee benefit.

The importance of the cashing-out policy is underlined by data showing that in the United States, 91 percent of all commuters drive to work and 92 percent of all cars driven to work have only one occupant. Of those who drive to work, 95 percent are given free parking, amounting to 85 million free parking spaces. Even in the largest cities, free parking is granted to the majority of motorists—53 percent in Los Angeles and 54 percent in Manhattan (studies quoted in Shoup 1997).

Interestingly, when employees were given a choice between either subsidized parking or an equivalent amount of cash, a significant number of solo drivers took the cash equivalent necessitating their use of more environmentally friendly modes of transportation to work—for example, carpooling, public transit, walking, or bicycling. In a study of eight firms with a total of 1,694 employees, Shoup (1997) found that the parking cashing-out program reduced the number of solo drivers by 17 percent, or 220 drivers. Overall vehicle travel to work for these eight firms was reduced by 12 percent—for every 100 cars originally commuting to work, 12 were removed from the road. This reduction in the number of vehicles traveling to work led to an average decrease of 652 miles per year (1,052 kilometers per year) in the number of vehicle miles traveled per employee and an average decrease in gasoline consumption of 26 U.S. gallons (99 liters) per year.[5] Thus, fewer cars on the road and the related decrease in vehicle miles traveled per employee led to less traffic congestion and less vehicle emissions.

The reduction in gasoline use was calculated as the average decrease in vehicle miles traveled per employee per year divided by the average number of miles per gallon for light-duty passenger vehicles.[6] Once the reduction in gasoline consumption per employee was determined, a value for emissions reduction was calculated—estimated by Shoup to be 5.2 cents per mile (3.2 cents per kilometer) based on the "maximum allowed control cost of proposed emission-reduction measures" (Shoup 1997, 209).[7] In addition, Shoup estimated the cost of congestion to be 10 cents per vehicle mile traveled. His estimate was based on a study by Cameron (1991), who calculated that these costs for Los Angeles ranged from 10 cents to 37 cents per vehicle mile traveled.

Using the results and cost information found in Shoup's study, an organization could report its impact on the environment in the Socioeconomic Impact Statement, as shown in Table 5.5 (numbers shown are based on per employee per year figures). The impact on traffic congestion of the reduction of the 652 vehicle miles traveled was estimated by multiplying 652 by 10 cents, or $65.20. The reduction in emissions was estimated at $33.96 (652 vehicle miles traveled multiplied by 5.2 cents/mile). As tax-exempt parking subsidies were exchanged for taxable cash, federal and state tax revenues were increased by $65 per employee per year. Employees also reduced gasoline consumption on average by 26 U.S. gallons per year, which at $1.26 per gallon[8] amounted to $32.76.

Table 5.5 adapts the Shoup data and presents the Socioeconomic Impact Statement for an organization. As with the preceding presentation for Junior Achievement of Rochester, the inflows, outflows, and net impact are associated with stakeholders. The employees experience an inflow of $32.76 from their reduced gasoline costs and an outflow of $65 from increased taxes resulting from the cash bonus they receive for changing their driving habits.

Suppliers experience a decrease in gasoline sales of $32.76 as a result of reduced purchases by employees who have cashed out. The impact on government is increased federal taxes of $48 and state taxes of $17 (the breakdown of the $65 additional taxes). For each employee, the state government also receives a $65.20 benefit for reduced congestion and $33.96 benefit for reduced emissions, both resulting from 652 fewer vehicle miles traveled in a year.

In total, the net social profit was $99.16 from totaling the net impacts on society as a result of this program. Bear in mind, however, that this presentation is based on one employee only. If it were based on an organization with 1,000 employees, the net impact would be almost $100,000.

Table 5.5 Socioeconomic Impact Statement
Impact of Organization on Environment
California Commuters

	Inflows	Outflows	Net Impact
I. IMPACT ON THE SOCIAL ECONOMY			
EMPLOYEES			
Increased taxes		$65.00	
Reduced gasoline costs	$32.76		
	32.76	65.00	(32.24)
II. IMPACT ON THE PRIVATE SECTOR			
SUPPLIERS			
Decrease in gasoline sales		32.76	
	0.00	32.76	(32.76)
III. IMPACT ON THE PUBLIC SECTOR			
FEDERAL GOVERNMENT			
Federal income taxes	48.00		
STATE GOVERNMENT			
State income taxes	17.00		
Savings in reducing congestion	65.20		
Savings in reducing emissions	33.96		
	164.16	0.00	164.16
Total– Net social profit			$99.16

THE SOCIOECONOMIC RESOURCE STATEMENT

Whereas the Socioeconomic Impact Statement is analogous to an income statement, the Socioeconomic Resource Statement is analogous to a balance sheet, but it too combines the social and the economic. The balance sheet examines the equilibrium between an organization's assets, liabilities, and equity. The basic equation is assets minus liabilities equals equity.

Although the balance sheet, like other conventional accounting statements, tends not to include social information, attempts have been made to do this. One of the earliest ideas for a combined social and economic balance sheet came from Abt and Associates, Inc. (1974), who produced a Social and Financial Balance Sheet that analyzed assets and liabilities in relation to stakeholders such as staff, organization, stockholders, and the public. The Socioeconomic Resource Statement presented in this chapter is inspired by Abt's pioneering initiative but, as will be seen, moves this work in a somewhat different direction.

The Socioeconomic Resource Statement shows the resources and obligations of an organization at a certain point in time. It consists of the three main elements of a balance sheet, albeit renamed to fit the redefined context. These elements become resources (assets), obligations (liabilities), and net resources/obligations (equity—that is, assets less liabilities). It also differs from a balance sheet in that, in addition to reporting economic capital and obligations, it also reports an intangible asset known as intellectual capital.

Capital

Capital is a term associated with the creation of wealth—most commonly, tangible economic items such as financial and physical capital. More recently, it has been used with intangible items that are knowledge based and referred to as "intellectual capital" (Figure 5.2).

Intellectual Capital

Intellectual capital is an umbrella term that includes three different forms of knowledge-based capital—human, organizational, and relational (Dzinkowski 1998). In this regard:

➤ **human capital** consists of the know-how, capabilities, skills, and expertise of an organization's employees and volunteers;
➤ **organizational capital** refers to items within the organization such as its culture, management philosophy, information systems, copyrights, and patents; and
➤ **relational capital** refers to items outside of the organization, including client loyalty, distribution channels, perceptions due to brands, and relations with clients, suppliers, and the local community.

Although intellectual capital is used most often in relation to profit-oriented businesses, it is just as relevant to organizations in the social economy.

The impetus for much of the discussion around intellectual capital has come from the rise of the "knowledge economy" where employee know-how, skills, and innovative capabilities play a leading role in an organization's success and competitive advantage. It is estimated that as much as 50 to 90 percent of the value created by a profit-oriented business today comes from the management of intellectual capital, not physical and financial capital (Hope and Hope 1997). In other words, physical and financial capital only account for 10 to 50 percent of the value created by these organizations. In the social economy, similar percentages of unreported value can be found (see Chapter 7).

Building on insights from the intellectual capital literature (see, for instance, Dzinkowski 1998; Guthrie, Petty, and Johanson 2001; Roslender and Fincham 2001; Seetharaman, Soori, and Saravanan 2002), the Socioeconomic Resource Statement reports the resources the organization has available to create value in the future. This statement includes the items on the organization's balance sheet (economic and physical capital), as well as several new components—human capital, organizational capital, and relational capital. The obligations of the organization are subtracted from its total available resources, and the result is either a net resource position or a net obligations position for both intellectual and economic capital. These amounts are reported separately to give a fuller picture of the organization's resources and to indicate clearly from where they are derived.

Figure 5.2 Value Creating Resources of an Organization

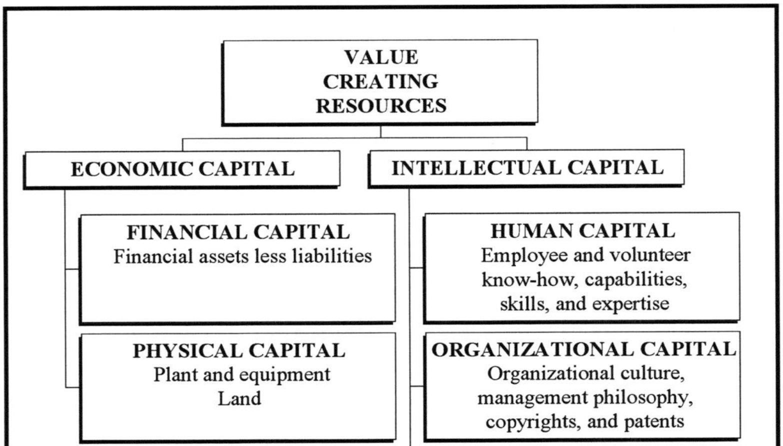

Junior Achievement of Rochester

Table 5.6 presents the Socioeconomic Resource Statement for Junior Achievement of Rochester for June 30, 2001. For that date, it shows the resources—"intellectual" and "economic"—available to produce future value. These resources are adjusted for the obligations or liabilities of the organization, and the result is a net asset position for intellectual capital and a net liability position for economic capital. As this was the first year of the study, the value of intellectual capital for the previous year was not available. However, in subsequent years, the previous year's figures should be shown so that the change in each of these items can be measured and analyzed.

Resources Available

This section of the Socioeconomic Resource Statement shows the value of the various categories of capital available to produce future services by Junior Achievement of Rochester. The following presentation will go through each category in Table 5.6, discussing how the associated amounts are derived. Intellectual capital will be dealt with first and followed by economic capital.

Intellectual Capital

As noted previously, under intellectual capital, three items are shown: human capital (the skills and know-how of employees and volunteers); organizational capital (the knowledge and expertise embedded in the Junior Achievement brand); and relational capital (the value of relationships with the schools that Junior Achievement of Rochester serves).

Human Capital

Human capital consists of two items—employee resources and volunteer resources. From this perspective, human resources are considered revenue generators rather than costs of production (Dzinkowski 1998). The estimate of Junior Achievement of Rochester's human resources available to create value in the coming year was based on the amount paid to its employees in salaries and benefits and the comparative market value of its unpaid volunteer labor for the previous year. This estimate assumed that the level of staffing and programming in the coming year would be similar to the previous year. Therefore, as in the Socioeconomic Impact Statement (previously), this amounted to $304,876 for paid employees and to $358,136 for volunteers.

For this particular illustration, comparative information from the previous year was not used. If it were available, the analysis would attempt to understand the reasons for any change in the organization's capital. For employees, the ability of the organization to be more productive could have been influential, as could societal changes in the cost of living. For volunteers, there was an additional factor—the ability of the organization to mobilize more volunteers and, thus, offer more programs.

Table 5.6 The Socioeconomic Resource Statement
Junior Achievement of Rochester, New York Area, Inc.

As of June 30, 2001	Intellectual	Economic
Resources Available		
Human Resources		
Employees	$304,876	
Volunteers	358,136	
Organizational		
Junior Achievement brand	32,576	
Relational		
Schools	239,850	
Current Assets		
Bank		$4,356
Petty cash		150
Pledges receivable		108,936
Prepaid expenses		1,209
Property and Equipment		
Office equipment		16,041
Furniture and fixtures		1,751
Total Resources	935,438	132,443
Obligations		
Financial		
Accounts payable		84,468
Accrued expenses		15,765
Refundable advance		
Note payable–Officer		
Note payable–Bank		13,591
Due to Junior Achievement, Inc.		109,288
Human		
Employees	304,876	
Organizational		
Junior Achievement brand	32,576	
Total obligations	337,452	223,112
Net Assets (Liabilities)	$597,986	($90,669)

The impact of Junior Achievement of Rochester in mobilizing volunteers and increasing their productivity is shown in Table 5.7. The total hours estimated for 2001 were 12,005, resulting in an average contribution of 12.92 hours for each of the 929 activities performed by the core group of 636 volunteers. Estimates for the previous year show a total of 11,351 hours for 834 activities performed by 562 core volunteers, for an average of 13.61 hours per volunteer activity (Table 5.8). Thus, in this example, Junior Achievement of Rochester increased its volunteer base by 74 volunteers and the total number of hours volunteered by 654. Volunteers in the previous year also contributed on average approximately 40 minutes more, as there were more programs delivered in middle schools and high schools in that year. As a result, the comparative market value of volunteer hours contributed increased in total by $27,611 over the previous year. It was estimated that 71 percent of the change in the volunteer contribution was due to Junior Achievement of Rochester's increased recruitment and 29 percent of the change was a societal influence—an increase in the hourly rate used as a comparative wage for volunteers.

Table 5.7 Changes in the Value of Volunteer Hours
Junior Achievement of Rochester, New York Area, Inc.

Year	Number of Volunteer Placements	Number of Hours	Hours per Volunteer	FTE	Avgerage Rate*	Value
2001	929	12,005	12.92	5.77	$29.83	$358,136
2000	834	11,351	13.61	5.46	29.12	330,525
Change	95	654	-0.69	0.31	$0.71	27,611
Change due to increase of hourly rates					29.34%	8,100
Change due to increase of hours					70.66%	19,510
Total Change						$27,611

* Including fringe benefits.

Table 5.8 Volunteer Hours Contributed for the Year Ended June 30, 2000
Junior Achievement of Rochester, New York Area, Inc.

	Number of Volunteer Placements	Number of Hours	Hours per Volunteer	FTE	Avgerage Rate	Value
Elementary school consultants	621	7,452	12	3.58	$26.19	$195,168
Middle school consultants	31	682	22	0.33	26.19	17,862
High school consultants	26	910	35	0.44	26.19	23,833
Company coordinators	45	990	22	0.48	28.06	27,779
Special events	75	525	7	0.25	11.74	6,164
Governance	36	792	22	0.38	30.69	24,306
Subtotal	834	11,351	13.61	5.46	26.00	295,112
Fringe benefits (12%)						35,413
Total including fringe benefits					$29.12	$330,525

Organizational Capital

The item in this category is the value of using the name Junior Achievement—as a benefit of being a franchise of Junior Achievement, Inc. and the expertise that goes into the copyrighted materials. This value is estimated to be the amount of franchise fees paid in the previous year ($32,576).

Relational Capital

In this example, relational capital refers to the value of the relationships set up with each of the 60 schools in which Junior Achievement of Rochester operates its programs. These relationships were estimated to take approximately 150 hours to set up, consisting of multiple meetings over a three- to six-month period. The value is estimated at almost $4,000 per school, based on the approximate cost of the hours involved in setting up such relationships. Using an hourly rate based on the amount of wages and benefits paid to Junior Achievement of Rochester employees, this amounts to 60 schools × 150 hours × $26.65, for a total of $239,850.

Economic Capital

Financial Capital

On the economic side, the information is taken from the organization's audited balance sheet. Current assets include cash and those items that could be turned into cash within a period of one year. For Junior Achievement of Rochester, these were money in the bank ($4,356), petty cash ($150), pledges receivable ($108,936), and prepaid expenses ($420). Pledges receivable are recognized when the donor makes to the organization a commitment that is unconditional and is considered to be fully collectible. If the pledge becomes uncollectible, it is charged to operations at the time when that determination is made.

Physical Capital

Property and equipment are tangible assets that are either purchased by or donated to the organization. Normally, the original cost or value of these assets is expensed over their estimated useful life. This is called depreciation or amortization—the process of matching the cost of an asset against revenues.[9] Thus, as outlined in the Notes to Financial Statements: "The preparation of financial statements in conformity with generally accepted accounting principles (GAAP) requires management to make estimates and assumptions that affect certain reported amounts and disclosures. Accordingly, actual results could differ from those estimates" (Junior Achievement of Rochester 2001, 7).

At the beginning of the fiscal period, Junior Achievement of Rochester's office equipment was valued at $27,322.95.[10] During the fiscal period, an additional $1,000 of office equipment was donated to the organization (a social contribution), bringing the total to $28,322.95. However, the office equipment was also used and, therefore, depreciated by $12,282.00. Thus, at the end of the period, the value of office equipment available for use in subsequent years was $16,040.95.

Similarly, Junior Achievement of Rochester also had furniture and fixtures, with a book value of $2,541.13, available to be used at the beginning of the period.[11] The estimated use of these assets during the period was $790.22, leaving a resource valued at $1,750.91 available for use in the next fiscal period.

Obligations

After arriving at the total resources available under the intellectual and economic columns, the organization's obligations are calculated, as shown in the second part of the Socioeconomic Resource Statement. As for resources available, these are estimated separately under the categories intellectual and economic.

Intellectual Capital

Human Capital

The primary obligation of Junior Achievement of Rochester is $304,876 for salaries and benefits for employees. This is payment for the skills and know-how that they will be providing over the next year to create value.

Organizational Capital

The amount shown here, $32,576, is the estimated cost of franchise fees that Junior Achievement of Rochester will have to pay to its national office in order to use the name Junior Achievement and to adopt its copyrighted materials. This amount assumes that donations to the organization, on which the fees are based, will remain the same.

Economic Capital

Financial Capital

In carrying out its activities, Junior Achievement of Rochester incurred certain obligations that would have to be covered in subsequent years. These included:

➢ obligations to suppliers (accounts payable $84,468);
➢ accrued expenses ($15,765) broken down as follows: to employees (salaries payable $2,313); to the government (employee taxes and benefits payable $2,558); and accrued franchise fees ($10,894);
➢ to the bank (note payable $13,591); and
➢ to the head office of Junior Achievement, Inc. ($109,288).

The total of these obligations at the end of the period was $223,112.

Net Resources (Obligations)

The Socioeconomic Resource Statement presents Junior Achievement's net balance for intellectual and economic capital separately. For economic capital, the statement shows a net obligations balance of ($90,669). For intellectual capital, however, it is a different story—Junior Achievement of Rochester had a net resource balance on June 30, 2001, of $597,986 (an amount that does not appear on the balance sheet).

DISCUSSION

As shown in Table 5.6, the Socioeconomic Resource Statement presents a more complete story of the resources that Junior Achievement of Rochester has available to create future value than does its Statement of Financial Position (balance sheet). The Statement of Financial Position (balance sheet) shows only the financial resources that Junior Achievement of Rochester has available, without any reference to its human resources (Table 5.9). Therefore, it grossly underestimates the resources that Junior Achievement possesses when entering the next fiscal year. Table 5.9 shows that as of June 30, 2001, Junior Achievement of Rochester had a net liability balance of $90,669 (the same as in the economic column of the Socioeconomic Resource Statement).

Table 5.9 Statement of Financial Position, June 30, 2001
Junior Achievement of Rochester, New York Area, Inc.

	2001	2000
Assets		
Cash	$4,506	$60,866
Pledges Receivable	108,936	88,149
Property, net of accumulated depreciation	17,792	29,864
Prepaid expenses	1,209	420
	132,443	179,299
Liabilities and Net Assets (Liabilities)		
Accounts payable	84,468	126,967
Accrued expenses and other liabilities	15,765	36,535
Refundable advance	—	600
Note payable—Officer	—	8,750
Note payable—Bank	13,591	24,544
Due to Junior Achievement, Inc.—Currently payable	109,288	69,463
	223,112	266,859
Commitments		
Net (Liabilities)—Unrestricted	(90,669)	(87,560)
	$132,443	$179,299

Source: Audited financial statements, 2001, p. 2.

However, the Statement of Financial Position does not include the net balance in the intellectual column, shown in the Socioeconomic Resource Statement. Therefore, by including its intellectual capital, the Socioeconomic Resource Statement tells a different story of the organization. It shows that even though the organization's economic resources are in deficit, it has a sizable stock of intellectual capital available for its services. In addition to highlighting the net intellectual capital of Junior Achievement of Rochester, the Socioeconomic Resource Statement focuses attention on other intangible items—namely, the added value of the Junior Achievement name and programs and the value of its relationships with its clients.

All the examples presented in this chapter are a first attempt at applying these models and can be expanded.[12] For example, the impact of tax credits for donations could certainly be included on the Socioeconomic Impact Statement. Likewise, the impact of the loss of gasoline tax revenue from the reduction in gasoline sales could also be calculated. Nevertheless, the examples shown here represent an important step forward in recognizing the full performance story of an organization, one that is not told by conventional financial statements.

QUESTIONS FOR DISCUSSION

1. What does the Socioeconomic Impact Statement tell us about an organization that a conventional income statement does not? How can this new information help us to understand the role of nonprofits and cooperatives?
2. Provide at least three examples of environmental impacts that could be considered on a Socioeconomic Impact Statement.
3. What does the Socioeconomic Resource Statement tell us about an organization that a conventional balance sheet does not? How can this new information help us to understand the role of nonprofits and cooperatives?
4. In this chapter, the Socioeconomic Resource Statement based the value of the human capital component on the prior year's market value. Can you think of a different way to calculate human capital?
5. What items could be considered as organizational capital on the Socioeconomic Resource Statement? How could these items be valued?
6. Similarly, what items could be included as relational capital on the Socioeconomic Resource Statement? How could these items be valued?
7. Take an existing organization and construct a Socioeconomic Impact Statement and Socioeconomic Resource Statement. Compare these to the income statement and balance sheet. What new insights arise?
8. What are the contributions and limitations of the Socioeconomic Impact and Socioeconomic Resource Statements?
9. How can stakeholder input be gathered and applied in the construction of these two statements?
10. What audiences might be interested in these two statements and why?

NOTES

[1] This information available from the Web site at data.bls.gov

[2] www.independentsector.org

[3] www.bls.gov/data.

[4] The complete audited financial statements, including the Notes to Financial Statements and Independent Auditors' Report can be found as an attachment to the organization's Form 990 at www.guidestar.com.

[5] In another study of transit use in the New York City and Philadelphia areas prepared for the U.S. Federal Transit Administration (FTA), it was estimated that for every commuter who travels to work by public transit instead of driving a car, about 400 U.S. gallons of gas per year are not consumed. This information is taken from the Federal Transit Administration. 1995. TransitChek® in the New York City and Philadelphia Areas.

[6] In California, for instance, in 1996 the average miles per gallon for a light-duty passenger vehicle was 25.

[7] "If the cost per kilogram of emissions reduced by a proposed measure is less than this value, the control measure is considered to be cost effective" (Shoup 1997, 209). In another study, which looked at the cost of pollution considering only health costs, it was estimated that vehicle emissions imposed a cost of 3.3 cents per vehicle miles traveled (Small and Kazimi 1995).

[8] Based on the average cost per gallon for all grades in California for 1995 (from the U.S. Department of Energy Web site: www.eia.doe.gov.

[9] Thus, as outlined in the Notes to Financial Statements, "the preparation of financial statements in conformity with generally accepted accounting principles (GAAP) requires management to make estimates and assumptions that affect certain reported amounts and disclosures. Accordingly, actual results could differ from those estimates" (Junior Achievement of Rochester 2001, 7).

[10] The office equipment was originally valued at $52,098.99, but the depreciation accumulated from previous years of $24,776.04 was subtracted from the original value. The remaining amount is office equipment resources available to be used.

[11] This was equal to their original cost of $20,538.83 less accumulated depreciation of $17,997.71.

[12] See Laurie Mook and Jack Quarter, 2006, Accounting for the social economy: The Socioeconomic Impact Statement, *Annals of Public and Cooperative Economics* 77 (2): 247–269 for another example of the Socioeconomic Impact Statement as applied to the Jane/Finch Community and Family Centre.

Chapter 6

An Expanded Value Added Statement

In this chapter we present a Value Added Statement model for determining the economic and social value added of an organization. To construct the model, we used information from audited financial statements of a nonprofit student-housing cooperative and then added quantified social data in order to make explicit the social and economic impact of the organization. Although the model is based on a student-housing cooperative, it can be applied more generally—to other nonprofits and cooperatives, to public sector organizations, and to conventional businesses.

The Value Added Statement supplies valuable information not found in other financial statements. As Burchell, Clubb, and Hopwood (1985, 388) state: "Value added has the property of revealing (or representing) something about the social character of production, something which is occluded by traditional profit and loss accounting. Value added reveals that the wealth created in production is the consequence of the combined effort of a number of agents who together form the cooperating team." By contrast to profit, which is interpreted as the wealth created for owners or shareholders, value added represents the wealth created for a larger group of stakeholders.

Income statements that analyze the return to shareholders may be logical for a private sector firm, but they are not an ideal fit for nonprofits and cooperatives because, as stated in Chapter 2, the mission of such organizations is to fulfill a social purpose rather than to earn profits for shareholders. By comparison, the Value Added Statement assumes that an organization is based on a group of stakeholders whose combined efforts create additional value (Riahi-Belkaoui 1999). Indeed, value added is distributed in its entirety to the different stakeholders necessary to sustain an organization in accordance with its goals and values. Thus, the Value Added Statement focuses attention on the wider implications of an organization's activities beyond the profits for its shareholders, or in the case of a social organization, beyond the surplus that it generates. Value added emphasizes that the organization also employs people, contributes to societal costs through taxes, rewards investors and creditors for risking their funds, and sets aside funds to ensure that it can continue functioning in the future.

Figures 6.1 and 6.2 depict the difference between profit and value added. Figure 6.1 presents a simple graphic illustration of an income statement, which equates wealth with profit—or revenues less expenses. The expenses may include payments for such items as external goods and services, wages and benefits to employees, interest on loans, taxes, and depreciation.[1] Revenues received (in other words, the market value of the organization's outputs) are shown on the left-hand side of Figure 6.1, while the expenses and profit that correspond to those revenues are shown on the right.

Figure 6.1 A Graphic Illustration of Profit

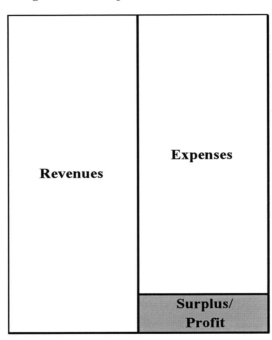

Value added, on the other hand, is a much broader definition of wealth. As can be seen in Figure 6.2, value added looks beyond the wealth (profit) created for shareholders and includes the wealth for a wider group of stakeholders such as employees, creditors, government, and the organization itself. Thus, value added can be thought of as revenues less purchases of external goods and services.

To create a Value Added Statement for a social organization such as a student-housing cooperative, the typical Value Added Statement (which we refer to as a Restricted Value Added Statement) has been adapted to include the accounting of social value that such an organization generates. The new framework is referred to as an Expanded Value Added Statement. Whereas the Restricted Value Added Statement is based on information from audited financial statements only, the Expanded Value Added Statement also includes social inputs (for example, volunteer contributions) that normally do not involve financial transactions. For these inputs to be included in a financial statement, market value comparisons are made (a point that will be dealt with in greater detail later). Therefore, the Expanded Value Added Statement builds upon (or expands) the information of a Restricted Value Added Statement and also attempts to calculate social value added by attributing a market value to non-monetized inputs such as volunteer contributions.

Figure 6.2 A Graphic Illustration of Value Added

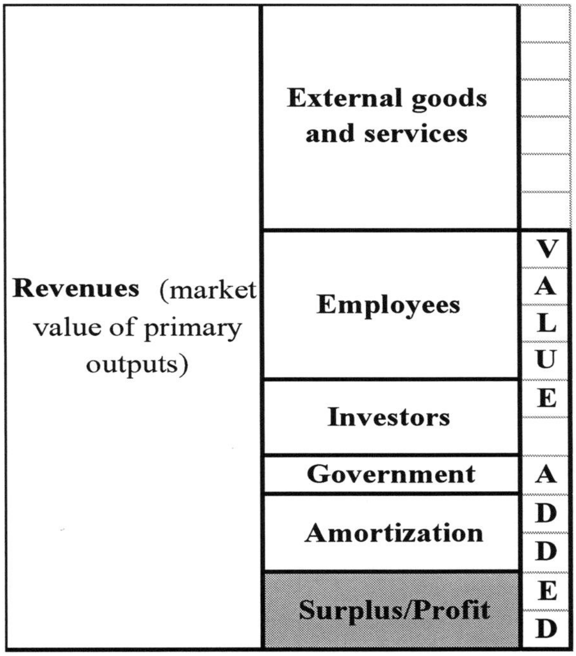

Revenues (market value of primary outputs)	External goods and services	
	Employees	V A L U
	Investors	E
	Government	A
	Amortization	D D
	Surplus/Profit	E D

WHAT IS VALUE ADDED?

Value added is a measure of wealth that an organization creates by "adding value" to raw materials, products, and services through the use of labor and capital. It is not a new concept; rather it has been used in the calculation of the gross domestic product since the turn of the twentieth century (Haller 1997). At the organizational level, it was used in the United Kingdom during the reconstruction following World War II, when cooperation between labor and capital and employee participation in decision making were seen as the keys to improving economic performance.

Value added resurfaced in the mid-1970s due to the growing power of labor, increasing recognition of consumer rights, and changing political conceptions of corporate accountability, especially with respect to the environment (Burchell et al. 1985). The renewed impetus for value added started in 1975 with the publication of

The Corporate Report by the U.K. Accounting Standards Steering Committee (Burchell et al. 1985; Haller 1997; Roslender 1992). This report (the findings of a committee that was reexamining "the scope and aims of published financial reports in the light of modern needs and conditions"), argued for a much wider view of accountability and recommended that a Value Added Statement be considered for new statutory disclosure requirements in the United Kingdom (Accounting Standards Steering Committee 1975, 48). Value-added statements became so popular in the United Kingdom that in the 1970s, one third of the largest companies included it in their corporate reports (Morley 1981, cf., Roslender 1992).

However, attention given to value added in the United Kingdom declined during the early 1980s as the political climate became more conservative. The election of Margaret Thatcher as prime minister resulted in a focus on free markets, competition, increased investment in technology, and reductions by corporations in their labor force (euphemistically referred to as "the elimination of surplus labor"). This political climate differed from the previous decade's emphasis on cooperation and participation (Burchell et al. 1985). As well, with the increase of oil prices in 1979, the related economic recession, and the focus on short-term financial results, social reporting all but disappeared until the mid-1980s. At that point, it was brought back as a result of the attention given to establishing environmental reporting standards—for example, by the Bruntland Report (UNWCED 1987).

The current wave of social reporting has also come with the recommendation by the American Accounting Association (1991) and the International Accounting Standards Committee (1996) for the inclusion of Value Added Statements in financial reporting. Although much, if not all, of the emphasis of value added reporting has been within the corporate sector, it is even more relevant to nonprofits and cooperatives because these organizations are established for a social purpose.

Typically, an organization's value added can be derived in two ways (Haller 1997). The first is called the indirect or subtractive method and is calculated as sales revenues less inputs (goods and services that are purchased externally). The second is the direct or additive method and is calculated by adding together remuneration to employees, government, and providers of capital, and those earnings retained by the enterprise through depreciation and profits. When we come to the case study of the student-housing cooperative, it will be seen that both methods are applied, and the process of deriving the value added will be explained in detail.

However, before coming to that point, a simple illustration is presented of what a typical corporate value added would look like (Table 6.1).

As shown in the table, there are two parts to the statement—the value added that is created and then its distribution to stakeholders. The first part utilizes a subtractive method in that the total of the firm's purchases of external goods and services is subtracted from its sales to arrive at the value added that is created. The second part distributes the value added to stakeholders. When the amount that is distributed to each stakeholder is added, it is equal to the value added created. As will be evident in the case study that follows, there is greater complexity to the process than is presented here; nevertheless, the example in Table 6.1 represents a simple introduction to the approach.

Table 6.1 Typical Corporate Value Added Statement

Sales		$XX
Less: Purchases of external goods and services		XX
Value Added		XX
Distributed in the following way:		
To pay employees		
Wages, pensions, and benefits		$XX
To pay providers of capital		
Interest	XX	
Dividends to shareholders	XX	XX
To pay government		XX
Taxes		
Reinvestment in the business		
Amortization of capital assets	XX	
Retained profits	XX	XX
Value Added		$XX

RATIONALE FOR AN EXPANDED VALUE ADDED STATEMENT

There are two shortcomings to the typical (or what we term Restricted) Value Added Statement. First, the restricted statement relies exclusively on financial data, which, as noted, can misrepresent the true performance of an organization. This is especially true of social organizations (nonprofits and cooperatives) that use social and volunteer labor as part of their resource base. Take, for example, a voluntary organization that mobilizes thousands of volunteer participants for a fund-raising event. First, a Restricted Value Added Statement utilizing audited financial statements only for information would not show the contribution of the volunteer participants as value added by the organization. Second, the restricted statement does not account for non-monetized indirect results of an organization's activities toward its mission. For example, a secondary output of an organization may be skills development for its volunteers through informal training. Likewise, the organization may furnish consultation services to other organizations. In order to overcome the limitations of this traditional approach, we developed an Expanded Value Added Statement that includes social variables that are normally ignored. The Expanded Value Added Statement also attributes a financial value to these social variables.

Nonprofits and cooperatives are natural choices for a Value Added Statement, as they define success in terms of more than just the bottom line. Additionally, cooperatives are guided by an explicit set of social principles—initially formulated in 1844 by the Rochdale pioneers (the founders of the first modern cooperative in England). Since then, the principles have been updated, most recently in 1995 in Manchester, England, by International Cooperative Alliance, the umbrella body for cooperatives in over 100 countries representing about 760 million members (International Co-operative Alliance 2001). These principles are:

1. open and voluntary membership (cooperatives are open to all persons willing to accept the responsibilities of membership and cannot engage in discrimination by gender or by social, racial, political, or religious criteria);

2. democratic control (cooperatives are democratic organizations controlled by their members according to the principle of one member, one vote);

3. member economic participation (members contribute equitably to financing the organization and are also the primary beneficiaries of the organization's services);

4. autonomy and independence (cooperatives are autonomous self-help organizations and must not jeopardize their independence through agreements with government or external lenders);

5. education, training, and information (cooperatives have an obligation to educate their members and employees about their organization);

6. cooperation among cooperatives (cooperatives are expected to work together, both to serve their members and to strengthen the cooperative movement); and

7. concern for the community (the obligation of cooperatives to work for sustainable development of their communities) (International Co-operative Alliance 1998).

The last principle, concern for the community, is fundamental to a value-added approach in that the community is viewed as a key stakeholder. Given the social principles that serve as their foundation, cooperatives are ideal for an Expanded Value Added Statement. Moreover, as discussed in Chapter 3, there is already a tradition in the cooperative movement in support of this type of accounting. Individual credit unions have developed social audits, and they are working together to develop protocols for future social audits (see Heritage Credit Union 1998; Metro Credit Union 1996, 1997, 1998, 2000, 2001, 2003; The Co-operative Bank 2004, 2005; VanCity 1998, 2000, 2002, 2004).

The Expanded Value Added Statement developed from our study (conducted in 1999–2000) was of the social impact of a student-housing cooperative. First, we discuss the organization that was used for the statements.

THE ORGANIZATION

Waterloo Co-operative Residence Incorporated (WCRI) supplies housing in dormitories and apartments for students of two major universities—Waterloo and Wilfrid Laurier. Its mission statement affirms that "WCRI aims to provide quality, affordable student housing, emphasizing member participation and superior service in the spirit of co-operation, while promoting pride, education, and diversity in a dynamic co-operative community" (WCRI n.d., 1). As a cooperative, WCRI is run by its members—that is, current students as well as former residents. The governance of WCRI is based on democratic and cooperative principles. Each resident becomes a member of the cooperative and is entitled to one vote at general membership meetings held each October. The general membership elects 10 directors for one-year terms, and directors may be reelected. Members can remove a director for non-performance of duties, but this is an unusual circumstance. The cooperative's democratic approach to decision making distinguishes it from other university residences.

WCRI is situated close to the main campuses of two universities and, therefore, is integrated into the surrounding university community. Nevertheless, its members still have a unique environment that includes:

➢ introduction to cooperative values and skills;
➢ participation in a democratic organization;
➢ experience in volunteer activities (both internal and external to the cooperative);
➢ leadership opportunities; and
➢ experience of teamwork.

In the Expanded Value Added Statement, these features of the cooperative experience are part of WCRI's social value added. In addition, there are a variety of services and facilities on the WCRI site that are not generally available in other university residences—such as common areas with barbecues and a large deck, as well as a customized meal-plan option.

Each resident of WCRI is required to perform social labor—that is, service to the organization that helps to reduce the housing charge. Common examples are food preparation, serving meals, dish and pot washing, common-space cleaning, snow shoveling, grounds maintenance, writing for the newsletter, participating in committees, and sitting on the board of directors. Residents may also become members of committees responsible for internal education, environmental education, and such practical issues as menu planning, conflict resolution, and special events. Again, these contributions from members are part of the value added of the organization and, therefore, are presented in the following Expanded Value Added Statement.

CREATING THE EXPANDED VALUE ADDED STATEMENT

As noted, there are two parts to a Value Added Statement: (1) the calculation of value added by an organization; and (2) its distribution to the stakeholders. For an Expanded Value Added Statement, the value added is broadened from financial transactions (that are part of the financial statements) to take into account non-monetized social contributions such as those referred to previously.

To prepare a Value Added Statement for WCRI, we needed to determine the financial and social value added. To do this, we started by examining WCRI documents and financial statements for the fiscal year under review. Then we visited the site, interviewed staff, and spoke with others in the cooperative movement who were knowledgeable about WCRI. As well, we surveyed current and former residents and held a focus group with residents who had been active either on WCRI committees or its board of directors. While the financial value added could be calculated by using the information on the audited financial statements, these steps were important in helping to understand the social value added.

The study found that, for the fiscal year examined, WCRI created financial and social wealth using both financial and non-financial resources. For its residents, it offered high-quality, well-managed social housing units. Residents also experienced secondary outputs such as learning skills from running the business of the cooperative and knowledge from functioning in a democratically run organization. The broader community also benefited from monies expended by the cooperative, cooperative leadership, the use of WCRI to house war refugees (at less than the going rate for such a service), and through payment of municipal property taxes.

The impact of these findings is shown in Tables 6.1 to 6.3. Although these tables may seem forbidding at first glance, as we go through them step by step, it should be apparent that the Expanded Value Added Statement is an accessible procedure.

**Table 6.2 Expanded Value Added Statement (Partial) for WCRI
for the Year Ended April 30, 1999**

Value Added Created		Financial	Social	Combined
Outputs	Primary	$3,964,031	$246,128	$4,210,159
	Secondary	65,192	424,808	490,000
	Tertiary		2,500	2,500
	Total	4,029,223	673,436	4,702,659
Purchases of external goods and services		1,538,561		1,538,561
Value Added Created		**$2,490,662**	**$673,436**	**$3,164,098**
Ratio of Value Added to Purchases		1.62	0.44	2.06

Table 6.2, which presents the value added by WCRI, has three columns that refer to different sources of value added:

➤ Financial, which represents information from audited financial statements only and which is also referred to as a Restricted Value Added Statement;
➤ Social, which represents information about non-monetized contributions and outputs for which market comparisons are estimated;
➤ Combined, which represents the total of the financial and social columns, and is also referred to as an Expanded Value Added Statement.

In order to calculate the amount of value added, the first step is to assess the total outputs of the organization and assign a comparative market value to them. Total outputs are the results of an organization's activities to accomplish its mission—all of the services that it offers. Total outputs, as noted in Table 6.2, are subdivided into primary, secondary, and tertiary, reflecting how directly the associated items are connected to fulfilling the organization's mission. Primary outputs are the direct services of the organization—in the case of WCRI, the housing for students. The secondary and tertiary outputs are the indirect results of an organization's activities to fulfill its mission. Secondary outputs are indirect outputs that accrue to the organization's members or customers; tertiary outputs are indirect outputs that accrue to those other than the organization's members or customers.

For WCRI, a secondary output was its provision of skills development for its residents. An example of a tertiary output was the consultations with other cooperatives. This was classified as tertiary because, unlike the skills training of residents, it was not related directly to WCRI's primary service. Rather it was a service to other organizations or, arguably, to the cooperative movement. Not all organizations would have all three categories of outputs, but for WCRI this division seemed logical.

Primary Outputs

For the fiscal year examined, the primary outputs of WCRI were housing units and services. To determine the market value for these housing units, three sources were considered:

➤ the revenues generated from members for the housing charges;
➤ the value of social labor that members contributed to operate the housing units; and
➤ the value of the services that the cooperative and its members donated to the community.

For WCRI, the primary outputs totaled $4,210,159. This amount, shown in the column "combined," consists of two parts: first, $3,964,031 from revenues received from such items as accommodation, food, and parking (shown under the columns "financial" since the amounts are taken from audited financial statements); and second, the value of social labor contributions and donated services ($246,128). With a combined total of $4,210,159, the related items are now discussed in greater detail.

Revenues

WCRI received revenues from fees for accommodation, meal plans, utilities, parking, laundry, and miscellaneous items, and also from its pub and restaurant. The amounts for these revenues are taken from the audited financial accounts and total $3,964,031, as shown in Table 6.2 for primary outputs in the column "financial." Technically speaking, revenues are not an output but rather a measure of outputs, or in this case, the primary outputs. There is an assumption involved that the market is an accurate measure of an organization's outputs. Although this is open to debate, for our purposes, we accept this premise and work with it.

Social Labor

For WCRI, social labor—the unpaid services of the members to the cooperative—reduces costs, creates opportunities for skills development, and also enhances the psychological sense of ownership among members. Social labor has an impact both on the market value of services and on the manner of payment by residents. For WCRI, dormitory residents contributed 40 hours of social labor a term. This figure was reduced by 50 percent to allow for inefficiencies and was valued at $8.00 per hour, an amount determined by the WCRI Market Subcommittee (1998). Therefore, the member contribution to the school term had an estimated financial value of $160 (40 hours × $8.00 × 0.50). Without this contribution, the residents of WCRI would have had to pay $2,360. With it, they paid only $2,200. On the Restricted Value Added Statement, only the portion received in cash ($2,200) would have been recorded as revenue and the $160 for social labor would have been ignored. Therefore, in order to record the true market value of the housing units and services in a Value Added Statement, an amount equivalent to the value of the social labor performed must be added to revenues obtained from the audited financial statements.

For the fiscal year studied, the estimated total hours of social labor were 58,632. As noted, this total was discounted by 50 percent to compensate for inefficiencies. At $8.00 per hour, this resulted in a total comparative market value of $234,528 (58,632 × 0.50 × $8.00).

On top of this, members of the board of directors contributed additional social labor. It was estimated that 10 members contributed 10 hours per month, which at $8.00 per hour totaled $9,600. The total of these two figures is $244,128 ($234,528 for the market value attributed to the contribution of the general membership and $9,600, the value attributed to the contribution of members of the board of directors). The $244,128 is the major part of the primary output, within the "social" column of Table 6.2.

Donated Service

In addition to revenues and social labor, donated service is a third component of WCRI's primary outputs. Although WCRI supplies services primarily to university students who are members of the cooperative, during the summer of the fiscal year examined, it housed approximately 50 war refugees. Based on the rate that WCRI charged students, the market value of these services was estimated at $14,000. However, WCRI charged immigration authorities at cost ($12,000), thereby forgoing a portion of revenues ($2,000) that it would have received at market value. In order to record the true market value of these services, an amount equal to the difference ($2,000) between its market value ($14,000) and its cost ($12,000) is treated as social value added and, therefore, is included as part of the primary outputs in the column "social." This item, a donated service, is treated as a primary output because it is directly related to the primary service of the organization, the provision of housing. It is social value added rather than financial because, unlike the $12,000 received from government for housing the war refugees (part of the $3,964,031, as a primary output in the column "financial"), it never appears on the audited financial statements. Yet this $2,000 is part of WCRI's contribution to a need in the community for social housing.

Therefore, this $2,000 of social value added is combined with the $244,128 of social labor to arrive at the total of $246,128 that appears in Table 6.2 as primary outputs in the column "social." All of these items represent WCRI's contribution to the service of housing. When the amount of financial revenues of $3,964,031 is added to the estimate of social value added of $246,128, we arrive at the total of $4,210,159, the amount of the primary outputs that appears in the column "combined," or in an Expanded Value Added Statement. In other words, to arrive at the total of WCRI's primary outputs in an Expanded Value Added Statement, an estimate of the market value of social labor and of donated housing service is added to the total revenues that appear on the audited financial statements.

Secondary Outputs

In addition to housing units and related services, WCRI also produced secondary outputs such as skills training.[2] To be included in the Value Added Statement, these also had to be assigned a market value. Like the primary outputs, secondary outputs are divided between financial and social. The secondary outputs appearing in the column "financial" are the expenditures of $65,192 taken from audited financial statements on such cooperative development items as meeting expenses, newsletter, and education. This part was relatively straightforward. The more demanding step was to estimate the social value for skills training. This item would not appear in a Restricted Value Added Statement but represents a genuine benefit (and, hence, added value) of the experience of living in WCRI and, therefore, appears in the column "social" and is part of the Expanded Value Added Statement.

Skills Training

The survey and the focus group indicated that a variety of skills were developed as a secondary benefit of living in the cooperative. These skills—a positive experience in the life of a university student—included independent living, as well as personal, organizational, and leadership skills. Skills development comes from a variety of experiences, and it was problematic to determine in a precise manner what portion should be attributed to living in the cooperative. However, by comparison to typical student dormitories or off-campus apartments, members of the cooperative acquire managerial skills and democratic experience—something that the participants in the focus groups emphasized. Members learn about running an organization with a $4 million budget and making decisions about both large and small matters.

In addition, through membership meetings, students experience member control and participate in democratic processes. These lessons occur in a highly personal context—that is, decisions affect members' living conditions and the quality of life. It requires the balancing of self-interest with the interests of the community as a whole and it also requires a maturity of judgment that students may find challenging.

Assigning a market value to these secondary outputs was not as straightforward as estimating the market value of social labor or donated service. Yet these were valuable benefits of living in the cooperative and should not be ignored in calculating the value added of WCRI. We assigned these benefits a comparative economic value equivalent to the cost of taking two undergraduate university courses at $500 each. Yet this benefit could not be assigned to all of WCRI's residents because from our survey, not all had participated actively in the governance. Therefore, it seemed reasonable to assign these benefits only to the 56 percent of residents who reported that they participated in management through the cooperative's meetings. Thus, the amount calculated for the market value of this portion of skills training was derived by multiplying the number of students active in the cooperative's management (56 percent of the total, or 460 students) by the cost of taking two university courses (at $500 each). This amounted to $460,000 (460 × $1,000).

While 56 percent of WCRI's residents were estimated to have gained this level of benefit, there was a small number who were especially active in the cooperative's governance. For this group, the additional enhancement of their skills as a result of extremely high participation in the running of the cooperative could be seen as a benefit not just to the students themselves but also to the community-at-large. The residents who benefited most from this type of learning experience were the 10 members of the board of directors as well as an additional 10 committee chairs and selected committee members. If these 20 students were to pay for this type of education, the equivalent was estimated to be an additional one theoretical and two practical courses in community development. Thus, the value assigned to this output was the cost of three university courses at $500 each, or $1,500, multiplied by 20 students, for a total of $30,000.

To arrive at the total value added of skills training, the $30,000 was added to the estimated value of $460,000 of the benefit experienced by the 56 percent of residents who participated in the governance but not as actively. This created a total social value added of $490,000 for skills training. However, to achieve these benefits, WCRI invested $65,192 (as shown in the column "financial," under secondary outputs). This amount represents such costs to the organization as meetings, education as it relates to living in and running a cooperative, and the production of a newsletter. To arrive at the net social value added of secondary outputs, the estimated market value of skills training has to be adjusted for financial expenditures. Therefore, the amount that WCRI spends ($65,192) is subtracted from $490,000, to arrive at the net social value for secondary outputs of $424,808, as shown in the "social" column of Table 6.2. In other words, in order to create these secondary outputs valued at $490,000, the organization spent $65,192.

To arrive at the value added of WCRI's secondary outputs, the expenditure of the organization on related items, as stated in the audited financial statements, is added to the estimated market value for skills training. This amount of $490,000 appears in the column "combined" and represents value added of secondary outputs for an Expanded Value Added Statement.

All of the outputs discussed to this point are directly related to the provision of housing for the residents of WCRI. However, WCRI also views itself as part of the cooperative movement and as such provides services for other cooperatives. Because these are external to WCRI's services to its members, they are labeled tertiary outputs.

Tertiary Outputs

Consultation with the Cooperative Sector

As a result of its achievements and leadership status, WCRI was able to transfer knowledge to other cooperatives, another component of social value added. In the fiscal year, WCRI supplied pro bono consultation services to three other cooperatives in various stages of development and with diverse management issues. These contributions were in the form of leadership development, cooperative consultation, and business consultation. To estimate a comparative value for these services, the number of days involved was multiplied by the daily amount that the cooperative would normally pay to a consultant. As shown in Table 6.2, this amount is estimated to be 5 days at $500 per day, or $2,500. This amount appears as tertiary output in the column "social" and also in the column "combined"—that is, as part of the Expanded Value Added Statement.

Total Outputs

Once the primary, secondary, and tertiary outputs are calculated, these are added together to arrive at the total outputs. The total outputs from the financial statements are $4,029,223, the amount that would appear in a Restricted Value Added Statement.

However, when the total outputs social of $673,436 are added to the total outputs financial, the total outputs combined are $4,702,659. This amount represents the total outputs for an Expanded Value Added Statement.

Subtracting External Purchases

Returning to our earlier definition, value added is a measure of wealth that an organization creates by "adding value" to the raw materials, products, and services through the use of labor and capital. The total outputs (combined) represent the value placed on the organization's services, but in order to provide those services WCRI has purchased goods and services externally. The cost of these purchases ($1,538,561) is taken from the organization's audited financial statements (see Table 6.3). As shown in Table 6.3, in order to arrive at this figure, the total expenses as recorded in the audited Consolidated Statement of Operations are adjusted for any labor and capital costs (in line with the definition of value added). These steps are taken because (as related to the preceding definition) labor and capital are the components used to add value to other purchases. As shown in Table 6.3, WCRI's total expenditures on its audited financial statements are $3,546,780, but in order to arrive at the amount expended externally on goods and services, the costs related to capital and labor have to be subtracted from the total. Therefore, $3,546,780 is reduced by the employee wages and benefits ($838,222), the municipal property taxes ($216,586), the loan interest ($519,961) and the amortization of capital assets ($433,450). In total, $1,538,561 is subtracted from the total outputs to arrive at the value added created by WCRI. For a Restricted Value Added Statement, the value added created is $2,490,662; for an Expanded Value Added Statement, the amount is $3,164,098 (see Table 6.2).

Table 6.3 Reconciliation of Expenditures on Audited Financial Statements to Purchases of External Goods and Services on a Value Added Statement

Expenditures per audited financial statements	$3,546,780
Less: Employee wages and benefits	838,222
Municipal property taxes	216,586
Loan interest	519,961
Amortization of capital assets	433,450
Purchases of external goods and services	$1,538,561

Ratio of Value Added to Purchases

The ratio of value added to purchases, indicated in the final row of Table 6.2, is established by dividing the value added by the cost of external goods and services. This ratio indicates that for every dollar expended on goods and services the organization generated $2.06 in value added. As noted, the Expanded Value Added

Statement includes a market estimate of non-monetized items such as social labor, donated service, skills training, and consultation to the cooperative sector. If those items had not been included, the ratio of value added to purchases would have been 1.62, as is indicated in the "financial" column. Therefore, the inclusion of non-monetized items increases this ratio by over 27 percent.

DISTRIBUTION OF VALUE ADDED

As mentioned, there are two sections to a Value Added Statement: the value added created and the distribution of value added. Whereas the former measures how much value added has been created, the distribution of value added analyzes how it was disseminated.

For the statement of distribution, the value added created by the organization (as shown in Table 6.2) is distributed to the stakeholders in its entirety. Stakeholders are selected on the basis of their contribution to the viability of the organization and its values. For a Value Added Statement, the stakeholders suggested by accounting regulatory bodies normally are employees, government, investors, and the organization itself. For purposes of the Expanded Value Added Statement of WCRI, one additional stakeholder was identified—residents; and one was modified—the stakeholder government was changed to the stakeholder society and expanded to include the nonprofit cooperative sector (as shown in Table 6.4).

As noted, the stakeholder-based approach of the Value Added Statement differentiates it from most other forms of financial statements that are oriented toward shareholders. The Value Added Statement not only is based upon the assumption that a broad group of stakeholders contribute to an organization but also attempts to analyze precisely how much value added each stakeholder receives from these combined efforts from year to year. Therefore, this form of financial statement not only acknowledges the importance of stakeholders, as so many organizations do in theory, but also in a very practical manner it attempts to assign a portion of the value added to them.

Table 6.4 presents the distribution of value added for these five stakeholders and also lists the items associated with each stakeholder.

Employees

The value added distributed to the stakeholder employees lists their wages and benefits at $838,222.

Residents

The residents of WCRI received a portion of the value added through a reduction in the cost of their housing and related services. This reduction results from their social labor (their unpaid service to WCRI) in the amount of $244,128 (as discussed previously). They also received value totaling $490,000 from skills training. Additionally, as WCRI does not receive the exemption from municipal property taxes accorded to university residences, eligible residents can claim 20 percent of their rental payments (not including meal portions) as an occupancy cost for the Ontario Property Tax Credit on their income tax form. If they had lived in a university residence, they would have been eligible for a deduction of only $25. Based on their rental payments and personal net income, this benefit is valued at $200 per person for 709 residents, or a total of $141,800. In Table 6.4, the $141,800 is shown as an economic benefit transferred from the government to the residents.

Table 6.4 Distribution of Value Added: Expanded Value Added Statement (Partial) for WCRI for the Year Ended April 30, 1999

Distribution of Value Added		Financial	Social	Combined
Employees	Wages and benefits	$838,222		$838,222
Residents	Value from social labor		$244,128	244,128
	Skills development	65,192	424,808	490,000
	Property tax credit		141,800	141,800
		65,192	810,736	875,928
Society	Government: municipal property taxes	216,586		216,586
	Government: property tax credit		(141,800)	(141,800)
	Government: housing of war refugees		2,000	2,000
	Cooperative sector: consultations		2,500	2,500
		216,586	(137,300)	79,286
Capital	Loan interest	519,961		519,961
Organization	Amortization of capital assets	433,450		433,450
	Operating surplus	417,251		417,251
		850,701		850,701
Value Added Distributed		**$2,490,662**	**$673,436**	**$3,164,098**

Society

The stakeholder referred to as society received value added in both the public and the nonprofit cooperative sectors. In the public sector, the government received municipal tax payments less property tax credits $74,786 ($216,586 minus $141,800), and the value of donated housing for war refugees ($2,000). The cooperative sector received value in the amount of $2,500 for consultations from other cooperatives. The support for the cooperative sector is an important difference between WCRI and other forms of student housing. WCRI contributes to the cooperative movement as a member of the North American Students of Cooperation (NASCO) and the Canadian Co-operative Association (CCA), and it also aims to educate others about cooperatives. In doing so, it adheres to the principles of the International Co-operative Alliance, as discussed earlier. The total of these contributions of $74,786, $2,000, and $2,500 was $79,286 (Table 6.4).

Providers of Capital

WCRI's interest payment of $519,961 was the portion of the value added distributed to the providers of capital.

Organization

Value added distributed to the stakeholder organization was for $433,450 for the amortization of capital assets and $417,251 from an operating surplus. For these items, the organization was viewed as the primary beneficiary.

Summary of Value Added Distribution

In total, the value added distributed corresponds to the value added created. Where the items were limited to those on audited financial statements, that amount was $2,490,662; where the items were expanded to include non-monetized social contributions, the amount was $3,164,098.

The value added created is distributed in total to a group of stakeholders who contribute to the organization's total outputs. For WCRI, these were employees, residents, society, providers of capital, and the organization. Table 6.4 shows the distribution of the value added to each of these stakeholders.

IMPLICATIONS

The Expanded Value Added Statement (Tables 6.1 and 6.3) indicates that $3,164,098 of value was added and distributed in the same period. If only the audited financial accounts were considered, WCRI appeared to create value added of $2,490,662 for the year ended April 30, 1999. The Expanded Value Added Statement shows that the financial information without the social value added did not tell the organization's whole performance story. The inclusion of the social value added in the calculation of value added led to an increase of over 27 percent. This is significant because there are few other indicators that the organization can use either to calculate the contribution of its residents or to assess the costs and benefits of managing such an extensive resource as 822 residents who contribute over 30,500 productive hours per year.

Furthermore, when considering the financial resources of the organization, resident hours accounted for over 6 percent of the total (Figure 6.3). This figure shows that resident contributions, both monetary and non-monetary, were a significant resource that should be counted in its overall performance.

Figure 6.3 Monetary and Non-monetary Contributions

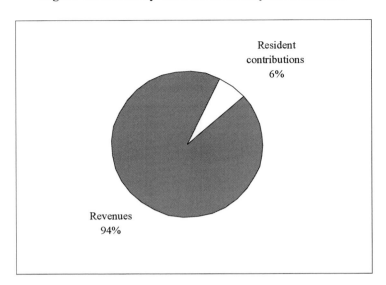

Another way of looking at the significance of resident contributions is to examine the proportion that residents contribute to the human resources of the organization. Resident activities accounted for over 35 percent of WCRI's human resources (Figure 6.4). Based on the estimate of 30,516 resident hours, residents contributed the equivalent of 17 full-time equivalent (FTE) positions for the year ended April 30, 1999. This means that WCRI had the equivalent of a total workforce FTE of 48, not just the paid staff FTE of 31. These figures are significant when considering issues related to managing the equivalent of an additional 17 FTE positions distributed over 800 residents.

Social goods and services that are not given a monetary value often represent a large part of a cooperative's operations. Without taking these goods and services into account, there is no clear picture either of a cooperative's performance or of the contributions made by its members. The Expanded Value Added Statement is an experimental methodology to broaden the accounting for nonprofits and cooperatives. In the case of WCRI, the Expanded Value Added Statement tells the story differently from the financial statements—and to a different audience. The Expanded Value Added Statement helps various stakeholders, particularly residents, to see what value they have added to WCRI—in this case, over 20 percent of the expanded value added—and what value they have received.

Figure 6.4 Proportion of Total Activity Hours by Residents and Staff

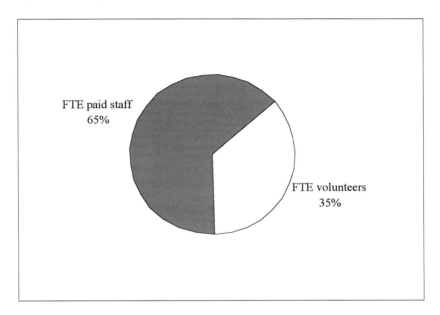

DISCUSSION

Figure 6.2 showed the Restricted Value Added Statement (based on financial information only). In Figure 6.5, this statement is modified to show the impact of volunteer labor and to include secondary outputs such as skills development of volunteers. Therefore, Figure 6.5 is based upon an Expanded Value Added Statement (using the information from audited financial statements; the valuation of social outputs, such as the skills development gained by volunteers as a benefit from their volunteering activities; and the valuation of social inputs such as volunteer contributions). Again, the value of the outputs of the organization is depicted on the left-hand side of the diagram; the right-hand side shows how this value is distributed. The portion above the line labeled "restricted" represents the value added from a financial statement only; the portion below the restricted line depicts the social value added normally excluded from a financial statement. As seen, the social value added is considerable.

The model developed in this chapter uses the format of a Value Added Statement to show both economic and social contributions to the value added by an organization. Many of the amounts in the Expanded Value Added Statements (Tables 6.2 and 6.4) can be found on the audited financial statements.[3] However, two important differences should be noted. First, the traditional financial statements are restricted to monetary transactions only, whereas the Expanded Value Added Statement allows for the inclusion of such items as social labor not entailing a cash outlay but still adding value to the organization.

Figure 6.5 Expanded Value Added Statement

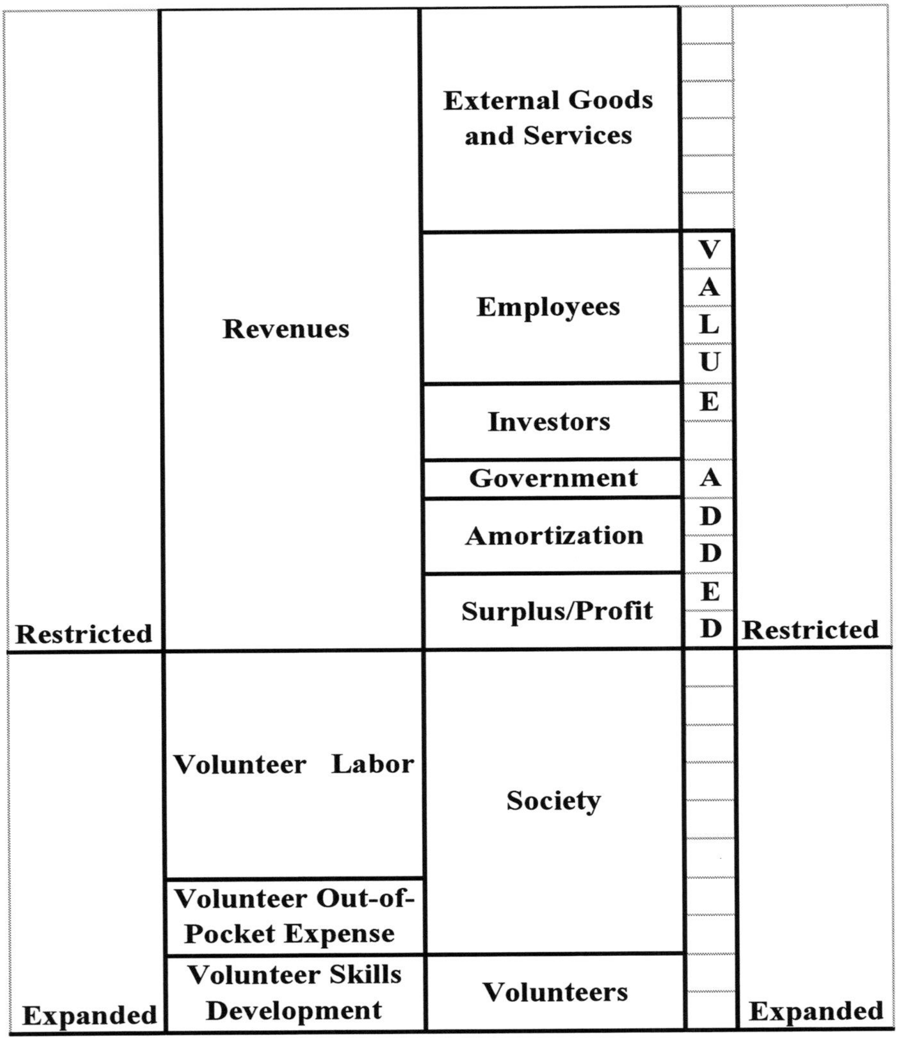

	Revenues	External Goods and Services	
		Employees	**V** **A** **L** **U** **E**
		Investors	
		Government	**A**
		Amortization	**D** **D**
Restricted		Surplus/Profit	**E** **D** Restricted
	Volunteer Labor	Society	
	Volunteer Out-of-Pocket Expense		
Expanded	Volunteer Skills Development	Volunteers	Expanded

Second, the objectives of each statement differ. For example, a Statement of Operations and Changes in Fund Balances is prepared to show financial position and impact on fund balances. It is similar to the income statement of a business where expenses are viewed negatively as a reduction of the bottom line (profits)—the larger the bottom line, the better for the firm and for the shareholders. By contrast, the objective of the Expanded Value Added Statement is to show how the value added by an organization—the result of a collective effort—is distributed to a wider group. The Expanded Value Added Statement suggests that all stakeholders are an important and integral part of the organization. For example, while employee wages are considered a reduction from surpluses on the Statement of Operations and Changes in Fund Balances, on the Expanded Value Added Statement they are considered a distribution of resources with benefit to a particular group that is an integral part of WCRI.

Another advantage of the Expanded Value Added Statement is its emphasis on the interactive and interdependent nature of the organization. As each stakeholder's share is relative, some may suggest that value-added reporting increases competition among stakeholders. However, for organizations that cooperate, the value-added approach can lead to more cohesiveness among the stakeholders, a more positive attitude to the organization, and a greater recognition of social impacts (Burchell et al. 1985; Meek and Gray 1988).

The Expanded Value Added Statement also addresses some concerns about applying accounting models developed for business enterprises to nonprofit organizations (Macintosh 1995; Macintosh, Bartel, and Snow 1999). Without question, nonprofit organizations are different from business enterprises in some very significant ways: They operate for purposes other than earning a profit; their efficiency and effectiveness cannot be determined by means of income measures; and they may receive large amounts of resources from donors who do not expect monetary benefits in return (Razek, Hosch, and Ives 2000). Nonprofits, particularly those that depend upon government funding and donors, are often viewed as users of others' wealth rather than as creators of additional wealth. Income statements show how nonprofits spend monies that others give to them. However, an Expanded Value Added Statement tells a different story. It shows how a nonprofit uses its resources to generate wealth. Our research using the Expanded Value Added Statement with nonprofits (in Chapter 7) clearly demonstrates that these organizations generate large amounts of value added from their donated funds and grants. This is true in general but even more so for organizations that rely heavily on volunteer labor. From the perspective of an income statement, they are users of others' capital and donated services; from the perspective of an Expanded Value Added Statement, they generate additional value, much of it for the surrounding community that is the beneficiary of their services. The Expanded Value Added Statement gives a different perspective, one that might be of interest to members of the organization and its funders.

For nonprofits depending upon donations and grants, an Expanded Value Added Statement shows that they generate added value with the dollars invested in them. By comparison, an income statement simply shows that they use funds that are granted to them.

Nonprofits are also uniquely different from profit-oriented businesses in that they have multiple stakeholders (for example, funders, regulators, clients, and community), involve volunteers, and have both economic and social goals. The Expanded Value

Added Statement recognizes this uniqueness by focusing on both economic and social impact, instead of the "bottom line"' of surpluses or deficits.

Thus, for WCRI, the Expanded Value Added Statement creates a greater awareness of:

> ➢ the collective effort needed to run an organization;
> ➢ the role of an organization in providing employment;
> ➢ the role of an organization in providing skills training;
> ➢ the impact of social labor and other contributions;
> ➢ the role of the organization in supporting the cooperative sector; and
> ➢ the role of an organization in contributing to society through taxes and donated services.

CONCLUSION

To be useful, the Expanded Value Added Statement should not simply be a rearrangement of existing financial statements. As Haller (1997) notes, it should present additional information for decision making that is not available from conventional financial statements. By synthesizing traditional financial data with social inputs, the Expanded Value Added Statement can be another mechanism for understanding the dynamics of an organization, one that shows great potential for enhancing the importance of social inputs and outputs.

The strengths of the Expanded Value Added Statement lie in its ability to take a broader look at the organization and the role of stakeholders within it and to put this in a larger social-economic perspective. By including non-monetary social inputs, the Expanded Value Added Statement presents a fuller picture of an organization's economic and social impact. Through this approach, benefits that are either unknown, undisclosed, or not measured are made explicit, allowing for different emphases in decision making. By combining financial and social variables, the Expanded Value Added Statement focuses attention on the interconnectedness and interdependence of the economy, community, and environment. The model particularly highlights the contribution of the organization to the community, something that is invaluable to nonprofits and cooperatives and is a key feature of a social accounting model.

The challenges faced by the Expanded Value Added Statement are shared by other forms of alternative accounting and economics—quantifying and placing a value on goods and services that are seen as "free." And yet, as the Expanded Value Added Statement for WCRI shows, free goods and services are utilized and produced in large measure by the organization and, therefore, need to be accounted for if the whole performance story of the organization is to be told. The Expanded Value Added Statement attempts to integrate financial information for which there are strict methods of accounting with non-financial or social information, and to develop a methodology that supports this.

In addition, it is necessary to assess not only value added but also value subtracted. This category might be pertinent to variables like the environment where citizens, through the taxes paid to government, have to bear the costs of cleaning up pollution. Such an approach might be threatening to large corporations, particularly those engaged in industrial production and resource extraction; however, it is important for accounting statements to illuminate rather than to obscure important relationships.

The limitations of the Expanded Value Added Statement are those that affect the many social organizations: There are few resources to track "free" goods and services. The Expanded Value Added Statement attempts to place a reasonable market value on items and activities that do not pass through the market. Much more research and application will be required to refine this process. However, as the report of WCRI shows, the Expanded Value Added Statement captures and displays information that other forms of accounting or evaluation do not. The procedures undertaken to create the Expanded Value Added Statement are not unlike those used in cost/benefit analyses, but the EVAS also creates an accounting framework that is based on actual results. This information can be used by the organization and its stakeholders to understand better the role and value of its residents.

Social accounting is in its infancy compared with traditional accounting, which itself took hundreds of years to develop. The Expanded Value Added Statement offers a beginning step toward understanding the links between the success of an organization and its social and democratic structure.

QUESTIONS FOR DISCUSSION

1. What additional information does an Expanded Value Added Statement provide over a Restricted Value Added Statement? How does this new information help us to understand the role of nonprofits and cooperatives?
2. What additional information does an Expanded Value Added Statement provide over an income statement? How does this new information help us to understand the role of nonprofits and cooperatives?
3. "While income statements focus on one stakeholder, value added statements allow us to understand the relationship between several stakeholders." Discuss.
4. In addition to those described in this chapter, present three examples of secondary outputs that an organization could create. How would you measure them? How would you put a value on them?
5. What are the possibilities and limitations of the Expanded Value Added Statement?
6. How can stakeholder input be gathered and applied in the construction of the Expanded Value Added Statement?
7. What audiences might be interested in the Expanded Value Added Statement and why?
8. Give three examples of "value subtracted" that could be included on the Expanded Value Added Statement.

9. What skills were gained by the resident members of the housing cooperative? What are some alternative ways for putting a value on the development of these skills?
10. By synthesizing financial data with social inputs, the Expanded Value Added Statement presents additional information for decision making that is not available from conventional financial statements. Illustrate this point with an example.

NOTES

[1] Depreciation or amortization is the process of matching the cost of an asset against revenues based on its estimated useful life. Thus, instead of expensing the entire cost of an asset when it is purchased, it is expensed according to how long it is estimated to be useful in producing value. In a simple example, if the asset were estimated to last five years, one fifth of its cost would be expensed every year for five years.

[2] Another secondary output identified for WCRI was a sense of community for its residents, and although there were initial attempts to put a value on this, it is not included here as the authors felt the valuation need further refinement.

[3] In fact, an organization does not have to make any significant changes to its accounting system to prepare a Restricted Value Added Statement and can go back to previous years' data to look at trends in how the value added was distributed.

Chapter 7

Volunteer Value Added: Five Nonprofits

Even though volunteers in the United States and Canada contribute the equivalent full-time work of almost 10 million people per year (Hall et al. 2001; Independent Sector 2001a), the value of this work, estimated to be over $250 billion, is not recognized in conventional accounting. This chapter presents an empirical study that measured the impact of volunteers on the value added created by five nonprofit organizations and that accounted for this value added in an Expanded Value Added Statement (EVAS). Each of the organizations studied has a strong volunteer base without which the mission of the organization could not be fulfilled. As a detailed explanation of the Value Added Statement was already provided in Chapter 6, this chapter will not repeat the procedures in the same detail. Rather, it will highlight the creation of value added by and for volunteers in these organizations.

The Volunteer Value Added project started as a one-year International Year of the Volunteer (IYV) research project that was sponsored by a Canadian federal government department, Human Resources Development Canada, in conjunction with the Canadian Centre for Philanthropy (forerunner to Imagine Canada), the primary advocacy organization for nonprofits in Canada. Four nonprofit organizations were initially researched—the Jane/Finch Community and Family Centre, the Toronto Region of the Canadian Red Cross, Canadian Crossroads International, and the Ontario Chapter of the Canadian Breast Cancer Foundation. The research was then extended to another nonprofit organization, Junior Achievement of Rochester, New York, Inc. In addition, we have conducted workshops on social accounting and the Expanded Value Added Statement with more than 700 staff and Board members of nonprofits and cooperatives. The principal objectives of the project were to assess the value of volunteer contributions and to demonstrate how the Value Added Statement could be adapted for use by nonprofits. It follows the general framework outlined in the previous chapter; however, the focus of the study was on measuring the contributions of volunteers to the value added created by each organization as well as on exploring the benefits that volunteers received from their efforts. This impact is presented in a partial Expanded Value Added Statement. (The statement is partial as it only focuses on the impact of volunteer contributions and does not show a full comparative market valuation of all outputs.)

As defined in Chapter 6, value added is a measure of wealth that an organization creates by "adding value" to externally purchased raw materials, products, and services through the use of labor and capital. In a conventional Value Added Statement, the only labor considered is that of paid employees. However, volunteers constitute a major portion of the workforce of a voluntary organization, and it seems absurd to report that they have zero impact on the value added by that organization simply because their service does not involve a monetary transaction.

This study addresses this inequity by measuring the contributions given and received by volunteers and by including this value in the Expanded Value Added Statement. The strength of the EVAS lies in its ability to take a broader look at the organization and the role of volunteers within it and to put this in a larger social-economic perspective. The challenges faced by the EVAS are shared by other forms of alternative accounting and economics—quantifying and placing a value on goods and services that are seen as "free." And yet, as the EVAS shows, free goods and services are utilized and produced in large measure by the organization and, therefore, need to be accounted for if the whole performance story is to be told. The EVAS attempts to integrate financial information, for which there are strict methods of accounting, with non-financial or social information, and to develop a methodology that supports this.

Another important feature of the Value Added Statement is the assumption that value is created by and distributed to many stakeholders, including volunteers. Therefore, it differs from the income statements used in conventional accounting that focus on one stakeholder, the shareholders, and the return on their investment. The EVAS in this chapter shows how the value added by volunteers and the organization they volunteer for is distributed both to the recipients of the nonprofit's services and also to the volunteers themselves.

In these five voluntary organizations, the EVAS tells a much different story than the financial statements alone—and to a different audience. The EVAS helps various stakeholders, particularly volunteers, see what value they have added to their organization—in these five cases, increases of between 40 to 233 percent over the value added calculated using only financial variables. The EVAS also makes explicit the value received by volunteers as a result of their volunteer activities. This chapter presents the EVAS for each of the five voluntary organizations and also draws out lessons that are special to each case.

CASE ONE:
JANE/FINCH COMMUNITY AND FAMILY CENTRE

The Jane/Finch Community and Family Centre, located in a low-income area of Metro Toronto, serves an ethnically and racially diverse community of people, many of whom are recent immigrants to Canada. In many respects, it is typical of community-based organizations serving low-income communities and relying upon a combination of government grants, United Way and other donations, and volunteer contributions from area residents. The stereotype of such organizations is that they are users of public funds. However, the EVAS that follows tells a different story.

The Jane/Finch Community and Family Centre was founded in 1976 when it received a three-year government grant. By 1980, it had received United Way membership. Over the next 20 years, the centre expanded greatly, and it currently operates the following programs and services, either independently or in partnership with other community organizations:

> child–parent programs—creative arts, nurseries, child care, Tiny Tots;
> parent support programs—a resource center, home visiting, parenting workshops;
> Cambodian, Vietnamese, and Spanish-speaking women's groups;
> community mental health programs—women's wellness workshops, health fairs;
> youth substance abuse—Glue Sniffing Prevention Committee;
> community development programs—support for neighborhood and tenant groups;
> community office programs—résumé writing, photocopying, referrals.

Each of the programs also does outreach in the community. In addition, the Jane/Finch Community and Family Centre runs a Volunteer Coordination program to recruit and place volunteers and students for many of the foregoing services. For these initiatives, in partnership with other local organizations, the Jane/Finch Community and Family Centre received the prestigious 1998 Caring Communities Award from the Ontario Trillium Foundation.

Human Resources

As with all of the organizations in this study, the human resources at Jane/Finch consist of both volunteers and paid staff. Volunteers make up the governance structure as well as contributing to programs and the organization in general.

The board of directors of Jane/Finch is made up of volunteer members of the community and consists of the president, vice president, treasurer, and secretary, and six members-at-large. They are elected by nomination for a three-year term. The board meets at least 11 times a year and also holds retreats once or twice a year for the purpose of strategic planning and skills building. New members also attend training programs where they are introduced to the centre and its programs as well as to the policy governance model.

In addition to the board of directors, volunteers also contribute hours to all of the programs at Jane/Finch as well as to the community office. A breakdown of the number of volunteers and the hours they contributed for a one-year period is shown in Table 7.1. For the purposes of the Expanded Value Added Statement, these hours were adjusted to reflect contributions for nine months, the period of time covered by its financial statements.[1]

The Jane/Finch Community and Family Centre also has a paid staff of 40, comprising an executive coordinator, a volunteer coordinator, and 5 office and 33 program staff. In addition, a number of students are hired to help out with each of the programs, especially Child–Parent and Mental Health.

Table 7.1 Staff Estimate of Volunteer Hours for the Year 2000
Jane/Finch Community and Family Centre

Area	Number of Volunteers	Volunteer Hours	Average Hours
Mental Health	15	3120	208
Mental Health practicum	3	1800	600
Cambodian Youth Group	25	7200	288
Community Development	76	15448	203
Community Office	2	600	300
Child–Parent Program	10	3000	300
Board	8	670	84
Total	139	31838	229

One way of looking at the significance of volunteer contributions is to examine the proportion of human resources that volunteers contribute to the total human resource base of the organization. For Jane/Finch, volunteer activities accounted for 30 percent of its human resources, corresponding to 17.5 full-time equivalent (FTE) positions. This means that Jane/Finch had the equivalent activities of a total FTE workforce of 57.5, not just those of the paid staff FTE of 40. Furthermore, when considering the financial and in-kind resources of the organization, volunteer hours accounted for 27 percent of the total. (This estimate is based on the value for volunteer activities as detailed further on in this chapter.) Therefore, volunteer contributions provide the organization with a significant resource that should be counted in its overall performance.

COLLECTING THE INFORMATION FOR THE EVAS

Information needed to create the EVAS was collected through a variety of methods: the review of documents, including audited financial statements; interviews with staff and volunteers; and surveys administered to volunteers (see Chapter 8 for examples of the survey questions). Collecting information at Jane/Finch presented a challenge in that for many of the residents, English or French (the languages used in the surveys) is not their first language. Group sessions for conducting surveys proved most effective. Surveys were also handed out at a board meeting, and a focus group was held with a cross section of staff, volunteers, and board members.

Our goal was to include the value added of volunteers in the performance story of the organization. The next section details the impact of volunteer contributions on the value of the primary and secondary outputs of the organization.

Primary Outputs

As mentioned in the previous chapters, primary outputs are directly related to the mission of the organization. In the case of Jane/Finch, these are the programs it offers. To establish a market value for its programs, two sources of inputs were considered: (1) financial expenditures and (2) volunteer hours contributed (see also Chapter 8 for more details on assigning a comparative market value to outputs). For Jane/Finch, financial expenditures totaled $866,641 from the audited financial statements, as they related to primary outputs for the nine-month period under study. This was the first component of the value of primary outputs.

However, these expenditures did not include any value for volunteer contributions. These contributions were measured and added to the financial expenditures to arrive at a total value of primary outputs. As is detailed next, the estimated value of the volunteer contributions was $324,077, which was added to the amount of expenditures to end up with a total of $1,190,718 (an increase of over 37%).

Volunteer Hours Contributed

The volunteer contributions to the primary outputs consisted of the hours volunteers contributed to the organization: For the year 2000, this was estimated to be 31,838 hours (Table 7.1). These hours were adjusted to reflect a nine-month reporting period. Thus, the total hours became $31,838 \times 9/12 = 23,879$.

The comparative market rates used in this study were obtained from Statistics Canada, which provided hourly wage rates organized according to the North American Industry Classification System (NAICS). This classification system (jointly developed by the statistics agencies of Canada, the United States, and Mexico) classifies organizations such as businesses, government institutions, unions, and charitable and nonprofit organizations according to economic activity. The activities of the majority of the volunteers of the Jane/Finch Community and Family Centre were classified as NAICS sub-sector 624, social assistance. This sub-sector includes organizations engaged in a variety of services such as food and housing within the community and emergency and other forms of relief both to the individual and family. The NAICS classification combines all the tasks for a sub-sector such as social services (including executive and administrative) and puts forward an average wage rate for all levels of occupation in that category, making its subsequent use straightforward. For the nine months ending December 31, 2000, the hourly wage rate in this category for Ontario, the province where the organization is located, was $13.38.[2]

However, the NAICS rates do not take into consideration governance tasks such as those performed by the board of directors. Therefore, a second source of wage rates was chosen as an equivalent for the hours contributed by the Jane/Finch board of directors. These hours were valued separately at an hourly rate of $22.50, based on responses by board members to the Volunteer Value Added survey as to what hourly rate they perceived their contributions were worth. While such estimates should not be accepted uncritically, given the nature of the services provided, this rate was determined to be reasonable.

The total comparative market value for the hours contributed by core volunteers through specific programs of the Jane/Finch Community and Family Centre is presented in Table 7.2. The total of $324,076 is obtained by taking the total hours contributed by volunteers within a program and multiplying them by the appropriate hourly rate.[3,4]

Table 7.2 Calculation of Market Value of Volunteer Hours Contributed
Jane/Finch Community and Family Centre

	Hours	Rate	Amount
Board	502.5	$22.50	$11,306
Community Office	450	13.38	6,021
Subtotal administrative	952.5		17,327
Mental Health	2,340	13.38	31,309
Mental Health Practicum	1,350	13.38	18,063
Cambodian Youth Group	5,400	13.38	72,252
Community Development	5,793	13.38	77,510
Child–Parent Program	2,250	13.38	30,105
Subtotal programs	17,133		229,239
Community Development	5,793	13.38	77,510
Subtotal volunteers	5,793		77,510
Total	23,878.5		$324,076

Secondary Outputs

Secondary outputs are those that are not directly related to an organization's mission but, nonetheless, are important and should be considered as part of the value added of an organization. For example, as part of volunteering, participants develop skills and other strengths that are of value to them and to wider society. In some respects, estimating the value of these benefits is more challenging than attributing a value to volunteer tasks. However, we would have been remiss to ignore this form of value.

Personal Growth and Development

Our survey included a section on benefits received by volunteers from their volunteering experiences. It included choices regarding the development of new skills, the strengthening of existing skills, social interaction, improvement in well-being, and opportunities to try new things. At least one of these benefits was chosen by 92.3 percent of the respondents, and 76.9 percent chose at least three out of five of these benefits. The high rates of response indicated that volunteers perceived themselves as receiving strong positive benefits through helping others and that this aspect of volunteering should be included in the Expanded Value Added Statement (EVAS).

Estimating the Market Value for Personal Growth and Development

To calculate the market value of volunteer personal growth and development, the total number of volunteers (139) was multiplied by the 76.9 percent of respondents who indicated strongly that they had benefited. After determining how many volunteers had benefited from their experience, it was necessary to assign a surrogate value (see Chapter 3). The surrogate value selected was the average cost at the time the study was done of a community college course for personal growth and development ($151.50). This seemed a conservative estimate of the market value of the volunteers' personal benefits and resulted in a total value of $139 \times 76.92\% \times \$151.50 = \$16,198$. This calculation assumes that the personal growth and development experienced by the respondents to the survey reflects the experience of volunteers as a whole at Jane/Finch. This figure was then adjusted to reflect the nine-month term for the statement—$\$16,198 \times 9/12 = \$12,149$.

Calculating Volunteer Value Added

The value added by the Jane/Finch Community and Family Centre for the nine-month term is presented in Table 7.3. As discussed in Chapter 6, one method of calculating the value of the outputs of an organization is to use the following three components:

➢ total expenditures for the fiscal period (for Jane/Finch this was $866,641 for primary outputs such as labor and external purchases and $1,746 for secondary outputs such as staff training);
➢ comparative market value of volunteer contributions ($324,077); and
➢ the social component of the comparative market value of secondary outputs such as personal benefits. This is the total comparative market value of personal benefits adjusted for financial expenditures for training ($12,149 less $1,746 = $10,403). Jane/Finch's expenditure on training is subtracted from the comparative market value for personal benefits because it is an investment by the organization in its volunteers and their development.

This resulted in a total value of outputs of $1,202,867. In order to determine the value added that an organization creates, it is necessary to measure the increase in the value of its expenditures on goods and services purchased externally in relation to the value of its total outputs. Therefore, to arrive at this amount, the goods and services that were purchased externally ($127,549) were subtracted from the total outputs, resulting in a total value added of $1,075,318 (column labeled "combined").[5] Note that if the value added were based on the audited financial statements only, it would have been $740,838. However, volunteer contributions for which market values were estimated (social value) added another $334,480, to arrive at the total of $1,075,318.

As the bottom row in Table 7.3 indicates, there is another piece to the Value Added Statement—that is, presenting the value added that the organization creates as a ratio to the goods and services purchased externally. For Jane/Finch, the ratio indicates that for every dollar spent on external goods and services, the organization generated value added of $8.43. If this calculation were based on the financial statements only, the ratio would be 5.81. However, by including the volunteer contributions, the ratio increases by 45 percent. This ratio presents a very different picture of Jane/Finch and illustrates that it generates much value for the resources that are invested in it.

Table 7.3 Expanded Value Added Statement (Partial)
Jane/Finch Community and Family Centre

Value Added		Financial	Social	Combined
Outputs	Primary	$866,641	$324,077	$1,190,718
	Secondary	1,746	10,403	12,149
	Total	868,387	334,480	1,202,867
Purchases of external goods and services		127,549		127,549
Value added		**$740,838**	**$334,480**	**$1,075,318**
Ratio of value added to purchases		5.81	2.62	8.43

Note: For the nine months ended December 31, 2000.

DISTRIBUTION OF VALUE ADDED

The value added created by the organization is distributed in its entirety to its primary stakeholders. These stakeholders may vary according to the nature of the organization's services, but for Jane/Finch those that seemed most appropriate were employees, volunteers, society (recipients of its services), and the organization itself. Table 7.4 presents the Distribution of Value Added for these four stakeholders and also lists the items associated with each stakeholder.

For the stakeholder employees, value added is received in the form of wages and benefits in the amount of $724,583. For the volunteers as a stakeholder group, the value added distributed to them is based on what they receive from the experience. In the case of Jane/Finch, the amounts distributed to volunteers were $4,054 on recognition and awards and $12,149 representing the value of their personal growth and development. In addition, there was one other item.

The value added associated with volunteer hours generally is not distributed back to the volunteers but rather to other stakeholders—primarily, society. However, there was one exception—the $155,020 of comparative market value generated by tenant groups volunteering for Jane/Finch. The members of that group felt that their hours were contributing both to the broader community and to themselves personally. The tenant group participants felt that the hours they contributed for personal benefit assisted those who otherwise would have had to pay on the market. Therefore, in this case, the volunteer contribution was analogous to social labor, as in the student-housing cooperative in Chapter 6. To recognize that the hours from tenant group participants differed from the other volunteers at Jane/Finch, these were split 50/50 between the volunteer and stakeholder society. Therefore, for the contribution by tenant group volunteers, $77,510 was distributed to the stakeholder volunteers and an equal amount to the stakeholder society. In Table 7.4, that $77,510 brings the total distribution to the stakeholder volunteer to $93,713 and the total to the stakeholder society to $229,240. Although the stakeholder society receives much more value from the organization as a whole, this portion is the amount contributed by volunteers directly. All of the components in the $229,240 allocation also appear in Table 7.2.

Table 7.4 EVAS (Partial)—Distribution of Value Added
Jane/Finch Community and Family Centre

Distribution of Value Added		Financial	Social	Combined
Employees	Wages and benefits	$724,583		$724,583
Volunteers	Personal growth and development	1,746	10,403	12,149
	Recognition and awards	4,054		4,054
	Tenant volunteers		77,510	77,510
		5,800	87,913	93,713
Society	Recipients (from volunteer hours)		229,240	229,240
Organization	Amortization of capital assets	10,455		10,455
	Programs (from volunteer hours)		17,327	17,327
		10,455	17,327	27,782
Value Added		$740,838	$334,480	$1,075,318

Note: For the nine months ended December 31, 2000.

Organization is the other case where some volunteer hours were distributed to a stakeholder other than society. For organization, the allocation includes volunteer contributions that were specifically administrative. Two volunteer roles are included for the distribution of volunteer hours to the stakeholder organization—$11,306 (the comparative market value for the services of the board of directors) and $6,021 (the comparative market value of services of volunteers who undertake administrative tasks in the community office). Together these amounts come to $17,327, the value of the volunteer contribution to the stakeholder organization. In addition, as shown in Table 7.4, the stakeholder organization also received value added from the amortization of its capital assets in the amount of $10,455, bringing to $27,782 the total distributed to it.

Overall, the total value added distributed corresponds to the value added created. Where the items are limited to those on audited financial statements, the amount is $740,838; where the items are expanded to include non-monetized social contributions, the amount is $1,075,318.

The Expanded Value Added Statement (Tables 7.3 and 7.4) indicates that by including the contribution from Jane/Finch volunteers, the reported amount of value added created by the organization increased by over 45 percent as compared to the amount calculated using financial information only. Thus, the EVAS shows that the financial information without the social misses part of the organization's performance story.

CASE TWO:
CANADIAN RED CROSS, TORONTO REGION

The inspiration for the Red Cross began in 1859 when Henry Dunant, a Swiss businessman and philanthropist (and winner of the first Nobel Peace Prize), helped the wounded from three armies at an Italian battlefield (Solferino) using volunteers. Over the next five years, Dunant and his friends developed the idea of a humanitarian volunteer group to provide relief to the wounded during a time of war. As a result of their efforts, the International Red Cross was formed in 1864, and that same year the first Geneva Convention was approved outlining humanitarian principles for the treatment of wounded soldiers during war. Today, throughout the world, there are Red Cross/Red Crescent societies—both national societies and regional affiliates—which, according to the International Federation, have 97 million members and volunteers, and 300,000 employees, assisting 233 million beneficiaries (International Federation of Red Cross and Red Crescent Societies 2006).

As with Red Cross Societies throughout the world, the Canadian Red Cross, Toronto Region (hereafter referred to as the Red Cross), focuses on one goal: to improve the situation of the most vulnerable. Programs include:

➤ International Services—tracing and reunion, fund-raising, educational programs;
➤ Community Services—Meals on Wheels, transportation, home health care;
➤ First Aid and Safety Services—education in CPR, water safety, first aid;
➤ Disaster Services—emergency response team, fire recovery program, hot lunch;
➤ Community Initiatives—food bank, child drop-in, emergency needs program.

The Red Cross office receives funding from a variety of sources—primarily the United Way but also program fees, donations, grants, and government contracts. The procedure in putting together an Expanded Value Added Statement for the Red Cross was similar to Jane/Finch. However, at least one feature of the Red Cross differed. Volunteers, in addition to contributing hours, also paid for expenses related to their volunteering and sometimes were not reimbursed. These contributions become an important source of value added.

Estimating the Volunteer Hours

Making an estimate of the volunteer hours is the first step in expanding the Value Added Statement beyond the information from the audited financial statements. For the Red Cross fiscal period, April 1, 1999, to March 31, 2000, staff estimated from volunteer tracking sheets that 1,506 volunteers contributed 63,568 hours (Table 7.5). Based on this estimate, volunteers contributed 32.6 full-time equivalent (FTE) positions, which, in addition to the Red Cross's paid staff FTE of 62, means that there was a total workforce FTE of 94.6. Thus, volunteer activities accounted for over one third of the organization's human resources. Furthermore, when considering the financial and in-kind resources of the organization, volunteer hours and non-reimbursed out-of-pocket expenses together accounted for 15 percent of the total. Again, volunteer contributions, both monetary and non-monetary, provide the organization with a significant resource that should be counted in its overall performance.

Table 7.5 Estimate of Volunteer Hours for the Social Accounting Year
Canadian Red Cross, Toronto Region

Estimated Number of Volunteer Hours	Number of Volunteers	Volunteer Hours
Congregate Dining	20	340
Community Services	772	9,680
Disaster and Emergency Services	150	2,800
Transportation	113	14,574
Fun and Fitness	2	1,716
First Aid	3	1,464
Employee and Volunteer Resources	2	350
Summer Students	110	6,800
International Services	40	320
Home Health Care and Equipment Services	21	1,586
Finance and Administration	2	1,856
Meals on Wheels	260	20,982
Regional Council (Board)	11	1,100
Total	1,506	63,568

Determining a Comparative Market Value

In determining a comparative market value for volunteer contributions for the Red Cross, the activities were broken into two broad groupings: council (board of directors) and programs. For the council, the volunteer hours were valued at a midpoint hourly rate of $40.24 for senior managers of health, education, social and community services, and membership organizations (Standard Occupational Code 0014), as determined by Human Resources Development Canada (HDRC) for the York region.[6] Hours contributed to the programs and administrative departments were valued at the rate for North American Industry Classification System (NAICS) sub-sector category 624, social assistance (the same as for Jane/Finch). For the year ending March 31, 2000, the hourly wage rate in Ontario for this sub-sector was $14.33. The value of these volunteer contributions is shown in Table 7.6.

Out-of-Pocket Expenses

Red Cross volunteers also contributed to the organization by paying for items out of their own pocket and not requesting reimbursement. These included travel, meals, supplies, and parking expenses related to volunteering. The amount of these out-of-pocket expenses was determined from the responses to a survey in which volunteers were asked to indicate whether or not they had non-reimbursed out-of-pocket expenses and to break this amount down into categories on the survey. The total of these non-reimbursed out-of-pocket expenses is shown in Table 7.7. Overall, excluding 110 summer-student volunteers, 56 percent of the volunteers had expenses averaging $125.64 each, or a total of $98,218, as shown in Table 7.7.[7] In making this calculation, it is important to exclude expenses reimbursed by the organization.

Table 7.6 Calculation of Market Value of Volunteer Hours Contributed
Canadian Red Cross, Toronto Region

	Number of Volunteers	Rate	Amount
Council	1,100	$40.24	$44,264
Office	2,206	14.33	31,612
			75,876
Programs	60,262	14.33	863,554
Total	63,568		$939,430

Table 7.7 Calculation of Volunteer Out-of-Pocket Expenses
Canadian Red Cross, Toronto Region

	Number of Volunteers	% with Expenses	Amount per Volunteer with Expenses	Totals
Community Services	772	40	$75.00	$23,160
Disaster and Emergency Services	150	84	111.19	13,956
Transportation	113	92	235.92	24,438
Home Health Care and Equipment Services	21	33	163.26	1,143
Meals on Wheels	260	68	145.00	25,582
Finance and Administration	2	50	105.00	105
Council	11	67	225.00	1,650
Other	67	75	163.26	8,183
Summer Students	110	NA	NA	0
Total	**1,506**			**$98,218**

Estimating the Market Value for Personal Benefits

Just over half of the respondents (53.38%) to the survey indicated that their volunteering activities benefited them in terms of personal growth and development. Assuming that the personal growth and development experienced by the respondents to the survey reflected the experience of volunteers as a whole at the Red Cross, the value of this benefit was determined to be $121,791 (1,506 volunteers × 53.38% × $151.50). As with Jane/Finch, the survey established that the surrogate value of $151.50 for this benefit was based upon the average cost of a community college course in personal development.

Calculating Volunteer Value Added

Overall, volunteer contributions of hours and out-of-pocket expenses and the benefits received by volunteers resulted in an increase of value added of $1,154,349—from $2,812,517 to $3,966,866. Of this increase, $939,430 came from hours contributed by volunteers, $98,218 additional from non-reimbursed out-of-pocket expenses, and another $116,701 from secondary value added through personal growth and development. As a result, the value added due to these contributions was over 40 percent more than would have been reported using financial information only (Table 7.8).

Table 7.8 Expanded Value Added Statement (Partial)
Canadian Red Cross, Toronto Region, for the Year Ended March 31, 2001

Value Added		Financial	Social	Combined
Outputs	Primary	$5,741,634	$1,037,648	$6,779,282
	Secondary	5,090	116,701	121,791
	Total	5,746,724	1,154,349	6,901,073
Purchases of external goods and services		2,934,207		2,934,207
Value added		**$2,812,517**	**$1,154,349**	**$3,966,866**
Ratio of value added to purchases		0.96	0.39	1.35

DISTRIBUTION OF VALUE ADDED

As with Jane/Finch, the value added created by the organization was distributed in total, as shown in Table 7.9. The same set of stakeholders was used as with Jane/Finch, and the distribution followed the same pattern. Therefore, the details are not repeated. However, it should be noted that, unlike Jane/Finch, no volunteer hours were distributed to the stakeholder volunteer. The distribution of a portion of the hours to the stakeholder volunteer was anomalous. Normally, volunteer hours are distributed to the stakeholder society, since these involve a service to the community; or if the volunteer were engaged in administration, the volunteer hours would be distributed to the stakeholder organization.

Table 7.9 EVAS (Partial)—Distribution of Value Added
Canadian Red Cross, Toronto Region, for the Year Ended March 31, 2001

Distribution of Value Added		Financial	Social	Combined
Employees	Wages and benefits	$2,608,957		$2,608,957
Volunteers	Personal growth and development	5,090	$116,701	121,791
	Recognition and awards	8,515		8,515
		13,605	116,701	130,306
Society	Recipients (from volunteer hours)		863,554	863,554
Organization	Amortization of capital assets	189,955		189,955
	Programs (from volunteer hours)		75,876	75,876
	Programs (from volunteer out-of-pocket expenses)		98,218	98,218
		189,955	174,094	364,049
Value Added		**$2,812,517**	**$1,154,349**	**$3,966,866**

The other way in which the Red Cross's distribution of value added differed from Jane/Finch is that the out-of-pocket expenses that were not reimbursed are shown under the stakeholder organization. In other words, this is value that the volunteers added to augment the organization's services.

CASE THREE:
CANADIAN CROSSROADS INTERNATIONAL

Canadian Crossroads International (CCI) is an international nonprofit that recruits, trains, and places volunteers from Canada and over 15 "partner" countries in international development projects and internships in those countries as well as in community development projects within Canada. CCI is funded primarily through the Canadian International Development Agency (CIDA) and through fund-raising.

CCI grew out of its American counterpart, Operation Crossroads Africa, founded by Dr. James H. Robinson in the 1950s. Robinson believed that all people are "fundamentally more similar than dissimilar" and that by living and working together could create a "crossroads" of cultures and personal experience leading to individual and societal change. This ideal led Robinson to develop a volunteer work program for Americans in Africa, one of the first programs of its kind (Canadian Crossroads International 2002).

Robinson's vision received international recognition and quickly caught on in Canada. Throughout the 1960s, small groups of Canadian volunteers who shared the objective of creating a more equitable and sustainable world coordinated international placements. In 1969, CCI became an independent, federally chartered organization. Ever since then, CCI has pursued Robinson's "one world" vision, arranging two-way volunteer placements and internships in more than 70 Canadian communities and over 15 countries in Africa, Asia, South America, and the Caribbean.

Each year, CCI recruits, trains, and sends over 300 volunteers on international development projects and internships in partner countries and Canada. Participants are matched to a variety of community-based activities run by local non-governmental organizations working to address community needs in the areas of health (HIV/AIDS), basic education, sustainable resource management, youth/children, and capacity building of local organizations. Pre-departure orientation, post-placement debriefing and reentry training, fund-raising, civic engagement, and education on development issues are all integral components of a CCI placement or internship. Travel, accommodation, and related costs are paid by CCI.

Volunteers also serve as animateurs (trainers), on the board of directors, and on 80 different national, regional, local, and country committees governing the various programs. A breakdown of the number of volunteers and the hours they contributed for the 15-month fiscal period studied is shown in Table 7.10.[8] In addition to its volunteers, CCI has a paid staff of 27: nine in its national office and from three to nine in each of its four regional offices.

Six hundred and nine (609) volunteers contributed 67 full-time equivalent (FTE) positions for the 15 months ending December 31, 2001. This was based on an estimate of 152,643 volunteer hours (see Table 7.10). This means that CCI had the equivalent of a total workforce FTE of 94, not just the paid staff FTE of 27. In other words, volunteers contributed over 70 percent of Canadian Crossroads International's human resources. Furthermore, when considering the financial and in-kind resources of the organization, volunteer hours and non-reimbursed out-of-pocket expenses together accounted for almost 50 percent of the total.

Primary Outputs

Creating an Expanded Value Added Statement for CCI involved steps similar to Jane/Finch and the Red Cross. Therefore, we will skip over some of the details and highlight issues unique to this organization. As with the two other cases, once the expenditures were taken from the audited financial statements, a key step was estimating the volunteer hours and establishing a comparative market value using the North American Industry Classification System (NAICS).[9]

The activities of the majority of the volunteers of CCI were classified under NAICS sub-sector 54, "professional, scientific and technical services." This category includes organizations engaged in activities in which knowledge and skills are the major input and in which much of the expertise requires a university or college education. For the 15 months ending March 31, 2001, the wage rate for hourly paid employees in this category for Canada was $19.08. For salaried employees in this job category, the hourly equivalent was $25.85. For volunteer activities requiring a high level of professional skills, the rate for salaried employees was used. For those activities requiring basic skills, the rate for hourly employees was used. For those activities using a mixture of skills, the two rates were averaged at $22.465.

As the NAICS rates do not take into consideration governance tasks performed by boards, a different source of market comparisons was used for these. Volunteer board service was valued at a midpoint hourly rate of $28.39 for "senior managers of health, education, social and community services and membership organizations" (Standard Occupational Code 0014), as determined by Human Resources Development Canada (HDRC).[10] Based on interviews with staff, this rate best reflected the type of leadership and management skills that were required by board members responsible for governance of the organization.

Using these rates, the total value of hours contributed by CCI volunteers was $3,618,772 (Table 7.10). For those volunteers who participated in placements (in Canada or overseas), travel, accommodation, and related expenses are provided by CCI. The total of these expenditures was $818,961. There are different ways to handle these costs on the EVAS, depending on the assumptions made. If these expenditures are considered as a partial "wage" paid to these volunteers, then the total value for volunteer hours used in the EVAS needs to be adjusted to reflect only the "free" contribution of hours—in other words, the total value of $3,618,772 less $818,961 = $2,799,811. Alternatively, if these costs are considered as external expenses of the program (in other words, purchases of external goods and services), then the full value of the hours contributed is used in the EVAS. Both scenarios will be considered later in the section "Calculating Volunteer Value Added."

Table 7.10 Hours Contributed and Market Value, by Volunteer Task
Canadian Crossroads International

	Number of Hours	Rate	Amount
Board	2,048	$28.39	$58,129
Committees	45,990	22.47	1,033,165
Animateurs	1,750	19.08	33,390
Subtotal	49,788		1,124,684
Overseas	69,400	25.85	1,793,990
To Canada	23,645	19.08	451,147
Interflow	685	19.08	13,070
Net Corps	9,125	25.85	235,881
Subtotal programs	102,855		$2,494,088
Total	152,643		$3,618,772

Sources: Hours: staff estimates. Rates: board—HDRC;
Others—CANSIM database.

Out-of-Pocket Expenses

CCI volunteers had sizable out-of-pocket expenses and substantial portions were not reimbursed. Based on survey results, 71 percent of board members indicated that they had non-reimbursed expenses, and these averaged $638 in the year under consideration. Similarly, 81 percent of the remaining volunteers spent an average of $204.23 in the year. These figures were adjusted to reflect expenditures for 15 months, resulting in a total of $131,029.

In addition, there were host families who supplied accommodation for the volunteers on placements and who also spent money out of their own pocket that was not reimbursed. This non-reimbursed portion was estimated conservatively at $36,143 by taking the number of weeks that a family served as a host and by allocating a value of $20 per week for those in Canada and of $10 per week for those overseas.

Secondary Outputs: Personal Benefit

For secondary outputs, just over 80 percent of respondents indicated strongly that they benefited in terms of personal growth and development by volunteering for CCI. Assuming that the personal growth and development of the surveyed volunteers reflects the experience of all CCI volunteers and using a surrogate measure of a community college course, this secondary output was valued at $74,263 (609 volunteers × 0.8049 × $151.50). This figure was then adjusted to reflect 15 months, resulting in a value of $92,829. The financial cost of training in this period was $34,028, so the social value added by CCI for volunteer personal development becomes the difference ($92,829 less 34,028 = $58,801).

Calculating Volunteer Value Added

To determine the organization's value added, first the value of outputs has to be calculated. Two examples are provided, depending on how the expenditures for travel, accommodation, and related items for placement volunteers are handled. As noted, one way is to consider them as a partial wage for the volunteers; the second is as an external expense of the program.

In the first example (Table 7.11) where these expenses are considered as a partial wage payment, the expenditures ($3,912,720) are added to the social contributions ($2,799,812 in hours contributed, $131,029 in out-of-pocket expenses from volunteers, $36,143 in out-of-pocket expenses from host families, and $58,801 from secondary outputs) to arrive at a total of $6,938,504. From this total is subtracted the goods and services that are purchased externally, $1,436,883, leading to a total of value added of $5,501,621 (column labeled "combined").

Table 7.11 Expanded Value Added Statement (Partial)—Example 1
Canadian Crossroads International

Value Added		Financial	Social	Combined
Outputs	Primary	$3,878,692	$2,966,983	$6,845,675
	Secondary	34,028	58,801	92,829
	Total	3,912,720	3,025,784	6,938,504
Purchases of external goods and services		1,436,883		1,436,883
Value added		**$2,475,837**	**$3,025,784**	**$5,501,621**
Ratio of value added to purchases		1.72	2.11	3.83

Note: For the 15 months ended March 31, 2001.

In the second example (Table 7.12), where these expenses are considered as purchases of external goods and services, the expenditures ($3,912,720) are added to the social contributions ($3,618,773 in hours contributed, $131,029 in out-of-pocket expenses from volunteers, $36,143 in out-of-pocket expenses from host families, and $58,801 from secondary outputs) to arrive at a total of $7,757,465. From this total is subtracted the goods and services that are purchased externally, $2,255,844, leading to a total of value added of $5,501,621 (column labeled "combined").

In both examples, the combined value added is the same ($5,501,621). However, the ratio of value added to external goods and services differs because, in the first example, the $818,961 for travel, accommodation, and related expenses is considered as a payment for labor and, thus, a distribution of value added to volunteers, while in the second example, these expenditures are considered as an external program expense. Since the ratio of value added is based on the value added created divided by the amount of external goods and services, the change in the latter figure affects the ratio.

In the first example, the ratio of value added to purchases indicates that for every dollar expended on goods and services, the organization generated $3.83 in value added. If the market estimate of non-monetized items such as volunteer contributions and personal growth and development had not been included, the ratio of value added to purchases would be 1.72, as indicated in the "financial" column (Table 7.11). Therefore, the inclusion of non-monetized items increases this ratio by over 122 percent. In the second example (Table 7.12), the ratio of value added to purchases is $2.44, whereas if only the financial contributions had been considered, it would have been $0.73.

Table 7.12 Expanded Value Added Statement (Partial)—Example 2
Canadian Crossroads International

Value Added		Financial	Social	Combined
Outputs	Primary	$3,878,692	$3,785,944	$7,664,636
	Secondary	34,028	58,801	92,829
	Total	3,912,720	3,844,745	7,757,465
Purchases of external goods and services		2,255,844		2,255,844
Value added		$1,656,876	$3,844,745	$5,501,621
Ratio of value added to purchases		0.73	1.70	2.44

Note: For the 15 months ended March 31, 2001.

DISTRIBUTION OF VALUE ADDED

In contrast to the stakeholders for the two previous organizations, CCI has a fifth stakeholder—the CCI Foundation to which loan interest is paid. Therefore, the CCI Foundation is analogous to an investor in the organization's services. For the other stakeholders—employees, volunteers, society (including government), and the organization itself—the distribution is similar to the two other case studies.

Again, the two scenarios are presented. Table 7.13 presents the Distribution of Value Added for the first example. In this scenario, as payments for travel, accommodation, and related items ($818,961) are considered as a partial wage, this amount is considered as a distribution of value added to volunteers, similar to the payment of wages and benefits to employees. The remaining "free" labor contributions ($2,494,088 less 818,961 = $1,675,127) are distributed to the stakeholder society (that is, partner organizations where the volunteers provide their services).

In the second scenario (Table 7.14), the payment for travel, accommodation, and related items is treated as a purchase of external goods and services. Thus, the full value of volunteer hours contributed by placement volunteers ($2,494,088) is distributed to the stakeholder society (partner organizations). Therefore, in the first case, $947,933 is distributed to the stakeholder volunteer because the reimbursement for expenses is treated as a payment similar to wages allocated to volunteers. In the second case, without the distribution of $818,961, the stakeholder volunteer is allocated only $128,972 of the value added. In the second case, the $818,961 is distributed to the stakeholder society, and the total distribution to that group increases from $1,712,579 to $2,531,540.

Table 7.13 EVAS (Partial)—Distribution of Value Added—Example 1
Canadian Crossroads International

	Distribution of Value Added	Financial	Social	Combined
Employees	Wages and benefits	$1,491,450		$1,491,450
Volunteers	Personal growth and development	34,028	$58,801	92,829
	Travel, accommodation, allowances, etc.	818,961		818,961
	Host families (out-of-pocket expenses)		36,143	36,143
		852,989	94,944	947,933
Society	Recipients (from volunteer hours)		1,675,127	1,675,127
	Government (GST)	37,452		37,452
		37,452	1,675,127	1,712,579
FCCF	Loan interest	46,604		46,604
Organization	Amortization of capital assets	47,342		47,342
	Programs (from volunteer hours)		1,124,684	1,124,684
	Programs (from volunteer out-of-pocket expenses)		131,029	131,029
		47,342	1,255,713	1,303,055
Value Added Distributed		**$2,475,837**	**$3,025,784**	**$5,501,621**

Note: For the 15 months ended March 31, 2001.

Is one of these procedures preferable to the other? There isn't a simple answer to this question. Creating an EVAS requires following rules, but it also involves judgments where differing interpretations are possible. For Jane/Finch, that was the case when the tenant volunteers claimed that not just the community centre benefited from their contribution but that they also grew personally. Therefore, those particular volunteer hours were divided 50/50 between the stakeholder groups, society and volunteer rather than allocating them in total to society. Similarly, for CCI, as shown, the expenditure made by the organization for travel, accommodation, and related items for placement volunteers can be interpreted differently. Our inclination is to favor the interpretation that treats this expenditure as the purchase of external goods and services because, if paid employees were in a similar circumstance, they would not be expected to pay for their own travel and living expenses. Their employer would normally cover them. Although volunteers are not employees, given the circumstances, it is likely that most employers would interpret such items as an organizational expense.

In both examples, the total value added distributed corresponds to the value added created. Where the items are limited to those on audited financial statements, that amount is $2,475,837; where the items are expanded to include non-monetized social contributions, the amount is $6,320,582.

Table 7.14 EVAS (Partial)—Distribution of Value Added—Example 2
Canadian Crossroads International

Distribution of Value Added		Financial	Social	Combined
Employees	Wages and benefits	$1,491,450		$1,491,450
Volunteers	Personal growth and development	34,028	$58,801	92,829
	Host families (out-of-pocket expenses)		36,143	36,143
		34,028	94,944	128,972
Society	Recipients (from volunteer hours)		2,494,088	2,494,088
	Government (GST)	37,452		37,452
		37,452	2,494,088	2,531,540
FCCF	Loan interest	46,604		46,604
Organization	Amortization of capital assets	47,342		47,342
	Programs (from volunteer hours)		1,124,684	1,124,684
	Programs (from volunteer out-of-pocket expenses)		131,029	131,029
		47,342	1,255,713	1,303,055
Value Added Distributed		**$1,656,876**	**$3,844,745**	**$5,501,621**

Note: For the 15 months ended March 31, 2001.

CASE FOUR:
CANADIAN BREAST CANCER FOUNDATION—ONTARIO CHAPTER

The fourth organization is the Ontario Chapter of the Canadian Breast Cancer Foundation (hereafter referred to as the Breast Cancer Foundation). The Canadian Breast Cancer Foundation is the largest charitable organization in Canada dedicated exclusively to the support and advancement of breast cancer research, education, diagnosis, and treatment. The Breast Cancer Foundation is an example of a "voluntary" organization in that it is funded almost entirely through fund-raising or donors and its volunteers heavily outweigh the paid staff.

The Breast Cancer Foundation was established in 1986 by a group of eight community leaders, and since its inception it has awarded grants and fellowships in excess of (Cdn.) $9.6 million for breast cancer research and educational initiatives in Canada. In order to achieve its goals, the Breast Cancer Foundation raises funds in many ways, including several high-profile fund-raising events such as its annual Run for the Cure and its awareness days. The first run took place in 1992 with 1,500 participants and raised $83,000. It has since grown to be Canada's largest single-day fund-raising event, with more than 170,000 participants in 51 communities.

In addition to funding research initiatives, the Foundation funds many community-based breast cancer projects and programs through its chapters and branches across Canada. The Ontario Chapter also provides Research and Advanced Practice Fellowship Awards for physicians and health care professionals in related disciplines.

For the fiscal year ending March 31, 2001, staff estimated that the chapter was assisted by the efforts of 2,564 core volunteers. These served on regional committees and boards, standing committees that reported to the board (such as grant review committees), as well as in planning and organizing special events. In total, they contributed 38,891 hours. In addition, an estimated 41,000 runners participated in the Run for the Cure in Ontario, contributing over 83,000 hours to this event. Including run-day participants, a total of 44,303 volunteers contributed an estimated 122,361 hours to the Breast Cancer Foundation, Ontario. Table 7.15 shows the estimates of volunteer numbers and hours by role.

Based on this estimate, volunteer activities accounted for 84 percent of the Breast Cancer Foundation's human resources and contributed 67 full-time equivalent (FTE) positions for the fiscal year ending March 31, 2001. Thus, the Breast Cancer Foundation, Ontario, had the equivalent of a total workforce FTE of 80, not just the paid staff FTE of 13. Furthermore, when considering the financial and in-kind resources of the organization, volunteer hours and non-reimbursed out-of-pocket expenses together account for 30 percent of the total.

Table 7.15 Staff Estimate of Volunteer Hours
Canadian Breast Cancer Foundation, Ontario Chapter

CBCF Ontario	Number of Volunteers	Volunteer Hours
Board of directors	16	1,369
Committees	77	1,876
Subtotal BOD/Committees*	89	3,245
Office administration	24	900
Regional offices	76	8,250
Run planning	212	11,450
Run day	1,999	13,707
Other events	164	1,339
Subtotal events	2,375	35,646
Subtotal (without runners)	2,564	38,891
Runners	41,735	83,470
Total	44,299	122,361

Source: Staff and regional director interviews.

* Subtotal is adjusted for four committee chairs also on the board of directors.

Comparative Market Value for Volunteers

As with the other cases presented in this chapter, establishing a comparative market value for the volunteers was an important piece of the EVAS. As shown in Table 7.14, volunteer hours contributed were valued primarily according to NAICS sub-sector 813 "grant-making, civic, professional and similar organizations." This sub-sector includes organizations engaged primarily in awarding grants from trust funds, or in soliciting contributions on behalf of others, to support a wide range of health, educational, scientific, cultural, and other social welfare activities. For the year ending March 31, 2001, the wage rate for hourly paid employees in this category for Ontario was $14.51. For salaried employees it was $19.72, and the midpoint of the two rates was $17.11. Committee members and run-day planning organizers were assigned the $19.72 value, based on salaried employees. Office administration, run-day volunteers, and runners were allocated a comparative market value of $14.51, based on hourly paid employees. Volunteers in regional offices or those assisting with awareness days and other special events were assigned a value of $17.11, based on the average of hourly paid and salaried employees.

For the volunteers who were members of the board of directors, the rate was taken from Human Resources Development Canada (HDRC) Standard Occupational Code 0014, "senior managers of health, education, social and community services and membership organizations." For the time period studied, the midpoint hourly rate for this category was $35.56 per hour.

The total comparative market value for the hours contributed by core volunteers through specific programs is presented in Table 7.16. These values were obtained by taking the total hours contributed by volunteers within a program and multiplying them by the appropriate hourly rates. As seen, the estimated market value of these contributions is $1,898,635.

Out-of-Pocket Expenses

Breast Cancer Foundation volunteers also incurred out-of-pocket expenses that were not reimbursed. Based on survey responses, 86 percent of board and committee members indicated non-reimbursed expenses of $402.12 per year, while 83 percent of office administration and regional office volunteers indicated average expenses of $75. Seventy-seven percent of the remaining volunteers indicated having out-of-pocket expenses averaging $75 for event planners and $12.50 for event-day assistants and participants. The total of all these expenses amounted to $481,112.

Secondary Outputs: Personal Benefits

Sixty percent of survey respondents (excluding runners) indicated strongly that they benefited in terms of personal growth and development by volunteering for the Breast Cancer Foundation. This percentage was multiplied by the core volunteer base of 2,564 and the value of a community college course ($151.50) to arrive at a value of $233,068.

Table 7.16 Calculation of Market Value of Volunteer Hours Contributed

	Number of Hours	Rate	Amount
Board of directors	1,369	$35.56	$48,682
Committees	1,876	19.72	36,995
Office administration	900	14.51	13,059
Regional offices	8,250	17.11	141,158
	12,395		239,893
Run planning	11,450	19.72	225,794
Run day	13,707	14.51	198,889
Runners	83,470	14.51	1,211,150
Awareness day	498	17.11	8,521
Great White North	841	17.11	14,390
	109,966		1,658,743
Total	122,361		$1,898,635

Calculating Volunteer Value Added

As in the other four nonprofits presented in this chapter, to calculate the organization's outputs, the expenditures ($5,319,931) are added to the social contributions ($2,612,815) to arrive at a total of $7,932,746. Then, in order to measure the value added by the organization, the goods and services that were purchased externally, $1,350,453, are subtracted from the total outputs of $7,932,746, leading to a total of value added of $6,582,293 (column labeled "combined"). The ratio of value added to purchases, indicated in the final row of Table 7.17, is established by dividing the value added by the cost of external goods and services. This ratio indicates that for every dollar expended on goods and services, the organization generated $4.87 in value added. Without the social contributions, the value-added ratio would have been $2.94 for every dollar expended. In other words, by including the volunteer contributions and the benefits they receive, the value-added ratio is increased by almost 66 percent.

As noted, the Expanded Value Added Statement includes a market estimate of non-monetized items such as volunteer contributions and personal growth and development—one of the benefits that the Breast Cancer Foundation volunteers indicated strongly that they had received. If those items had not been included, the ratio of value added to purchases would have been 2.94, as is indicated in the "financial" column of Table 7.17. The inclusion of non-monetized items increases this ratio by almost 66 percent.

Table 7.17 Expanded Value Added Statement (Partial)
Canadian Breast Cancer Foundation, Ontario Chapter

Value Added		Financial	Social	Combined
Outputs	Primary	$5,319,931	$2,379,747	$7,699,678
	Secondary		233,068	233,068
	Total	5,319,931	2,612,815	7,932,746
Purchases of external goods and services		1,350,453		1,350,453
Value added		$3,969,478	$2,612,815	$6,582,293
Ratio of value added to purchases		2.94	1.93	4.87

Note: For the year ended March 31, 2001.

DISTRIBUTION OF VALUE ADDED

The distribution of value added to the primary stakeholders of the Breast Cancer Foundation is shown in Table 7.18. The value added distributed to employees represents their wages and benefits of $571,656. For volunteers, the value added distributed was the $2,241 expended on recognition and awards and $233,068 representing the value of their personal growth and development.

The stakeholder referred to as society received value added from the programs of the organization—for example, grant disbursements for research totaling $3,034,217. The national office received value added in the amount of $344,762 for support of core programs. Value added distributed to the stakeholder organization was for three items: $16,602 for the amortization of capital assets; $1,898,635 from volunteer contributions of hours; and $481,112 for out-of-pocket expenses not reimbursed. In total, the value added distributed corresponds to the value added created. Where the items are limited to those on audited financial statements, that amount is $3,969,478; where the items are expanded to include non-monetized social contributions, the amount is $6,582,293.

Fund-Raising: A Different Perspective

It is also possible to create an EVAS based on individual program or activity, as shown in Table 7.19. In the case of the Breast Cancer Foundation, the major activities of the organization are fund-raising and program delivery, including community awareness, grant allocation, volunteer development, and chapter/branch development.

Table 7.18 EVAS (Partial)—Distribution of Value Added
Canadian Breast Cancer Foundation, Ontario Chapter

Distribution of Value Added		Financial	Social	Combined
Employees	Wages and benefits	$571,656		$571,656
Volunteers	Personal growth and development		$233,068	233,068
	Recognition and awards	2,241		2,241
		2,241	233,068	235,309
Society	CBCRI	506,000		506,000
	Grant disbursements	2,528,217		2,528,217
		3,034,217		3,034,217
National Programs	Internal transfer	344,762		344,762
Organization	Amortization of capital assets	16,602		16,602
	Volunteer hours (administrative)		239,893	239,893
	Volunteer hours (fund-raising/awareness)		1,658,742	1,658,742
	Programs (from volunteer out-of-pocket expenses)		481,112	481,112
		16,602	2,379,747	2,396,349
Value Added Distributed		**$3,969,478**	**$2,612,815**	**$6,582,293**

Note: For the year ended March 31, 2001.

Table 7.19 EVAS (Partial)—By Fund–raising and Programs
Canadian Breast Cancer Foundation, Ontario Chapter

Value Added	Fund-raising	Programming	Combined
Revenues raised	$5,664,278	$3,912,521	$5,664,278
Surplus retained		344,347	344,347
	5,664,278	3,568,174	5,319,931
Volunteer contributions (hours and out-of-pocket expenses)	2,244,106	135,641	2,379,747
	7,908,384	3,703,815	7,699,678
Secondary outputs (volunteer personal growth and development	225,328	7,740	233,068
	8,133,712	3,711,555	7,932,746
Purchases of external goods and services	1,258,058	92,395	1,350,453
Value Added	**$6,875,654**	**$3,619,160**	**$6,582,293**
Distribution of Value Added			
Employees	$474,856	$96,800	$571,656
Volunteers–recognition	2,241		2,241
Volunteers–personal growth and development	225,328	7,740	233,068
Total volunteers	227,569	7,740	235,309
National office		344,762	344,762
Canadian Breast Cancer Research Initiative		506,000	506,000
Grant disbursements: research		1,585,000	1,585,000
Grant disbursements: education		559,126	559,126
Grant disbursements: other		384,091	384,091
Total programs		3,378,979	3,378,979
Organization: depreciation	16,602		16,602
Organization: volunteer contributions	2,244,106	135,641	2,379,747
Surplus available for programming	3,912,521		
Total organization	6,173,229	135,641	2,396,349
Value Added Distributed	**$6,875,654**	**$3,619,160**	**$6,582,293**

Looking first at fund-raising activities, the Breast Cancer Foundation raised $5,664,278 and mobilized tens of thousands of volunteers who contributed hours and out-of-pocket expenses valued at $2,244,106. It also created secondary outputs valued at $225,328 for personal growth and development of its fund-raising volunteers. The total value of all outputs, therefore, was $8,133,712. From this total, $1,258,058 of external goods and services was subtracted, leaving a total of value added created of $6,875,654. Of this amount, $3,912,521 remained as a surplus available for program activities. However, $344,347 of this surplus was carried forward to the subsequent fiscal year and, therefore, the Breast Cancer Foundation had $3,568,174 available to spend on programs.

Thus, the EVAS specific to programs, as presented in Table 7.19, starts with the revenues that are transferred from fund-raising to programs and adjusted for the $344,347 carried forward. The next step is to add the volunteer contributions specific to programs. For hours, these were valued at $98,725, and for out-of-pocket expenses at $36,906, resulting in total volunteer contributions to programs of $135,641. Secondary outputs received by the program volunteers were valued at a total of $7,740. To arrive at the total program outputs, these amounts—$135,641 and $7,740—were added to the total the Breast Cancer Foundation had available for programs—$3,568,174—resulting in an overall value of $3,711,555. The purchases of external goods and services specific to programs, $92,395, was then subtracted from the total outputs to end up with the value added associated with programs of $3,619,160.

To arrive at the total value added created by the organization, it is necessary to add together the value added from fund-raising and the value added from programs and to subtract any internal transfers. In the case of the Breast Cancer Foundation, the amount of its internal transfer was the surplus resulting from fund-raising that was transferred to programs ($3,912,521). Thus, for the Breast Cancer Foundation, the total value added created is calculated as $6,875,654 from fund-raising, plus $3,619,160 from programs, less the internal transfer of $3,912,521. This resulted in a final total of value added of $6,582,293 (see also Table 7.17).

CASE FIVE:
JUNIOR ACHIEVEMENT OF ROCHESTER, NEW YORK AREA, INC.

As mentioned previously in Chapter 5, Junior Achievement of Rochester, a nonprofit franchise of Junior Achievement, Inc., runs 640 economic-education programs yearly in 65 elementary, middle, and high schools using over 480 core volunteers. Details of the calculation of the value of its contributions for the year ended June 30, 2001, were shown previously in Chapter 5, in Tables 5.1 and 5.2. These contributions amounted to $345,606 for over 12,000 hours contributed and $12,530 for out-of-pocket expenses.

For the year ended June 30, 2001, Junior Achievement of Rochester volunteers contributed over 51 percent of that organization's human-resource hours and almost 40 percent of the total of financial and social contributions. Contributions by and to volunteers accounted for over 54 percent of the organization's expanded value added. The Expanded Value Added Statement for Junior Achievement of Rochester is presented in Table 7.20.

Table 7.20 Expanded Value Added Statement (Partial)
Junior Achievement of Rochester, New York Area, Inc.

Value Added		Financial	Social	Combined
Outputs	Primary	$630,513	$358,136	$988,649
	Secondary		24,232	24,232
	Total	630,513	382,368	1,012,881
Purchases of external goods and services		306,363		306,363
Value added		**$324,150**	**$382,368**	**$706,518**
Ratio of value added to purchases		1.06	1.25	2.31

Note: For the year ended June 30, 2001.

To calculate the value of the organization's outputs, the expenditures for programs, fund-raising, administration, and special events ($630,513) were added to the social contributions ($382,368)—representing the value attributed to volunteer hours, out-of-pocket expenses, and the secondary output of personal growth and development—to arrive at a total of $1,012,881. As in the other cases in this chapter, volunteer personal growth and development was calculated based on survey responses, which indicated that 38.1 percent of respondents felt strongly that they received this benefit. Using an average cost of a community college course of $100 and a core base of volunteers of 636, the comparative market value of this output was calculated as 636 volunteers × .381 × $100 = $24,232.

Purchases of external goods and services amounting to $306,363 were then subtracted from total outputs of $1,012,881, to arrive at a total for expanded value added of $706,518. The ratio of expanded value added to purchases was 2.31, but when considering only financial items, the ratio was 1.06. This means that volunteer contributions increased the value added of Junior Achievement of Rochester by almost 118 percent.

Table 7.21 presents the Distribution of Value Added for Junior Achievement of Rochester. Four stakeholders are shown—employees, volunteers, creditors, and the organization. The value added distributed to employees represents their wages and benefits of $304,876. For volunteers, the value added distributed was the $24,232 representing the value of their personal growth and development. Creditors received $6,202 in interest payments.

Table 7.21 EVAS (Partial)—Distribution of Value Added
Junior Achievement of Rochester, New York Area, Inc.

Distribution of Value Added	Financial	Social	Combined
Employees: wages and benefits	$304,876		$304,876
Volunteers: personal growth and development		$24,232	24,232
Creditors: Interest paid	6,202		6,202
Organization:			
Amortization of capital assets	13,072		13,072
From volunteer hours		345,606	345,606
From volunteer out-of-pocket expenses		12,530	12,530
	13,072	358,136	371,208
Value Added	**$324,150**	**$382,368**	**$706,518**

Note: For the year ended June 30, 2001.

Value added distributed to the stakeholder organization was for three items: $13,072 for the amortization of capital assets; $345,606 from volunteer contributions of hours; and $12,530 for out-of-pocket expenses not reimbursed (Tables 5.1 and 5.2). In total, the value added distributed corresponds to the value added created. Where the items are limited to those on audited financial statements, that amount is $324,150; where the items are expanded to include non-monetized social contributions, the amount is $706,518.

SUMMARY AND CONCLUSION

The EVAS tells a much different story for these five organizations than do the financial statements alone. The EVAS helps various stakeholders, particularly volunteers, to see what value they have added to the organization in which they participate. When viewed in relation to the financial information only, volunteer contributions at Jane/Finch added 44 percent more to the value added created by the organization. For the other organizations, the increases in value added from volunteers were: the Red Cross—37 percent; CCI—118 or 226 percent (depending on the scenario); the Breast Cancer Foundation—60 percent; and Junior Achievement of Rochester—almost 118 percent. In addition, each organization added value by making available opportunities for personal growth and development for its volunteers. In dollar terms, the total of these contributions ranged from $334,480 for Jane/Finch, to $1,154,349 for the Red Cross, $3,844,745 for CCI, $2,612,815 for the Breast Cancer

Foundation, and $382,368 for Junior Achievement of Rochester. In each case, these are significant contributions not accounted for in conventional accounting.

Volunteers account for a major portion of each organization's human resources (Figure 7.1). In the case of Jane/Finch and the Red Cross, volunteers made up about one third of the labor pool. In the case of the other three organizations, volunteers provided more resources than paid staff—for CCI, volunteers accounted for over 70 percent of the organization's human resources, for the Breast Cancer Foundation, this contribution was over 84 percent, and for Junior Achievement of Rochester it was over 51 percent. It must also be noted that not only do volunteers contribute significantly, but also these contributions are spread out over hundreds, if not thousands, of people.

Most of the value added by and for volunteers to voluntary nonprofit organizations go unreported because it is not monetized and, therefore, is not included in conventional accounting statements. For the five organizations discussed in this chapter, the amount of value added that was unreported ranged from about 30 to 70 percent of the total value added calculated (Figure 7.2). As was seen in this chapter, the EVAS is one way for organizations to present the value of this important resource and relate it to their economic performance.

These figures make the assumption that the financial expenditures and volunteer contributions of each organization represent an efficient use of resources. To gauge the accuracy of this valuation, it would be necessary to do a complete assessment of the organization's outputs, based on similar goods and services in the private sector. While that was beyond the scope of the Volunteer Value Added project, it is one of the next steps in carrying this research forward.

Figure 7.1 Human Resources

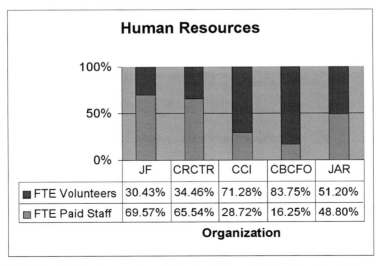

Legend: JF = Jane/Finch Community and Family Centre; CRCT = Canadian Red Cross, Toronto Region; CCI = Canadian Crossroads International; CBCF = Canadian Breast Cancer Foundation, Ontario Chapter; JAR = Junior Achievement of Rochester.

Figure 7.2 Value Added Reported and Unreported

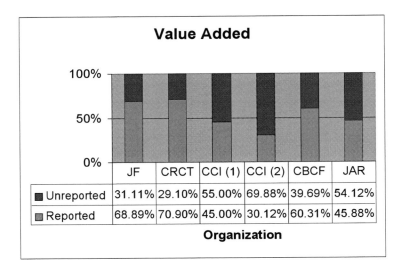

Legend: JF = Jane/Finch Community and Family Centre; CRCT = Canadian Red
Cross, Toronto Region; CCI = Canadian Crossroads International; CBCF = Canadian
Breast Cancer Foundation, Ontario Chapter; JAR = Junior Achievement of Rochester.

QUESTIONS FOR DISCUSSION

1. What are some of the barriers faced by nonprofits and cooperatives to including
    volunteer contributions and social labor on their financial statements? How can
    they be overcome?
2. What are some of the barriers faced by accountants and auditors to including
    volunteer contributions on financial statements? How can they be overcome?
3. "The hours that paid employees may work beyond their regular workday and for
    which they do not get paid are similar to 'volunteer time contributed' and,
    therefore, should be included in the Expanded Value Added Statement." Do you
    agree or disagree with this statement and why?
4. What are the potential risks and benefits of putting a value on volunteer
    contributions? In your view, do the benefits outweigh the risks?
5. List five benefits that volunteers can gain from volunteering. How would you
    measure them, and how would you assign a value to them?
6. What additional information does the Expanded Value Added Statement tell us by
    including volunteer contributions or social labor? How can this information help
    an organization?
7. Until recently, volunteer contributions to the economy were seldom recognized.
    Emerging research shows that these contributions are significant. What are the
    implications of these findings for research, policy, and practice?

8. Which audiences might find it useful to put a value on volunteer contributions and why?
9. Take an existing organization, calculate the volunteer contributions, and include them in an Expanded Value Added Statement. Compare the Expanded Value Added Statement to the income statement of the organization. What new insights arise?
10. Using existing information on the Internet or in annual reports, calculate the number of hours volunteers contribute to two or more nonprofits and compare the full-time equivalents of these hours to the full-time equivalents of the organizations' paid employees. Present the data graphically. What is the impact of knowing this information?

NOTES

[1] At the time of the study, Jane/Finch was in the process of changing its fiscal year-end; therefore, the period studied was nine months, not the usual 12 months.

[2] These data and all subsequent NAICS data originate from the Statistics Canada CANSIM Data Base. CANSIM is an official Mark of Statistics Canada.

[3] For the four Canadian case studies, fringe benefits were not included in the Expanded Value Added Statement because determining an appropriate percentage was beyond the scope of this project. However, for Junior Achievement of Rochester, an amount equal to 12 percent of wages was included for fringe benefits, as suggested by the Independent Sector (2006) as an appropriate rate for volunteer contributions in the United States.

[4] About half of the volunteers surveyed at the Jane/Finch Community and Family Centre had out-of-pocket expenses, but those participating in the focus groups indicated that all such expenses were reimbursed. Given the practice of reimbursement, out-of-pocket expenses are not included in Expanded Value Added Statement (EVAS) for Jane/Finch (although they have been included for the other sites in this project).

[5] This is still only a partial Value Added Statement, showing the impact of volunteer contributions. A full Value Added Statement would involve a deeper examination of all the outputs of the organization and their comparative market value.

[6] A salary range was not available for the greater Toronto region; so the salary range for a similar region was used. See Web site: lmi-imt.hrdc-drhc.gc.ca.

[7] To arrive at this figure, the 110 summer-student volunteers were subtracted from the total of 1,506. Then the remaining 1,396 were multiplied by 56 percent (the percentage that had non-reimbursed out-of-pocket expenses) leading to 781.76. That figure was then multiplied by $125.76, the average out-of-pocket expense, leading to a total of $98,314.

[8] At the time of the study, CCI was in the process of changing its fiscal year-end date; therefore, the fiscal period studied was 15 months, not the usual 12 months.

[9] Salary ranges were obtained for the following regions: York, London, Quebec, and Nova Scotia. See Web site: lmi-imt.hrdc-drhc.gc.ca.

[10] Salary ranges were obtained for York and London. See Web site: lmi-imt.hrdc-drhc.gc.ca.

Chapter 8

A Social Accounting Toolkit

To prepare a social accounting statement, basic information is required. Some of the information comes from audited financial statements, but collecting information on social items that do not involve a market exchange requires different techniques. Chapters 4 to 7 presented social accounting statements but did not describe the procedures for collecting data related to social items, which is the focus of this chapter. These procedures are prerequisites for preparing social accounting statements, but for organizations not yet ready to get into social accounting, they can also be used to collect basic information that can help tell the organization's story more powerfully. The toolkit presented in this chapter will be of assistance in accounting for the value of social outputs, improving upon the record keeping of volunteers, and even attributing a dollar value to volunteers' contributions.

Our primary objective in this chapter is to ease the way for organizations to collect the information needed for social accounting. Social accounting has the advantage of highlighting the value an organization adds to its community. The approaches to social accounting presented in earlier chapters were:

➢ a Community Social Return on Investment Model;
➢ a Socioeconomic Impact Statement;
➢ a Socioeconomic Resource Statement; and
➢ an Expanded Value Added Statement.

These statements differ but all include social impacts that are normally not found in financial statements. Once those responsible have chosen the approach to social accounting that best suits their organization, the toolkit in this chapter can be used in conjunction with the statement format (as presented in the earlier chapters) to gather information and make the required calculations. The statement format provides information about what is included in inputs and outputs and how calculations are completed.

As discussed previously, social accounting statements can be presented along with the organization's other financial statements at the annual general meeting. They also can be presented to funders and are of particular use by organizations which rely on donors and government grants to assist in measuring their social impact. Even without preparing a social accounting statement, the toolkit can be used to help with funding applications, to report to funders, and to attract potential supporters.

This chapter is directed mainly to managers of nonprofits and cooperatives, but it should be of use to researchers, instructors, and students with an interest in these organizations. The last section on background information was written for small- and medium-sized organizations with limited staffing. Suggestions that cost money are not practical for many organizations, and so the tools that follow are designed to assist them in telling their story. The toolkit is presented in three sections:

➢   accounting for the value of volunteer contributions;
➢   identifying and evaluating social outputs and value; and
➢   collecting background information.

ACCOUNTING FOR THE VALUE OF VOLUNTEER CONTRIBUTIONS

The statements in Chapters 4 to 7 included estimates of volunteer value. This section offers a step-by-step method for collecting information on volunteer participation, including costs and benefits and how to calculate volunteer value. It also includes two calculations that show how volunteering extends organizational resources: volunteer hours as a percentage of an organization's total human resources and volunteer value as a percentage of an organization's overall resources.

As discussed in Chapter 2, an important characteristic of social organizations is volunteer participation—essentially, these organizations rely upon unpaid labor in order to make their services available. When unpaid labor comes from the members of either a nonprofit mutual association or a cooperative and is oriented toward lowering the costs of service to members, we have referred to it as social labor. Regardless of the label, it is helpful for social organizations to have tools at hand that measure these unpaid contributions.

To estimate the dollar value of volunteer contributions, information about tasks and hours needs to be collected and valued, as described in Step 3. Steps 2 and 4 provide a larger picture of volunteer resources within the organization, and Step 1 begins the process. Additionally, for organizations with the capacity to do so, the picture of volunteer contributions can be completed by calculating the out-of-pocket expenditures absorbed by volunteers. These expenditures can be added to the value of volunteer work. In other words, for valuing the overall contributions of volunteers, their hours of work can be combined with the related out-of-pocket expenditures they absorb. Instructions provided in the sections that follow can be used to complete any or all of the steps outlined.

Step 1. Calculating Volunteer Tasks and Hours

An organization that uses volunteers in only one or two roles (for example, to serve on its board of directors or for a particular service) will find it easier to gather the information than one in which volunteers play multiple roles. Those latter organizations will have to set up more detailed record-keeping procedures, which can be done on a computer using either a simple spreadsheet program or specialized volunteer-management software.[1] If computer tracking of this information is beyond an organization's means, volunteer hours can still be recorded on paper.

The following information should be gathered:

➢ the tasks performed by volunteers in the organization (for example, sitting on the board of directors, planting trees, disaster relief);
➢ the number of volunteers who perform each task;
➢ the number of hours each volunteer contributes to each task;
➢ the number of hours each volunteer spends preparing for volunteer activities (for example, reading documents, preparing reports, training for a special event); and
➢ the number of hours each volunteer spends traveling during volunteer activities. (Traveling time might not seem important, but it is part of a volunteer's contribution, and over a full year it can add up.)

There are two ways to gather this information:

➢ either staff or volunteers assigned to this task can keep records throughout the year and prepare monthly reports; or
➢ each volunteer can be asked to fill out a questionnaire once a year.

The first option is preferable. While volunteers may find it easy to report on what tasks they performed during a year, they may have trouble remembering the precise number of hours they spent. To minimize error, it is better to collect this information on an ongoing basis. The information, as with all information discussed in this chapter, should be collected for the same period that is covered by the organization's financial statements (that is, the organization's regular fiscal year). For organizations that diversify volunteer tasks, the questionnaire that is used to collect this information should have items reflecting the options that are available. The prompts will vary according to the organization—therefore, the following sample will need to be modified for organizations with a different array of tasks.

➢ **Sample Item for Tracking Volunteer Tasks**: Please list the volunteer activities you undertook for our organization during the past year (for example, sitting on the board of directors, sitting on a fund-raising committee, providing office administrative support, delivering meals in the community, counseling clients, doing friendly visiting, planting trees, mentoring a child, disaster relief). Please list all tasks, even those with a relatively minor time commitment.

For nonprofit mutual associations and cooperatives in which the primary service of members is to the organization, the preceding sample might be adapted slightly so that the prompts better reflect the types of contributions that the members make to the organization.

➤ **Sample Item for Social Labor**: Please list all of the unpaid tasks that you undertook for our organization during the past year (for example, sitting on the board of directors, sitting on a fund-raising committee, maintenance, providing office administrative support). Please list all tasks, even those with a relatively minor time commitment.

Some organizations might mobilize thousands of volunteers for a particular event—for example, a run to raise funds for research on breast cancer. For such an event, it would be impractical to survey all of the volunteers. The information needed could probably be obtained from pledge forms; but if a survey were required, it would be best to sample randomly and generalize from the sample to the entire group.

For most organizations, knowing the tasks volunteers perform is relatively straightforward. The bigger problem is estimating the number of hours associated with each task. If a volunteer task involves a regular pattern (for example, assisting with readings for an hour twice a week), estimating the total hours should not be a problem. However, for volunteers who have a variety of tasks and who do not follow a regular pattern, arriving at estimates of hours could be challenging. Where feasible, organizations with such patterns might consider using software that either tracks volunteer tasks and times or compiles this information on paper monthly rather than annually. For organizations that track volunteer contributions manually, an annual survey of volunteer hours should suffice. Here are some sample items that can be used:

➤ For each of these volunteer roles, please estimate the number of hours you spent volunteering in the past year;
➤ Please estimate the number of hours you spent preparing for your volunteer activities (for example, reading documents, preparing reports, training for a special event) in the past year;
➤ Please estimate the number of hours you spent traveling on behalf of (not to and from) your volunteer activities in the past year.

The first of these three items is the most critical, but the others are also of importance because the hours of volunteering are not simply those associated with the actual execution of tasks but also the preparation and travel time while undertaking the tasks. As with the preceding question on the type of task, the prompts related to hours will vary by organization.

Once the information on volunteer tasks and hours has been gathered, it needs to be totaled, as shown in Table 8.1 for the Canadian Breast Cancer Foundation. Note that prior to arriving at the total for volunteer hours, it is useful to have a breakdown by task. Having this record will make it easier to update the information subsequently and to undertake year-to-year comparisons.

Table 8.1 Staff Estimate of Volunteer Hours
Canadian Breast Cancer Foundation, Ontario Region

CBCF Ontario	Number of Volunteers	Volunteer Hours
Board of directors	16	1,369
Committees	77	1,876
Subtotal*	89	3,245
Office adminintration	24	900
Regional offices	76	8,250
Run planning	212	11,450
Run day	1,999	13,707
Other events	164	1,339
Subtotal Events	2,375	35,646
Subtotal (without runners)	2,564	38,891
Runners	41,735	83,470
Total	44,299	122,361

*Some board members also sit on committees.

Step 2: Calculating Volunteer Hours as a Percentage of Human Resources

Volunteers make valuable contributions to the management and services of an organization. To find out what impact they have within the organization's total human resources, the total hours contributed by volunteers can be expressed as full-time (staff) equivalences (FTEs). For this calculation, you need the total volunteer hours over the fiscal period, as discussed in the previous section. To use an example where volunteers play a large role, let's consider a fictitious meals-on-wheels program, Senior Links, in which 100 volunteers assist 5,000 seniors in a highly populated urban area by contributing 10 hours each per week for 52 weeks of the year, for a total of 52,000 hours per year ($52 \times 10 \times 100$). The program is part of a countywide operation that has 20 staff on a 37.5-hour workweek—in other words, each full-time staff member works 1,950 hours per year (37.5×52).

As shown in Table 8.2, in order to express the volunteer hours as full-time positions, divide the total volunteer hours by 1,950 for a total of 26.7 full-time equivalent positions (FTEs)—in this case, rounded off to 27. The figure of 27 full-time staff equivalents can be used to see how volunteer time fits into the total human resources of the organization. Knowing that the full-time paid workforce of the meals-on-wheels provider is 30 (as shown in Figure 8.1), we can add the full-time equivalence for volunteers (30 + 27 = 57) and then figure out what percentage to assign volunteer hours within the organization's total human resources—in this case (as shown in Figure 8.2), it is 47 percent (57 ÷ 27). This is a large percentage of our fictional organization's total human resources—almost one half. However, in many cases the percentages will be much smaller, particularly in nonprofits that rely heavily on staff. The calculation is not designed for comparisons among organizations but to take a snapshot of each particular organization within its own context.

Table 8.2: Calculating Volunteer Hours as a Percentage of Total Human Resources
Senior Links, a fictitious case

Calculating the Full-time Equivalents of Your Volunteer Hours	
What is the total number of hours contributed by your volunteers in the fiscal period?	52,000
What is the average number of hours worked in one year for one full-time paid staff? 37.5 hours/week × 52 weeks/year	1,950
Full-time equivalents of volunteer hours (*total volunteer hours divided by 1,950)*	26.7

Calculating the Percentage Contribution of Volunteer Hours to Total Labour Contributions	
What were your full-time equivalents for paid staff for the fiscal period?	30
Total full-time-equivalents (*volunteers plus paid staff)*	56.7
Percentage of volunteer resources to total human resources (total volunteer FTEs of 27 divided by total FTEs of 57 multiplied by 100)	47.1%

These percentages can easily be turned into a chart that illustrates them more graphically, as shown in Figure 8.1.

Figure 8.1 Volunteer Hours as a Percentage of Total Human Resources

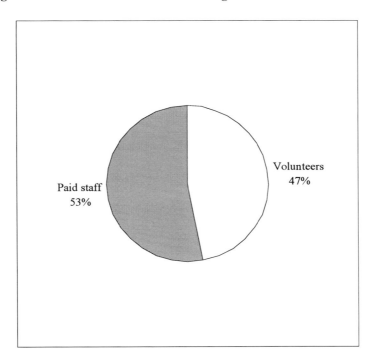

Step 3: Estimating a Market Value for Volunteer Hours

To estimate the value of volunteer contributions, it is necessary to assign a dollar value to the tasks. As discussed in Chapter 3, there are different procedures for doing this, but the two most popular are either to use an across-the-board hourly rate (treat all hours the same) or to vary the rate by task. We prefer a variable rate, as demonstrated in the case studies in Chapters 4 to 7. However, there is nothing wrong with applying the same rate to all hours, as is done by the Independent Sector (2006)—$18.04 based on figures from 2005, including 12 percent benefits. For organizations utilizing an across-the-board rate, it is important to consult with an apex organization in your area—the Independent Sector in the United States, the National Council of Voluntary Organisations in England, or Imagine Canada .

A variable rate is more demanding to apply, but it could be more precise. As in Chapters 5 to 7, there are differing options available in applying a variable rate. In the United States, check the Department of Labor, Bureau of Labor Statistics hourly wage rates from the National Compensation Survey.[2] There is a similar breakdown called the North American Industry Classification System (NAICS), an industry classification system developed by the statistical agencies of Canada, the United States, and Mexico. A manual listing all the different classifications can be found on the Statistics Canada Web site.[3]

Table 8.3 presents a task breakdown for volunteers in Junior Achievement of Rochester, the hours contributed by volunteers for each task, and the equivalent dollar values. Using the U.S. Department of Labor, Bureau of Labor Statistics, the rates assigned to volunteer tasks at Junior Achievement of Rochester were:

➢ board of directors—the $31.30 hourly wage rate for executives, administrators, and managers;
➢ company coordinators—the $26.85 hourly wage rate for managers in service organizations, not elsewhere classified;
➢ teachers of the Junior Achievement curricula—the $25.86 hourly rate for teachers, not elsewhere classified;.and
➢ for special event volunteers—the $12.22 hourly rate for administrative support occupations, not elsewhere classified.

Using these rates, the total value of volunteer hours was estimated to be $308,577. Then 12 percent was added for fringe benefits, as suggested by the Independent Sector (2002b)[4] as appropriate for volunteer contributions in the United States, resulting in a final total of $345,606.

Table 8.3 Volunteer Hours Contributed for the Year Ended June 30, 2001
Junior Achievement of Rochester, New York Area, Inc.

	Placements	Number of Hours	Average Hours	FTE	Rate	Value
Elementary school consultants	736	8832	12	4.25	$25.86	$228,395.52
Middle school consultants	33	726	22	0.35	25.86	18,774.36
High school consultants	4	140	35	0.07	25.86	3,620.40
Company coordinators	45	990	22	0.48	26.85	26,581.50
Special events	75	525	7	0.25	12.22	6,415.50
Governance	36	792	22	0.38	31.30	24,789.60
Subtotal	929	12005	13	5.77	$25.70	$308,576.88
Fringe benefits (12%)						37,029.23
Total						$345,606.11

As a second example, Table 8.4 presents the Canadian Breast Cancer Foundation breakdown, which involves a broader range of tasks—from members of the board of directors to runners in a fund-raising event. Using the North American Industry Classification System (NAICS), most volunteers of the Canadian Breast Cancer Foundation, Ontario Chapter, were classified as sub-sector 813, grant-making, civic, professional, and similar organizations. This sub-sector included organizations engaged primarily in awarding grants from trust funds or in soliciting contributions on behalf of others to support a wide range of health, educational, scientific, cultural, and other social welfare activities. For the year ending March 31, 2001, the wage rate for hourly paid employees in this category for Ontario was $14.51—for salaried employees it was $19.72, with a midpoint of $17.11.

As the NAICS rates do not take into consideration governance tasks performed by boards, these hours were valued at a midpoint hourly rate of $35.56 for senior managers of health, education, social and community services, and of membership organizations (Standard Occupational Code 0014), as determined by Human Resources Development Canada (now Human Resources and Social Development) in its National Occupational Classification code (HRSD 2006). The total comparative market value for the hours contributed by core volunteers through specific programs of the Canadian Breast Cancer Foundation, Ontario Chapter, is presented in Table 8.3. These values are obtained by taking the total hours contributed by volunteers within a program and multiplying them by the appropriate hourly rate.

Table 8.4 Calculation of Market Value of Volunteer Hours Contributed
Canadian Breast Cancer Foundation, Ontario Chapter

	Number of Hours	Rate	Amount
Board	1,369	$35.56	$48,682
Committees	1,876	19.72	36,995
Office administration	900	14.51	13,059
Regional offices	8,250	17.11	141,158
	12,395		239,893
Run planning	11,450	19.72	225,794
Run day	13,707	14.51	198,889
Runners	83,470	14.51	1,211,150
Awareness day	498	17.11	8,521
Great White North	841	17.11	14,390
	109,966		1,658,743
Total	122,361		$3,797,271

Step 4: Calculating Volunteer Hours Within Overall Resources

This calculation—volunteer hours within overall resources—expresses the total hours contributed by volunteers in a fiscal year: first by assigning a dollar value to them; and then as a percentage of the overall resources coming into the organization. Rather than ignore this resource (as standard accounting generally does), this set of calculations helps to estimate the contribution of volunteers to the overall resources. In the first calculation, we use the total value for volunteer hours as produced in the previous section of the toolkit. Our fictitious meals-on-wheels organization, Senior

Links, had overall revenues of $2.5 million in the last fiscal year. Sources of revenue were government grants at $1 million, foundations at $700,000, fees-for-service at $500,000, and fund-raising at $300,000. If volunteer value is calculated at $18.04 (using the Independent Sector amount discussed previously), the total estimated value contributed by volunteers is $938,080. As shown in Table 8.5, when this amount is added to the organization's overall resources of $2.5 million, the estimated combined amount totals $3,438,080. Volunteer resources are calculated as 27 percent of overall resources ($938,080 divided by $3,438,080).

Table 8.5: Calculating Volunteer Hours as a Percentage of Overall Resources
Senior Links, a fictitious case

Calculating the Dollar Value of Volunteer Hours	
What is the total number of hours contributed by your volunteers in the fiscal period?	52,000
What is the average hourly rate you estimate for the value of activities performed by your volunteers?	$18.04
Dollar value of volunteer hours (social resources) (*total hours multiplied by dollar rate per hour*)	$938,080

Calculating the Percentage Contribution of Volunteer Hours to Total Resources	
What were your total revenues for the fiscal period (financial resources)?	$2,500,000
Estimated value of total resources (*value of volunteer resources plus total revenues for the fiscal period*; $938,080 plus $2,500,000)	$3,438,080
Percentage of volunteer resources to total inputs (*value of volunteer resources divided by total resources multiplied by 100*; $938,080 divided by $3,438,080 multiplied by 100)	27.3%

This calculation in Table 8.5 can be expressed in a pie chart, as in Figure 8.2. The chart demonstrates that volunteer resources play a secondary role to government grants but are greater than foundation funding or fees-for-service contributions. This helps management of our fictitious organization evaluate the resources put into attracting, managing, training and retaining volunteers compared to the resources allotted to managing fees-for-service or seeking out foundation grants. As discussed by a nonprofit financial manager in the Afterword to this book, this type of information can help guide management decisions.

Figure 8.2 Volunteer Hours Within Overall Resources

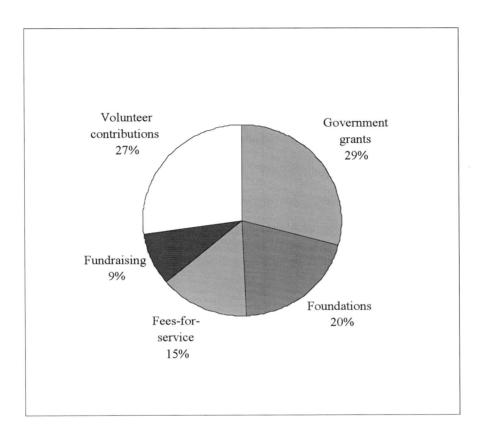

Additional Calculations: Volunteer Out-of-Pocket Expenses

In addition to contributing unpaid hours, volunteers sometimes pay for expenses related to their services, even though the organization has a policy of reimbursing them. Like their hours, these expenses were a contribution—analogous to a financial donation—and should be added to the dollar value of volunteer hours. Even with small amounts, if many volunteers are absorbing their own expenses, their value to the organization could be considerable. As shown in Table 8.6, volunteers associated with the Canadian Breast Cancer Foundation absorbed relatively modest amounts over the fiscal year, but the total projected for 44,299 volunteers reached $481,112. In making this calculation, note that not all volunteers reported having out-of-pocket expenses. Therefore, the average outlay should be adjusted for the percentage with expenditures. Also, it is important to differentiate between expenses that are reimbursed and those that are not. Expenses that *are* reimbursed do *not* count as volunteer contributions. For expenses that are partially reimbursed, only the non-reimbursed portion counts as out-of-pocket expenses.

Table 8.6 Calculation of Volunteer Out-of-Pocket Expenses
Canadian Breast Cancer Foundation, Ontario Chapter

	Number of Volunteers	% with Expenses	Expenses per Volunteer	Totals
Board and committees	89	86	$402.12	$30,677
Office administration	24	83	75.00	1,495
Regional offices	76	83	75.00	4,734
Run planning	212	77	75.00	12,286
Run day	1,999	77	12.50	19,308
Runners	41,735	77	12.50	403,108
Awareness day	102	77	75.00	5,911
Great White North	62	77	75.00	3,593
Total	44,299			$481,112

Finding Out About Out-of-Pocket Expenses

Figure 8.3 contains some sample items, used in our research with Junior Achievement of Rochester, to ask volunteers about their out-of-pocket expenses:

Figure 8.3 Sample Items from Survey

a.   In the past year, did you spend any money out of your own pocket to do your volunteer work with this organization?

[   ] No   [   ] Yes

b.   If you spent money out of your own pocket to do your volunteer tasks, please use the chart below to record how this money was spent and whether or not you were given any money back either from Junior Achievement of Rochester or your place of employment to cover your expenses. Approximate answers are fine.

Figure 8.3 Sample Items from Survey Continued

Type of Expense	Amount of Money Spent by You in the last Year	Amount Paid Back to You	
		By the Organization You Volunteer for	By Your Place of Employment
Travel/bus fare while performing volunteer activities	$	$	$
Parking			
Meals/food/coffee			
Phone/long-distance			
Resource materials/supplies			
Photocopying/printing			
Internet time			
Day care			
Other, please specify:			

It would be possible to obtain the amount without using the chart in Figure 8.1. If volunteers answer that they have absorbed expenses related to their tasks, then simply ask:

➤ Please estimate the total amount that you spent in the past year: $_____

However, in spite of this question's simplicity, our experience suggests that it is better to use the chart because volunteers may not be conscious of their expenses—for example, the baseball coach who treats the team to ice cream following a game. If a chart is applied, the categories could vary by organization according to the roles of volunteers. There is no point in using categories that definitely do not apply in your organization.

Arriving at an Amount

The procedures referred to above indicate how to calculate the volunteer/social labor contributions to an organization. This amount can be treated as a stand-alone descriptor that the organization uses in reports to the public and to funding agencies or it can also be treated as information that goes into social accounting statements, as illustrated in Chapters 4 to 7.

Value to Volunteers

In our research, we also estimated the personal growth and development experienced by volunteers. Technically speaking, this item is an indirect or secondary output of the organization; however, we discuss it here as part of the presentation on information-collection procedures for estimating the contribution of volunteers. Here are some basic items that can be used in making an evaluation of personal growth and development.[5]

Skills could include:

➢ fund-raising;
➢ technical or office;
➢ organizational/managerial;
➢ increased knowledge of a topic such as breast cancer or the environment;
➢ communication; and
➢ interpersonal skills such as how to deal with difficult situations.

Benefits could include:

➢ social interaction;
➢ an improvement in personal well-being;
➢ closer ties to a community; and
➢ increased participation in civic life.

When asking about the personal benefits derived from volunteering, be sure to include any negative impact because not everyone's volunteer experience is positive. If volunteers have a substantial number of negative experiences, these should be viewed as value subtracted. Figure 8.4 contains sample questions that can be used for assessing negative experiences.

Figure 8.4 Sample Items to Assess Negative Experiences

Have you experienced any negative impacts from volunteering?

[ ] No   [ ] Yes

If you have experienced negative impacts from volunteering, please list them here along with any explanation that you wish to provide:

a) _____

b) _____

If you experienced negative impacts, would you say that they outweighed the positive benefits?
[ ] No   [ ] Yes

If you answered yes, please explain.

Calculating a Value for Volunteers' Personal Growth and Development

This procedure was referred to in Chapter 7 but will be presented here in greater detail. Once the survey is completed, there are three steps to assigning a value to volunteers' personal growth and development:

Step 1: Using the information from the survey, calculate what percentage of volunteers derived benefits and/or learned skills. For this information, we used five questions on personal growth and development. If a respondent answered affirmatively to at least three of the five, this was taken as strong evidence of having benefited from volunteering.

➢ **Example**: The Canadian Red Cross, Toronto Region, surveyed a sample of 271 of its core volunteers. It found that 53.38 percent indicated strongly that they had benefited personally by volunteering for the organization. The response from the sample was used as a benchmark for personal growth and development for all of the Canadian Red Cross, Toronto Region's, volunteers—in other words, the organization assumed that the calculation of personal growth and development should be applied to 53.38 percent of its 1,506 core volunteers.

Step 2: Assign a dollar value to the personal growth and development reported by volunteers. It requires creativity to assign a dollar value to personal benefits such as "success in my job," "closer ties to my community," "learned fund-raising skills," or "learned interpersonal skills." As a surrogate, the cost of a personal growth and development course at a community college can be used. This seems like a conservative estimate of the personal benefit derived by volunteers. When the matter was researched, the average price was $151.50—based on five different personal growth courses at three community colleges in Toronto in March 2002.

> **Example:** The Canadian Red Cross, Toronto Region, had 1,506 volunteers. It multiplied this number by 53.38 (the percent who strongly indicated that they had benefited personally), and then multiplied by $151.50 (the cost of a personal development course at a community college). This gave a total dollar value of $121,791 for volunteer personal growth and development.

Figure 8.5 presents a sample worksheet for calculating the surrogate value of volunteer growth and development.

Figure 8.5 Calculating Volunteer Personal Growth and Development
Canadian Red Cross, Toronto Region: Year Ended March 31, 2000

1. Total number of volunteers: 1,506

2. Percentage of respondents who indicated strongly that they benefited in their personal growth and development by volunteering for this organization: 53.38%

3. Average cost of community college course for personal growth and development: $151.50

4. Total value of this benefit: 1,506   .5338 $151.50 = $121,791

Summary of Volunteer Measures

When we think of volunteers, the tendency is to focus on their contribution to the community and the organization. As shown, it is important to measure their hours and the out-of-pocket expenses they absorb. However, the impact of the organization upon the volunteers should also be taken into consideration. This is an important contribution of the organization to its volunteers. In a social accounting statement, the market value of this benefit should be adjusted for the costs that the organization absorbs for training and administering its volunteers.

IDENTIFYING AND EVALUATING SOCIAL OUTPUTS AND VALUE

The second section of this chapter focuses on identifying social outputs and assigning a value to them. This is one of the more challenging aspects of social accounting because social outputs do not involve financial transactions. For training organizations, a typical social output is the estimated market value of the wages for graduates that went on to find jobs.

Chapters 4 to 7 give some examples of how social outputs can be included in social accounting statements—for example, the personal growth and development of volunteers. In this section, we emphasize the information needed to assess social outputs. What questions should be asked? What are the various ways of collecting the information? How should the information be evaluated?

Identifying Social Outputs

Before initiating this part of the discussion, a point of clarification is needed. Many nonprofit funders focus on outcomes or organizational results, and they may have specific requirements about how these are to be counted. The organizational evaluation literature also differentiates between outputs and outcomes, referring to outputs as the services or products of an organization and outcomes as the effects of those outputs (Hatry 1999). While this distinction seems appropriate under some circumstances, we felt that it was adding to the complexity of our presentation—in part, this was because our models used different categories of outputs (primary, secondary, and tertiary) and, in part, because there were circumstances in which it was unclear whether an item was an output or an outcome. Since *outputs* is a more common term in accounting, we decided to simplify and bypass outcomes—albeit recognizing that we might be taken to task for doing so. For readers who prefer outcomes, we suggest that you substitute outcomes for outputs where the reference is to the results of an organization's services.

Measuring social outputs is crucial to social accounting and is invaluable in telling an organization's performance story. Given that social outputs do not involve market transactions, the tendency is to ignore them or to limit the account to qualitative descriptions. While qualitative descriptions can be worthwhile, this path should not be chosen by default. Even though social organizations may have difficulty agreeing upon methodologies for measuring social outputs, placing a value on social outputs can be important to an organization and can enhance its image in the eyes of funders. Even though the task may seem daunting, with perseverance and the sharing of knowledge among participants, it can become manageable.

In the accounting models in Chapters 4 to 7, three levels of output are referred to—primary, secondary, and tertiary.

Primary outputs refer to the direct effects of the organization's activities on clients.

➢ **Example:** At the Computer Training Center, described in Chapter 4, the primary outputs were employment acquisition—that is, employment training that led to a job—and employment enhancement—that is, training that led to improved chances of employment. For residents of Waterloo Co-operative Residence Inc., described in Chapter 6, primary outputs were the units of good-quality student housing.

Secondary outputs are the indirect effects of the organization's activities on its clients or members.

➢ **Example:** The personal growth and development of the volunteers (referred to earlier) is an example of a secondary output. This example was included for the five organizations in Chapter 7. These organizations were not set up to enhance the personal growth and development of their volunteers, but this was a secondary effect of the volunteers' experience.

Tertiary outputs are the effects of the organization's activities on those other than the clients, volunteers, or members of the organization.

➢ **Example:** Waterloo Co-operative Residence Incorporated donated consulting services to other cooperatives. This was viewed as a service in addition to its primary mission to supply affordable housing to its members. Similarly, as a result of obtaining employment, graduates of the Computer Training Center saved costs to society—for example, welfare costs as well as health care and dental benefits.

Although these three categories of outputs are useful, for organizations that desire greater simplicity, two categories (direct and indirect) might be sufficient.

Resources for Identifying Outputs

There are many methods for identifying and measuring outputs. Funders such as the United Way train nonprofit management for this task. However, the staff and members of social organizations can also generate ideas about determining and measuring outputs because they understand best what their organization is accomplishing.

➢ **Step 1:** Set aside an hour at a scheduled staff meeting to brainstorm all of the direct and indirect effects that might be measurable for an agency. For simplicity, start with one program and experiment with the possibilities. Frontline staff members tend to be keenly aware of program impacts on their clients, including the indirect effects.

➢ **Step 2:** Even though your staff may not be experts in measurement, they can have valuable insights into how particular organizational effects may be measured, bearing in mind that not all outputs are quantifiable. Many funders supply tools for measurement on their Web sites—for example, the United Way resources[6] and W. K. Kellogg Foundation's Evaluation Handbook.[7]

➢ **Step 3:** Once the anticipated outputs have been identified for one program, try the same exercise for another, taking time at each staff meeting. The process is likely to create its own momentum.

Let us consider a hypothetical organization, Applegrove Community Center, which provides sports and recreation programs, coaching training, and leadership training for youth in an inner-city setting. During the summer period, it runs a special program for youth-at-risk—the participants are 14 to 18 years of age and engaged in a combination of athletics and hanging out. On Friday and Saturday evenings, there is a drop-in with music, videos, and snacks. In total, there are 25 regular participants for the two-month period of the program. As an agency that receives funding from the United Way and the municipality, Applegrove Community Center does not charge its participants.

The staff undertook a brainstorming exercise to identify the outputs of this program. Their goals were modest and they decided to start with this specific program rather than the center as a whole. For primary outputs—associated directly with the organization's objectives with respect to its summer program for youth-at-risk—they came up with:

➢ recreation activities in a safe environment for 25 youth 14 to 18 years of age;
➢ enhanced social and conflict resolution skills; and
➢ enhanced leadership skills (learned as the youth help organize events).

For secondary outputs—indirect effects on the client group that the organization serves—the following impacts on youth were noted:

➢ wider social circle through meeting new friends;
➢ greater understanding of other cultures; and
➢ fewer instances of trouble with parents, neighbors, and police.

For tertiary outputs—impact on the local community—the staff proposed the following outputs:

➢ costs saved in community policing;
➢ improved family relations; and
➢ a safer, more pleasant neighborhood.

The next step was to determine whether the staff's intuition was supported by evidence and how many participants in the center were associated with each output. The first output—"recreation activities for 25 youth in a safe environment"—was researched from the center's attendance records. For the other primary and secondary outputs, evidence was gathered by surveying the 25 youth in this program. The survey was comprehensive and asked questions about each of the items under consideration—social skills, leadership skills, wider social circle, greater understanding of others' cultures, and fewer incidences of trouble.

For the tertiary outputs—relating to impact on the community—different evidence was needed—for example, police records on the number of times police were called to the neighborhood because of complaints about the youth, how that had changed over time, and also anecdotal information from officers. However, surveying family and neighborhood relations was a task too onerous for a small recreation center, and a student from a Master of Social Work program did this as a practicum. (Alternatively, this work might have been done as one of the center's activities by its youth as a skill-teaching and résumé-building activity.) This research determined what supportive evidence was available to document the outputs identified by staff.

Because the evidence was subjective, it would be important to apply a high threshold (for example, at least 75 percent agreement among those responding to surveys) before accepting that there was sufficient support for a particular output. After undertaking the research, the three tertiary outputs proposed by the staff were eliminated for lack of evidence. In addition, two of the primary outputs—enhanced social and conflict resolution skills and enhanced leadership skills—were combined, since the participants didn't seem to distinguish between them.

Assigning a Value to Outputs

Since the participants in this program did not pay for the service, there was no market value that could be associated with these outputs. Therefore, the next step, as discussed in Chapter 3, was to assign a surrogate value to them—that is, some item or service sold on the market that was of similar value. When choosing a surrogate value, it is important to find examples as close to the circumstance as possible and to use modest estimates. It must not appear that the surrogate value is being inflated.

For the primary outputs—recreation activities for 25 youth in a safe environment—a comparison was made to a similar camp where participants paid a fee. To find an appropriate comparison was challenging. Camps run by the municipality or by social organizations either did not charge or charged lower fees than a private camp because of subsidized costs. The private camps were more expensive than those offered either by the municipality or by social organizations, but they represented a clear market comparison. Of the two private day camps in the city, one that charged $500 per week offered a program quite similar to that of Applegrove Community Center. Therefore, it was used as a comparison.

➢ For the 25 participants in Applegrove Community Center summer program, the estimated value of this output—recreation for 25 youth in a safe environment—was $12,500 (25 × $500).

For the second output—enhanced social and conflict resolution skills and leadership skills—it was difficult to come up with an appropriate surrogate, but the student assistant discovered a course that was offered on leadership for youth at a cost of $100 for six three-hour workshops. It seemed an appropriate match.

➢ Therefore, for the 25 participants, the estimated value of this output was $2,500 (25 × $100).

For the three secondary outputs—wider social circle through meeting new friends; greater understanding of other cultures; and fewer instances of trouble with parents, school, neighbors, and police—there was compelling evidence from the surveys in support of these outputs, but it was difficult to arrive at an appropriate surrogate. For example, police statistics showed fewer reports on the participants in the program; but over the two months, the police did not adjust their staffing arrangements and so immediate costs were not lowered. Perhaps police would have shifted staff away from the neighborhood in the future, but there was no evidence at this point to indicate that there were cost savings to the community. Nevertheless, the evidence in support of these outputs was reported as a form of disclosure. Even though a surrogate value was not attached to an output, the anecdotal evidence was important documentation of the program's value and could have been included in the program's reports.

Most funders acknowledge that not all of an organization's outputs can be measured numerically. To capture more elusive secondary and tertiary outputs, self-reports by clients are one of the few tools available. This can be done through a general survey, as was used with the residents of the Waterloo Cooperative Residence Incorporated (Chapter 6), the volunteers of the five organizations in Chapter 7, and the participants of the programs of the Computer Training Center (Chapter 4). It can also be done by preprogram and post-program comparisons. As well, creative methods of capturing program feedback can be derived from videos, photographs, collages, plays, or other artistic presentations that can be documented in still photographs and text. Even though no numerical value can be assigned to some outputs, the feedback from participants is an important form of information that should be systematically organized.

For Applegrove Community Center's summer program for 25 youth-at-risk, a social accounting statement quantified two outputs with an estimated value of $15,000. The estimated value of these outputs represented a social return in the Community Social Return on Investment Model (Chapter 4) or a portion of the value added in the Expanded Value Added Statement in Chapters 6 and 7.

Summary of Social Outputs Measures

While determining and measuring social outputs may be forbidding to the staff of a social organization, it is a realizable goal. Staff should not underestimate their insights about the impacts of the programs in which they are involved or their ability to collect information as to whether there is support for these insights. Determining surrogates may seem challenging but, through brainstorming and creative thinking, that too can be a realizable goal.

COLLECTING BACKGROUND INFORMATION

The third section of this chapter deals with the background and context of a social accounting report. To understand the organization within its context, background information was collected for each of the case studies in Chapters 4 to 7. However, in addition to its use with social accounting statements, background information can also be used both internally to help with strategic planning and externally to position the organization so as to describe its uniqueness and to attract support.

To illustrate the importance of context for understanding an organization's use of resources, the high cost of training at the Computer Training Center (described in Chapter 4) can best be interpreted in relation to its client group, field, and mandate—to enable adults with physical disabilities to acquire and enhance the skills necessary to become employed in jobs with computers. This was a risky venture at the time. The students faced obstacles to mastering the course material and an uncertain employment market for people with disabilities. In addition, many of the students had primary challenges to overcome (such as managing complex health conditions) as well as secondary challenges (such as being newcomers to the country).

In order to fulfill its mission, the center's board of directors chose a structure that included intense volunteer input, mentoring, and assisting with job contacts. Without knowing the context—and particularly the high levels of unemployment for persons in these circumstances—it would have been difficult to undertake a fair accounting of the center's outputs in relation to its costs or to attribute a fair value to volunteer contributions. For the Computer Training Center, costs were high because the client group required a highly supportive context. Moreover, the volunteers were highly skilled and took on key roles in assisting the clients to acquire the skills needed to enter the job market. Background information and context were useful in interpreting the costs of the program and in assigning appropriate market values to volunteer contributions.

The Computer Training Center example is illustrative of the importance of background and context to social accounting. In general, to complete social accounting statements, the following information about an organization is required:

➢ niche;
➢ field;
➢ location;
➢ clients; and
➢ core programs and activities.

Niche

To identify an organization's outputs, it is helpful first to understand its niche. A well-crafted and substantiated statement about what makes an organization different can also help with strategic planning and social marketing. Applegrove Community Center (the hypothetical center referred to earlier) has evolved into a large recreation center in a low-income community and is situated in a city with many recent immigrants. The center describes its niche as follows:

> **Example:** We are the community's largest provider of recreation programs for youth from over five cultures; we teach sports, fellowship, and leadership skills, and the kids have fun. We provide a safe haven for young people to meet with each other and learn how to get along. And the neighbors support us—over 200 of our neighbors in the Applegrove-Highgate area volunteer here each year to coach, act as mentors, and organize special events.

There are many community centers, and so defining the organization's niche or specialized contribution is of importance and assists with preparing a social accounting statement. The center's niche helps to identify what makes it special and what to look for when beginning a social accounting process—a high degree of volunteer participation by neighbors and coaches, direct outputs such as youth skill development, and indirect outputs such as learning from people in other cultures.

Field

Wherever possible, the case studies in Chapters 4 to 7 identified potential impacts of the organization by understanding it within the context of its field. This information is also helpful to have on hand when applying for funds or reaching out to the community. When groups are affiliates of a larger organization, information about the field is often available from the parent organization, as with several of the case studies in Chapters 4 to 7. For example, the Canadian Red Cross, Toronto Region, is part of a broad field involving Red Cross and Red Crescent societies throughout the world. To understand that field, information from the parent organization, the International Red Cross, is informative:

> **Example:** The International Red Cross was formed in 1864, the same year that the first Geneva Convention was approved outlining humanitarian principles for the treatment of wounded soldiers during the war. Today, in more than 150 countries throughout the world, there are Red Cross/Red Crescent societies—both national societies and regional affiliates—which run or support programs that assist millions of the world's most vulnerable people. Like all Red Cross Societies, the Canadian Red Cross, Toronto Region, focuses on one goal: to improve the situation of the most vulnerable (see Chapter 7).

For the Red Cross, the local organization's reach—the numbers of people it helps through its services—needs to be interpreted against the backdrop of the massive structure and impact of Red Cross societies worldwide. In other words, the Toronto Region society is effective in mobilizing large cadres of volunteers because it is part of a broader field. The Toronto Region's services, though geared to its particular circumstances, are also best understood in relation to the general field established by the International Red Cross—humanitarian aid that it has undertaken since its inception in 1864.

Location

Along with information about an organization's field of operations, a description of its physical location is helpful in estimating its impact. The description can specify whether the organization operates in an urban, rural, or mixed setting and can refer to the size of the population around it as well as any distinguishing characteristics such as large numbers of youth, seniors, or particular cultural and linguistic groups. Depending on the type of service, other relevant information can be included—for example, rates of unemployment in the area; the quality of services available; and the kinds of cultural and recreational organizations.

➤ **Example**: Applegrove Community Center is located at 121 Applegrove Street, a mixed-income area. The area is residential, with two thirds of the residents living in rental accommodation—mostly high-rise apartments—and with home ownership for the remaining third. Family incomes are low and unemployment is high relative to the rest of the city. The area is made up of Anglo and Hispanic families (about 70 percent), most of whom have lived in the area for over 20 years, and newcomers from at least five different countries. The area currently experiences a high level of youth crime that disturbs the local population; consequently, residents and representatives of local agencies have begun meeting to discuss solutions.

This description of its location makes it clear that the center will have challenges that will stretch its resources and require a high degree of community input and involvement. The description of location also indicates that the community is likely to receive a significant benefit from the center's programs, and this benefit should be analyzed as part of the social accounts. The description of location provides indicators of what to consider when compiling information on social inputs and outputs for a social accounting statement.

Clients

Clients refer to the recipients of service, customers, or audiences. For a mutual association or cooperative, the members could also be the clients. A description of the clients helps to explain the context in which the organization produces its outputs.

➤ **Example**: For Applegrove Community Center, the clients could be described as youth from families in the surrounding community—about two thirds are from long-established Anglo and Hispanic families and about one third from families who have immigrated within the last 10 years from over five different countries. Family incomes in the area are low. Most of the clients are in the 14 to 18 age bracket, equally divided between males and females. Almost all are in high school, but there is a small subgroup of dropouts who are joining gangs and also having difficulties with the law. Based on feedback from the residents and from local services, the center has added informal programs such as Friday- and Saturday-night drop-ins to try to reach this group.

Information about Applegrove Community Center's clients adds to knowledge about potential impacts. Running a Friday night drop-in program at the center could be expected to produce a different impact than a similar program for affluent youth who are high achievers. Information on client groups feeds directly into the process of identifying outputs and placing a value on them. The goals for youth-at-risk may differ from those who are in school and functioning relatively well. Since program costs for such a group might be relatively high, having this background information will be important in determining the indirect impact of this program and interpreting the costs.

Core Programs and Activities

Information on core programs and activities is a primary source of data to determine social outputs of a social accounting statement. Many organizations do not have this information at their fingertips. But a short description of programs, a description that is free of jargon and acronyms and that identifies the numbers served, is also an effective tool when reporting to funders or requesting funds. Figure 8.6 presents an example of a partial program outline for Applegrove Community Center. As shown in the figure, there is a short outline for each program, the numbers of youth involved, their gender and ages, along with the program's duration—details often left out of descriptions.

Figure 8.6 Partial Program Outline
Applegrove Community Center

Sports Programs April 1, 2001 to March 31, 2002		
Program	**Activities**	**Participants**
Sports	Two coeducational and T-ball leagues	• 10 teams in all; ages 5 to 8; 80 children participated over 40 weeks
	Two baseball leagues	• 6 teams each; one league for boys, one for girls; 120 players in all; ages 14 to 18; over 5 months
	Four basketball leagues	• 4 teams each; 20 players per league—for boys ages 10 to 14; for boys ages 15 to 18; for girls ages 10 to 14; and for girls ages 14 to 18; over 40 weeks
	Pickup soccer	• 2 soccer camps each year—for 20 boys ages 8 to 18; for 10 girls ages 8 to 16; total 38 children participated; over 10 weeks

For a large recreation center, it is more likely that each program would have its own page in a broader collection of program descriptions. From information on activities and the numbers served, the center's primary outputs can be identified using the process described in the previous section.

Summary of the Background Section

An organization's context points to what information to gather, which stakeholders to survey, and what to ask. As well, context helps with the interpretation of the information collected. In many organizations, background information may not be reproduced in a systematic way. However, once the components have been collected, they can be used not only for social accounting but also to define the organization for a variety of audiences.

CONCLUSION

There is often a lack of resources in social organizations for information collection and management. However, the examples and templates in this chapter can help to set a basic structure in place. Information can then be updated regularly to produce social accounting statements.

Most social organizations are not in the habit of attributing a surrogate value to volunteer contributions and social outputs. While there is reason to be conservative about doing so, when there are appropriate comparisons, market values should be estimated. Often there is information available for making comparisons. For an arts festival, for example, there may be tangible benefits such as a boost to the local economy. Health benefits may accrue to members of social organizations such as the YMCA/YWCA or to participants in a breakfast program at school. Disaster relief programs such as those undertaken by Red Cross societies around the world also have tangible benefits that may be measurable: Supplies are purchased in the local economy and services are rendered for which it may be possible to make market comparisons. Similarly, values can be assessed for the environmental benefits of reclaiming lakes and rivers.

Nonprofits that belong to an umbrella organization may be able to obtain studies with benefit or cost figures relating directly to the nonprofit's program. With perseverance, useful information can be found.

Overall, social accounting and its tools can help to create a deeper appreciation of the contribution of nonprofits and cooperatives. Not only is that appreciation needed in the community at large, but also it can be enlightening for those who work, volunteer, or are members of social organizations. Creating value is one thing, but getting credit for it is important, too. The tools presented in this chapter are offered as a way of showing what counts.

QUESTIONS FOR DISCUSSION

1. What is the difference between social labor and volunteer labor? Is this an important distinction and, if so, why?
2. What information is required to calculate volunteer tasks and hours as well as volunteer hours as a percentage of human resources and overall resources? What kinds of system and resources are needed to gather this information regularly?
3. Why calculate volunteers' out-of-pocket expenses? What are the potential benefits and risks of doing this?
4. What are the differences between primary, secondary, and tertiary outputs? Provide one example of each and suggest ways to calculate them. Which of these outputs is the most difficult to calculate and why?
5. What are some of the direct and indirect benefits of an arts education program in which musicians from different cultures go into schools to teach students popular folk songs? How would you put a value on them?
6. Identify two direct and two indirect effects of a crime-prevention program aimed at youth and provide market comparisons for each.
7. What are some of the potential costs saved by a program for teen mothers held at an inner-city health center? What are the positive and negative aspects of reporting these costs?
8. How is background information on an organization of assistance in social accounting? What are other uses for this information?
9. What are some of the risks and benefits of assigning a surrogate value? In your view, how can the risks be overcome?
10. What roles can staff, board members, and volunteers play in preparing social accounting statements? What conditions need to be present for this process to work effectively?

NOTES

[1] As mentioned in the preface, the software package, *VolunteersCount* provides support for tracking volunteer contributions. As well, Imagine Canada's Knowledge Development Centre provides an on-line volunteer-value calculator (see www.kdc-cdc.ca).

[2] Department of Labor, Bureau of Labor Statistics hourly wage rate from the National Compensation Survey is available at data.bls.gov.

[3] The North American Industry Classification System (NAICS) Web site is cansim2.statcan.ca/cgi-win.

[4] The information on the rate for volunteering is posted at the Independent Sector's Web site www.independentsector.org.

[5] Our Web site home.oise.utoronto.ca/~volunteer has a sample survey for volunteers.

[6] For the United Way resources, see national.unitedway.org/outcomes/resources.

[7] W. K. Kellogg Foundation's Evaluation Handbook can be ordered from that organization's Web site www.wkkf.org.

Chapter 9

Making It Count

Social accounting is in an early stage of development. Much remains to be done to expand the work and increase its viability. Four issues are presented for consideration:

> ➢ broadening the domain of items that are considered when accounting for the impact of an organization;
> ➢ creating an accountability framework that includes multiple stakeholders;
> ➢ developing an infrastructure to support social accounting; and
> ➢ viewing social accounting as part of a broader exercise of reinterpreting what is valued.

BROADENING THE DOMAIN

Accounting's playing field circumscribes what should be considered and what should not. Every accounting framework includes some items and excludes others. As such, what counts should be perceived as something that is open to debate rather than as truths etched in stone. This point is underlined by the corporate scandals (Enron, WorldCom) related to accounting. It is not our intention to cast aspersions on the accounting profession but simply to underline the fact that within generally accepted accounting principles (or GAAP) there is broad latitude for interpretation.

Accounting frameworks are often presented as if they represent the full story but, in fact, they are but a glimpse at one perspective of reality. We have made this point in reference to the application of conventional accounting statements to social organizations, but the same is true with respect to profit-oriented corporations. Increasingly, accounting regulatory bodies have acknowledged the limitations of applying the so-called industrial paradigm to the new economy with dot-com companies and others that rely upon intellectual capital (Canadian Institute of Chartered Accountants 2000; Financial Accounting Standards Board 2002; McLean 1995; Upton Jr. 2001). These can be corporations with limited economic value but with enormous intellectual capital. The importance of intellectual capital was underlined in the accounting models presented in Chapter 5, with respect to Junior Achievement of Rochester, and is widely accepted in today's business world (Hope and Hope 1997). The talents of the workforce (an expense in conventional accounting—unlike bricks and cash) are seen as being of importance in modern business and a major resource for generating value (Flamholtz 1974, 1985, 1999).

As argued in Chapter 3, a common feature of all the approaches to and definitions of social accounting is to broaden variables that count. Much of the scholarly work on social accounting is a critique of the limited set of variables used in the financial accounting of profit-oriented businesses (for example, Gray et al. 1996; Mathews 1997; Mathews and Perera 1995). Financial accounting statements typically ignore the impact of corporations on the physical environment and on society and are confined to a narrow range of considerations internal to the organization. Automobile fuels, as is well documented, pass toxins into the environment, but the environmental costs associated with the product are not part of the financial statements of manufacturers. Assuming that the hydrogen fuel-cell technology currently in development takes hold, its value to society would be reflected to a degree in the increased stock value of the corporations owning the patents and manufacturing the products; but the accounting will not include the value of increased health, an important social benefit.

As a rule, the generally accepted accounting principles ignore impacts external to the organization. And despite the fact that environmental toxins involve a huge cost to the public and environmentally sustaining technologies involve a huge benefit, the accounting in each case is partial focusing only on the market transactions of the manufacturer. Therefore, financial accounting removes the organization from its context—society and the environment—or what economists label as externalities. To poke fun at this decontextualized viewpoint, we recall the Tom Lehrer folk song that satirizes the German American rocket scientist, Wernher von Braun: "Once the rockets are up, who cares where they come down? That's not my department, says Wernher von Braun" (Keaveny 2001, 14).

Organizations exist in relation to their surroundings. For a business corporation, the context is often defined narrowly as its owners—and its accounting statements reflect that relationship. Milton Friedman, the outspoken neoliberal economist, aptly summarized the primary corporate orientation when, in an interview with *The New York Times Magazine* (1970, 32), he stated: "There is one and only one social responsibility of business—to use its resources and engage in activities designed to increase its profits so long as it stays within the rules of the game, which is to say, engages in open and free competition without deception or fraud."

Friedman's interpretation of the organizational context is narrow but nevertheless reflective of the predominant dynamic in business and accounting. It attempts to extract the corporation from its surroundings (that is, externalities) and focus on its shareholders. While this is inappropriate for profit-oriented businesses in that it does not capture their full costs and benefits, it is completely unacceptable for social organizations in that they are created to fulfill a social mission. To some extent, financial transactions reflect an organization's relationship to its surroundings, but as noted throughout this book, financial transactions do not capture accurately the value of many social services and goods.

Even for social organizations with revenues earned from the market—cooperatives, market-based nonprofits, and nonprofit mutual associations—their financial transactions represent only a partial view of the organization's social impact. This problem is exacerbated for public sector nonprofits, particularly those that serve people with low incomes. For such organizations, most revenues are in the form of grants or contracts from government and their outputs are not monetized.

For social organizations in general, the exclusion of volunteer service and social labor from accounting statements is an oversight. Major accounting organizations (Canadian Institute of Chartered Accountants 1980; Financial Accounting Standards Board 1980, 1993) have sanctioned the inclusion of volunteer service but only under very specific conditions. However, as noted, accountants have been reluctant to include estimates in financial statements. For each of the organizations included in this book, volunteer labor was an important supplement to the paid staff, but only Canadian Crossroads International (CCI) included it on financial statements. For that organization, volunteers were the equivalent of 67 full-time positions or 71 percent of the human resources. On its 1998 Statement of Operations, Canadian Crossroads International's accountants included volunteers as a revenue item valued at $2,840,000, or nearly half of that organization's total revenues. The same amount was also included as an expense, called "contributions by volunteers."

By monetizing the contributions of all volunteers and including that estimate in its financial statements, CCI is unusual. But it ought to be commonplace because national surveys estimate the value of volunteers, and advocacy organizations such as the Independent Sector in the United States, Imagine Canada, and the National Council of Voluntary Organisations in England engage in the same exercise. For organizations that rely heavily on volunteers, an estimate of the market value of their contribution should be the rule for accounting statements rather than the exception.

The same is true for the social labor of mutual associations and cooperatives. The impact of this contribution on the cost of the service is an important savings to the members—for WCRI, the student-housing cooperative discussed in Chapter 6, the social labor of members reduced the cost of accommodation by nearly 7 percent. Without this social labor, the cooperative would have had to pay more for services such as cleaning, food preparation, serving meals, dish and pot washing, snow shoveling, grounds maintenance, and the costs of governance. Indeed, member service is a common feature of nonprofit mutual associations and cooperatives, and this unpaid labor contribution reduces the amount that the organization charges; yet accounting associations do not sanction a comparative market value for social labor. Whereas there is some flexibility from accounting associations with respect to volunteer contributions to the community, assigning a market value to social labor contributions to mutual associations and cooperatives is prohibited (Canadian Institute of Chartered Accountants 1980; Financial Accounting Standards Board 1980; 1993).

These points are made to underline our argument that accounting statements present a very partial analysis of an organization's performance—based upon market transactions only. By decontextualizing the organization from its surroundings, these statements ignore vital information about its social impact. By contrast, social accounting attempts to broaden the domain of accounting by attributing a market value to non-monetized items. The models presented in Chapters 4 to 7 have a broader array of variables than are found in conventional accounting, including such non-monetized items as:

➢ the value of volunteer services donated to the organization and the community;
➢ the value of social labor to the organization;
➢ out-of-pocket expenses absorbed by volunteers;
➢ the value of outputs such as employment acquisition and enhancement, savings from income benefits and related services, pro bono consultation services, and personal growth and development of volunteers and members;
➢ the value of intellectual capital; and
➢ the environmental impact of compensating employees for choosing public transport or car pooling to travel to work.

By way of illustration, let us look at the Jane/Finch Community and Family Centre in a low-income area of Toronto. The conventional financial statements prepared by Jane/Finch's accountants are adapted from those for a profit-oriented business. The income statement shows the categories of revenue and expenditure and then indicates that Jane/Finch spent slightly more than it received. When the revenues are broken down, the statement shows that about 62 percent comes from government grants and most of the remainder comes from charitable donations. The breakdown of expenditures illustrates that 83 percent is allocated to personnel. For both revenues and expenditures, the pattern is similar to that of the previous year. The balance sheet, or Statement of Financial Position, indicates that Jane/Finch started the year 2000 with net assets of $249,400 and finished with $238,181, reflecting its small deficit of $11,219, as shown in the income statement.

The information in these statements is important because it indicates that the organization is living within its means and has a modest amount of assets to fall back upon if there were a decrease in its revenues. However, these statements are silent on the contribution that Jane/Finch is making to the surrounding community. The balance sheet tells the reader what value or equity there is in a business after the liabilities are subtracted from the assets. This information is of importance to owners of a business because they can determine the value on paper of their holding. Even though the balance sheet is informative about the value in a business, it does not tell the complete story of its value, especially as it concerns intangible items such as intellectual capital (as illustrated in the discussion of Junior Achievement of Rochester in Chapter 5). Moreover, for Jane/Finch and for the many similar organizations that are set up to serve a community, the information from the conventional accounting statements is silent on social impact. The Expanded Value Added Statement, by contrast, indicates that for every dollar spent on external goods and services, Jane/Finch generated expanded value added of $8.43 (see Chapter 7). While this information may be far from complete, it nevertheless attempts to account for the social impact of Jane/Finch's services.

The same can be said of each of the approaches to social accounting presented in Chapters 4 to 7—the Community Social Return on Investment model in Chapter 4; the Socioeconomic Impact Statement and the Socioeconomic Resource Statement in Chapter 5; or the Expanded Value Added Statement in Chapters 6 and 7. Each analyzes social impact and thereby broadens the domain of accounting. While it is informative that social organizations are living within their means and have more economic assets than liabilities, this view of their assets ignores their important human resources, both paid staff and volunteers (intellectual capital, as labeled in Chapter 5), and is silent about their social impact. Arguably, there is more to say about the social impact of such organizations than is found in our social accounting statements, but at the very least these statements are opening up that issue. The Jane/Finches of the world are not simply users of others' resources but are generating an important return from that investment. Accounting must be reoriented to address that impact.

ACCOUNTABILITY FRAMEWORK WITH MULTIPLE STAKEHOLDERS

As noted in Chapter 3, an important theme in social accounting is to broaden the framework for accountability and to create an approach based on many stakeholders rather than one as in conventional accounting. The qualitative approach to social accounting, discussed in Chapter 3, is based on multiple stakeholders, as are many of the integrated approaches to social accounting that develop financial statements (Abt and Associates 1974; Estes 1976; Linowes 1972, 1973; Vaccari 1997). The same is true of the Socioeconomic Impact Statement and the Expanded Value Added Statement presented in this book.

It is relatively straightforward to build a stakeholder analysis into an accounting statement. However, within an organization one stakeholder normally predominates by virtue of its critical role (Jawahar and McLaughlin 2001). Within a profit-oriented corporation, it is the shareholders and other capital providers because financing is of such importance to the firm's development. Within member-based organizations—nonprofit mutual associations and cooperatives—the members dominate because their representatives form the board of directors and the members are also the users or consumers of the service. Therefore, they have multiple roles that are of critical importance to the organization. For public sector nonprofits, government is normally the key stakeholder since most financing comes from either government grants or contracts, and government policy places constraints upon the organization's services.

While it is relatively simple to theorize about the desirability of multiple stakeholders and about lateral rather than hierarchical relationships, the dominant role of one particular group places a constraint on accountability arrangements. Indeed, definitions of accountability often refer to it as hierarchical and dyadic. For example, Cutt and Murray (2000, 6) state: "All accountability frameworks are built around the core, hierarchical model involving two parties, one who allocates responsibility and one who accepts it with an undertaking to report on the manner in which it has been discharged." Using government as the focus on his analysis, Flinders (2001, 13) defines accountability as "the condition of having to answer to an individual or body for one's actions."

Like many other groups, the Panel on Governance and Accountability in the Voluntary Sector (1999, 11) in Canada does push for a broader conception of accountability—"downward, outward and upward." However, the panel's definition also implies that accountability involves a hierarchical relationship: "Accountability is the requirement to explain and accept responsibility for carrying out an assigned mandate in light of agreed upon expectations" (1999, 11). In general, the definitions acknowledge prevalent power dynamics in accountability relationships—that is, by virtue of their role in an organization some players assume greater influence than others. In some cases, the relationship is direct and personal, as in an employee–manager relationship; in other cases, accountability is anonymous, as when an organization is beholden to the public or to its clients, a distinction that is developed by Gagne (1996). The physical environment and society tend to be faceless stakeholders—in theory, they are of importance, but they may not have a presence within an organization.

Shragge et al. (2001, 14) suggest that multi-lateral accountability can be achieved by creating a democratic governance that builds "mechanisms of representation of interest into the structures." For organizations that attempt this—some public sector nonprofits, for example—most often members of the board of directors appoint persons whom they feel would represent designated groups. Shragge et al. (2001) argue for elected representatives but also point out that a small group of activists could dominate. "The lesson here," they suggest, "is that structures of accountability, no matter how good they look on paper, cannot work unless there is active participation in community life either because of local tradition or because of investment of the time and energy of the organization itself to promote citizen activity" (2001, 15).

Therefore, while multi-lateral accountability may be highly desirable, in practice it is difficult to achieve because the organizational role of one stakeholder can lead to it being dominant. The dominant stakeholder will create accountability mechanisms between it and representatives of the organization. This is not to suggest that the other stakeholders are unimportant and ought not to have a defined role in the governance and a defined accountability relationship. However, organizational dynamics often militate against those other groups being taken as seriously as the dominant stakeholder.

Accounting, and particularly social accounting, has an obligation to go beyond mirroring the power dynamics of an organization. The accounting analysis should present the organization within its broadest context and should examine its impact on a variety of stakeholders, including those with the least power. Employees, volunteers, society, and the users of the service may not be the dominant stakeholders in an organization's hierarchy, but their role is indispensable to the provision of services. Therefore, an accounting framework should take their contributions into consideration.

Existing social accounting frameworks have demonstrated that multi-stakeholder accounting is feasible. Qualitative forms of social accounting involve an elaborate process for stakeholder input as to how well the organization is fulfilling its mission. For integrated approaches involving financial statements, there are many multi-stakeholder examples, as discussed in Chapter 3 and previously in this chapter. Since not all the stakeholders are as involved in the organization as the dominant group, these analyses do not guarantee increased accountability. However, recommendations in the qualitative reports do lend themselves to follow-up. Among the principles of the Institute of Social and Ethical AccountAbility (2000) are a commitment to improve performance and embedding the related process within the organization.

Similarly, the Expanded Value Added Statement demonstrates that many stakeholders contribute to and benefit from the value added created by the organization. Whereas volunteers may not be dominant in the power dynamics of the organizations discussed in Chapter 7, the Expanded Value Added Statement indicates that volunteers contributed a major part of the value added—ranging from 29 to 70 percent in the five organizations discussed in that chapter.

Will this knowledge change the accountability dynamics of these organizations toward volunteers? It is difficult to answer to this question, but the Expanded Value Added Statement does more accurately reflect the contribution of volunteers than the Statement of Financial Position that would normally be undertaken. Moreover, the knowledge that volunteers create a major portion of value added inevitably will affect perceptions and attitudes not only of management but also of the volunteers. It should also influence funders who look at the contribution of volunteers as an indication of the resources the organization can muster in support of its mission.

In summary, while it is ideal to strive toward multi-lateral accountability, that objective differs from a multi-stakeholder social accounting framework. As demonstrated in this book, multi-stakeholder social accounting is achievable, but multi-lateral accountability is a more difficult challenge because in most organizations one stakeholder dominates. Moreover, the less dominant stakeholders such as volunteers or society usually are not organized and, therefore, their voice counts for less. The information from the accounting statements may portray stakeholder contributions more accurately, but this does not mean that the organization will be more accountable to them. Nevertheless, a multi-stakeholder accounting framework is an end worth pursuing because it does create a frame of reference for social accounting. As will be demonstrated in this next section, the efforts at moving social accounting forward are largely indistinguishable from those of creating better accountability. Both efforts involve infrastructure building.

BUILDING A SUPPORTIVE INFRASTRUCTURE

Since the early 1970s, major accounting organizations have considered whether nonprofits (often referred to as "not-for profits") require different treatment in accounting. Some modifications have been made in generally accepted accounting principles, but as noted, the prevailing rules for profit-oriented businesses have been applied to social organizations, including those that do not sell their services in the market. This latter practice is subject to much criticism (Macintosh 1995, 2000).

The American Accounting Association, representing researchers and educators of accounting, has flirted with a more fundamental departure from tradition and has suggested that accounting analyze the effects of nonprofits on society. In policy statements in 1972 and 1989, it proposed that nonprofits should establish a strategic plan of their intended social benefits over time that would be monitored in order to determine whether its objectives were being achieved (American Accounting Association 1972, 1989). The primary accounting is of actual expenditures related to these objectives over time.

However, the Financial Accounting Standards Board (1980, 1993) has taken a more conservative stand and has decreed that accounting statements have general application regardless of the type of organization. Its concept statements have influenced accounting bodies in other countries, including the Canadian Institute of Chartered Accountants (1980). In both countries, the approach to accounting for profit-oriented businesses has been applied with slight adaptations to nonprofits.

The accounting profession has resisted any fundamental departure from practice to accommodate social organizations, even proposals from accountants (Abt and Associates 1974; Estes 1976; Linowes 1972, 1973). Therefore, alternatives operate without the sanction of the primary governing bodies for the profession. For social organizations, the most widely used alternative is the qualitative approach that solicits feedback from primary stakeholders on the extent to which the organization is fulfilling its mission (see Chapter 3). This approach—also referred to as a social or ethical audit—has been used by socially oriented businesses (such as The Body Shop, Ben & Jerry's, and Traidcraft), credit unions, and nonprofits. However, it remains a supplement to the financial statements and may not even be viewed as accounting. Accountants prepare the financial statements—a consultant (not necessarily an accountant) prepares the social account. The problem, therefore, goes beyond the creation of appropriate alternatives in that the governing bodies for the accounting profession are determining the procedures.

In response, an infrastructure is being created to support social accounting and related accountability arrangements. In the United Kingdom, the Institute of Social and Ethical AccountAbility working closely with the New Economics Foundation has created guidelines to govern social accounting and the AA1000 Standards Guide that certify organizations (Institute of Social and Ethical AccountAbility 2000). In the United States, a leader has been the Council on Economic Priorities, a nonprofit specializing in research on corporate social responsibility. Although its work is not as directly related to social accounting as the Institute of Social and Ethical AccountAbility, it has had a major influence on creating an accountability infrastructure. In 1997, that agency founded an accreditation agency, since called Social Accountability International, which has created basic standards for workplace conditions (Social Accountability 8000 or SA8000) and a system of verifying compliance that is influenced by the international standards organization, ISO9000. Social Accountability 8000 is based on "international human rights norms as delineated by the Labour Organisation Conventions, the United Nations Convention on the Rights of the Child and the Universal Declaration of Human Rights" (Social Accountability 8000 2002, 2). These rights include prohibitions on child labor, forced labor, and discrimination, and in addition, the right to unionize and bargain collectively, and basic standards for working hours, compensation, and health and safety.

The growing influence of these organizations can be found in their participation in the Global Reporting Initiative (2000) whose mission was "to develop and disseminate globally applicable sustainability reporting guidelines for voluntary use by organisations reporting on the economic, environmental, and social dimensions of their activities, products and services" (Global Reporting Initiative 2000, 1). Interestingly, other participants were the Association of Chartered Accountants in the United Kingdom and the Canadian Institute of Chartered Accountants. Evidently, the infrastructure for social accounting and improved accountability is gradually intermingling with mainstream accounting organizations.

The work of the Council on Economic Priorities and the Institute of Social and Ethical AccountAbility is not oriented specifically toward social organizations. However, other forms of infrastructure building are so oriented. In part this thrust toward infrastructure building comes from within but also it is coming in response to invitations from state agencies to enter into compacts or accords with the "voluntary sector." The prototype in England is referred to as "an agreement between the Government and the Voluntary and Community Sector made in November 1998 to improve their relationship for mutual advantage. The Compact aims to build the partnership relationship between government and the sector" (National Council of Voluntary Organisations 2002, 2). These compacts involve official recognition by both the government and the public of the significance of nonprofits. Government's motivation for these compacts is that as part of downsizing, nonprofits have been drawn increasingly into partnerships with government. Since a subset of nonprofits has become providers of services that are funded largely through taxes, government has become more interested in defining the parameters of their relationships and ensuring accountability.

This point is underlined by the Prime Minister of Canada, Jean Chrétien (2001, 1), in a statement about the accord between his government and the voluntary sector: "I believe that this Accord is the blueprint for a strong and vibrant relationship between the voluntary sector and the Government of Canada. As such, it will show us how we can continue to work together to build a better country." The prime minister's statement acknowledges specifically the partnership that exists between government and nonprofits.

The accord in Canada was modeled after those created in England, Scotland, Northern Ireland, and Wales (Phillips 2001). Similar arrangements have been made in the Republic of Ireland, South Africa, and the provinces of Quebec and Newfoundland. In England, dozens of local agreements have been modeled after the national arrangement. Although the specifics of these many agreements differ, in general they are accountability arrangements that attempt to define the relationship between the participating parties.

With the exception of the Institute of Social and Ethical AccountAbility, these other organizations have not specifically confronted the issue of the accounting frameworks for social organizations. Moreover, as noted, compacts with government predominantly involve public sector nonprofits. Nevertheless, these compacts reflect an attempt at strengthening the infrastructure for nonprofits and are an indication of interest in a broader range of issues. In some jurisdictions, the apex organizations are representing a wider array of participants—as for example, in Quebec where the participants in the Compact included community organizations (Phillips 2001) and where there is an apex organization for the social economy, Le Chantier de l'économie sociale.

REINTERPRETING WHAT IS VALUED

The social accounting movement is an initiative to broaden accounting practices, but it can also be seen as part of a broader movement to reinterpret what is valued. Two additional manifestations of this trend are the movement to redefine national accounts (gross domestic product or GDP) and the social investment movement.

Redefining the National Accounts

A central theme in the GDP critique is that forms of productive labor such as housework are ignored because the people undertaking them (predominantly women) do not earn an income for their contributions. Economist Ernest Mandel pointed out this faulty evaluation of household labor. He sarcastically commented that the GDP would decline if bachelors en masse married their housekeepers, "who thenceforth no longer received wages for doing the same work as they were doing before they married" (Mandel 1968, 307). Economists refer to this contradiction as Pigou's paradox, after Arthur Pigou who first discussed it. This example underlines the illogic of how the national income is calculated—that is, if domestic labor is paid for, it counts; if it is unpaid, as is often the case, it does not count even though it involves services that are essential to social well-being. The parallels to accounting at the organizational level are unmistakable.

This same point is central to the feminist critique of economics (Mies 1986; Shiva 1989; Waring 1996, 1999). Waring juxtaposes the extensive domestic labor undertaken by married women in support of the family (labor that counts for nothing in estimates of the GDP) to the paid contribution of men and women who sit passively waiting for orders to detonate a nuclear missile. Waring states also that some nations impute value in their national accounts to activities such as pimping and drug trafficking. Even though these activities are illegal and hidden from official view (the hidden economy), they are known to exact a monetary value and known to be widespread—though not as widespread as housework. The fact that they are socially destructive, whereas unpaid household labor is of social value, is inconsequential to the evaluation of the GDP.

Internationally, work that does not receive a payment in the market (much of it domestic work by women) is estimated in the United Nations Human Development Report (1995) to have a value of $16 trillion. This unpaid work—that doesn't count in the GDP calculations—is estimated at about 70 percent of the paid global outputs of $23 trillion that do count.

Proponents of sustainable development (Daly and Cobb 1994; Ekins 1986; Schumacher 1973) have similar critiques. Fritz Schumacher, in particular, was one of the first economists to challenge the widely held view that increasing production was a worthwhile end in itself. In his influential book *Small Is Beautiful*, he argues that resources cannot be depleted indefinitely and that there has to be equilibrium among increasing production, using resources, and continuing to increase the population. Schumacher's approach to economics, in contrast to the predominant trend in his field, was explicitly value based rather than assuming value neutrality:

> The development of production and the acquisition of wealth have thus become the highest goals of the modern world in relation to which all other goals, no matter how much lip-service may still be paid to them, have to take second place. This is the philosophy of materialism, and it is now being challenged by events (1973, 293).

Like many others, Schumacher's critique of mainstream economics highlights the limitations of current national economic indicators such as the GDP. These critics point out that not only do current aggregates fail to take into account the value of the sustenance and renewal of life but they also overlook a key indicator of economic progress—the sustainability of growth (Daly and Cobb 1994; Mies 1986; Schumacher 1973; Shiva 1989). Essentially, mainstream economics fails to include the social and environmental costs of production, rendering accounts unbalanced and the long-term sustainability of production unanalyzed (Lintott, as summarized in Ekins 1986). This points to the need to include sustainability in new models of economics and to cost more realistically the use and depletion of natural resources in organizational accounting.

Like the alternatives presented at the organizational level, the reformulation of the national accounts expands the number of economic sectors to encompass non-monetized economic activity. Handy's (1984) three-layered model of unvalued work consists of the illegal, voluntary, and household economies. Sparrow (as summarized in Ekins 1986) adds to Handy's model a fourth layer of informal work exchange, which is estimated at 60 percent of the GDP (Ekins 1986). Like these other theorists, Ross (1986) attempts to broaden the number of economic sectors. His nine-sector model of the economy includes big business, public sector, small business, collectives and cooperatives, community enterprises, voluntary activity, barter and exchange, mutual aid, and household sectors.

In contrast to these aforementioned models, Henderson (1981) emphasizes that the environment is a resource that supports all economic activity. In Henderson's (1981) model, the private sector forms the smallest layer, followed in size by the public sector and unpaid work, with nature comprising the bottom layer that supports the rest of the structure. Henderson's (1981) model places the natural environment at the foundation because without food, water, clean air, and raw materials to sustain human life and production, economic activity would not take place.

Like these other theorists, Pietilä (1993) questions the apparent exclusions from what counts, but her conceptualization of the economy is portrayed as concentric circles. In this model, sectors of the economy are differentiated by their ability to act independently. The thin outer circle represents the "fettered" economy of large-scale regulated production that is bound to the fluctuations of world markets; the middle circle represents the protected sector, consisting of both private production for the home market and public services that are guided and protected by legislation; and the large inner circle at the core represents the free economy—work done voluntarily at home and in the community.

In her 1980 study of Finland, Pietilä (1993) measures time spent in labor, volume of output, and money value. She argues that the work done in the free economy, largely invisible and female, counts for 54 percent of the total time spent in work and 35 percent of the money value. By contrast, the fettered economy counts for 10 percent of the total work time and 19 percent of the money output.

Taken together, these alternative frameworks for depicting the national accounts highlight the same problem as do the proponents of social accounting at the organizational level—important forms of non-monetized work are excluded. Until social scientists develop standard measures for other activities such as barter, household work, volunteer work, and social labor, these items will not be included in the GDP.

Statistics Canada's decision to include household work in secondary statistical profiles points the way toward broader indices (Statistics Canada 1995), but this work is still viewed as experimental. Similarly, the United Nations has attempted to go beyond the limitations of GDP accounts based solely on financial transactions in creating its Human Development Index that combines an array of indicators within the broad categories of health and longevity, education, and standard of living (United Nations Human Development Report 2002).

From his study of alternative economic models, Ekins (1986) presents a useful summary of principles for a new economics:

➢ first, that natural resources and the environment are neither infinite nor, at current levels of usage, free;
➢ second, that all costs and benefits of production and consumption should be accounted for;

> third, that the distinction between economic and social values and motivations is both false and misleading; they are inextricably interlinked and should always be considered together; and

> fourth, that paid work per se is neither more valuable nor should it have higher status than unpaid work.

These guidelines for alternative measurement offer the basis for conceptualizing the integration of economic and social accounting.

Daly and Cobb (1994) move this work one step further by actually creating a measure of economic welfare. In effect, they produce an alternative index—the Index of Sustainable Economic Welfare (ISEW)—that takes into account such factors as the value of housework, the cost of resource depletion, whether increases of income lead to redistribution of wealth (the assumption being that "an additional thousand dollars in income adds more to the welfare of a poor family than it does to a rich family") (Daly and Cobb 1994, 444).

The reformulations of the national accounts give social organizations a higher profile than does the GDP because they include non-monetized labor. However, Ross (1986) argues that, in a market system, broader indices will still result in the systematic under-representation of useful activities because of the problems associated with attributing economic value to activities that do not fit the traditional concept of economic. Taking Ross's (1986) objections into account, it is still possible to develop indicators that can link economic and social progress, and at the same time be frank about their limitations. Controversy surrounding economic indicators and their predictive abilities suggests that they are generally incomplete and also open to interpretation. Developing social indicators can play a positive role in supplementing economic indicators, especially ones that omit social considerations.

Social Investment

As with the movement to redefine the national accounts, the social investment movement is also attempting to change what counts. Investors are increasingly directing their money to mutual funds with social and ethical screens (Becker and McVeigh 2001) and to targeted community investment (Calabrese 2001; Carmichael 2005; Carmichael and Quarter 2003). Social investment has become big business in many Western countries. In the United States, a 10-year study by the Social Investment Forum estimates the number of socially-screened mutual funds increased from 55 in 1995 to 201 in 2005 and the total assets under management by these funds increased from $12 billion to $179 billion (Social Investment Forum 2006). This report "identified $2.29 trillion in total assets under management using one or more of the three core socially responsible investing strategies—screening, shareholder advocacy, and community investing. ... Nearly one out of every ten dollars under professional management in the United States today—9.4 percent of the $24.4 trillion in total assets under management tracked in Nelson Information's Directory of

Investment Managers—is involved in socially responsible investing" (Social Investment Forum 2006, iv).

Nor is the trend in the United States unique. In Canada, the assets managed according to social responsibility guidelines as of June, 2004, reached $65.46 billion (Social Investment Organization 2005). In Europe, a 2003 report of eight Western European countries by Eurosif (European Sustainable and Responsible Investment Forum) states that "Social Responsible Investment has undergone tremendous developments in Europe in the last few years" (Eurosif 2003, 6). This report indicates further that in these countries 336 billion of assets are subject to some form of screening, and indicates that the U.K. and the Netherlands are the strongest in this regard.

Although social investment has its limitations in that the best practices in a particular industry are often far from ideal, it nevertheless indicates a growing desire of investors to know the social behavior of the firms in which they invest. The social investment movement has also actively attempted to alter corporate behavior by pushing social standards. An outstanding example of this is the Coalition for Environmentally Responsible Economies (CERES), a U.S. alliance of investment firms and pensions funds that promotes environmental friendly behavior among corporations. The CERES principles (originally the *Valdez* principles—after the Exxon *Valdez* oil spill in 1989) consist of 10 points to guide corporate conduct (CERES 2002). One of the key principles is corporate environmental reporting, one form of social accountability. CERES uses shareholder resolutions to put pressure on corporations to improve their environmental performance and some of CERES's institutional investors—for example, the Interfaith Center on Corporate Responsibility—have filed proxy resolutions asking firms in which they invest to endorse the CERES principles. In 2002, endorsers of the CERES principles included 13 *Fortune* 500 corporations—for example, Ford, General Motors, and American Airlines.

The CERES principles are part of a growing trend toward the creation of basic social standards for corporate behavior, a trend that has been spearheaded by community groups with the support of UN and government agencies. A variation of Social Accountability 8000 (referred to previously in this chapter) is the Worldwide Responsible Apparel Production (WRAP) that audits the behavior of member countries and their suppliers (Worldwide Responsible Apparel Production 2002). The WRAP principles were endorsed by the American Apparel Manufacturers Association in 1998 and, since then, have received international support.

The context has changed since the early 1970s, when integrated forms of social accounting were first introduced. Today, there appears to be greater interest in establishing basic social standards and creating evaluative procedures for them. This trend is a response to, or a minor correction of, the incredible power and economic wealth of modern corporations and of related concerns about exploitation of labor, including child labor, and the environment.

Even though the frame of reference differs between social accounting and these other movements for social investment and to alter the measurement of national accounts, all are critical of the narrowness of conventional approaches and the segregation of social from economic. Moreover, all seek to reinterpret what counts.

CONCLUSION

For many organizations, opting for a social accounting statement may seem forbidding. However, social accounting is not simply a procedure for producing accounting statements; it is also a mechanism for understanding the dynamics of an organization. Assembling such statements can create insights for stakeholders, an understanding of what has been accomplished and where improvements can be achieved. By synthesizing financial data with social inputs and outputs, social accounting can enhance the importance of the social items and give them meaning within the context of the organization's finances. The many Jane/Finches of the world know that they are serving their local communities well and can supply testimonials from the clients whom they serve. When these testimonials are systematically organized, they can be impressive. However, it is also impressive for funders to know that for every dollar invested in Jane/Finch $8.43 of value added is created, or that volunteers contributed almost 30 percent of its total resources. As illustrated in Chapter 7, the amount of value added and the contribution of volunteers to the total resources may vary by organization, but these figures are graphic illustrations of social impact. Our point is that a statistical summary of social impact can be helpful in presenting results, and this is one of the methods that social organizations should apply.

This comment should not be interpreted as a criticism of qualitative social accounting. Although we have not used that approach in this book, we view it as an important tool for expressing how the stakeholders of an organization perceive its functioning in relation to its mission. Qualitative social accounting has gained increased credibility as its format has been systematized by organizations such as the New Economics Foundation and the Institute of Social and Ethical AccountAbility. Entering into a debate about whether the quantitative approach is superior to the qualitative would be a pointless exercise in this context, as it has been in the social sciences more generally. That debate reflects dogmatic rigidities and seldom generates insight—to undertake qualitative analysis, it is necessary to count; to collect quantitative data, it is advisable to converse with the participants in the exercise and attempt to understand whether the measures are a good match with their experience.

Indeed, it is misleading to refer to the models presented in this book as quantitative since the data collection process involves qualitative techniques and even borrows from the procedures of fourth-generation evaluation (Guba and Lincoln 1989). It should be emphasized that we "borrow" from the procedures; we do not adopt the entire package and the accompanying philosophy. We make the point about applying qualitative procedures to the creation of financial statements to emphasize that our techniques are eclectic. Both qualitative approaches and integrated social accounting financial statements create understanding and insight.

Not everyone agrees with this view—for example, Traidcraft "rejected earlier approaches to social accounting which attempted to reduce social impacts to a list of financial credits and debits" (Evans 1997, 87). This viewpoint is consistent with critiques of statistics in the social sciences (Boyle 2000; Chambers 1997). While there is a point to such criticism, every technique—whether it is for accounting or for social science research more generally—has its limitations. The forms of social accounting that reduce organizational performance to financial values can miss the human element, as Traidcraft suggests; the qualitative approaches to social accounting can be unwieldy and shaped by unrepresentative sampling. Both approaches are subject to manipulation by management that wants a particular version of the organization's story to be told. The objective should not be perfection but having a variety of techniques that create valuable insights into an organization.

Producing actual accounting statements has been emphasized in this book because this approach speaks to a gap in the social accounting field—financial statements are the territory of conventional approaches to accounting. In this book, we have sought to demonstrate that there are credible approaches to creating accounting statements that better serve the needs of social organizations. Although these statements differ significantly from any in use, three social accounting statements presented in the book are adaptations of conventional accounting statements used with profit-oriented businesses:

➢   the Socioeconomic Impact Statement is an adaptation of an income statement;
➢   the Socioeconomic Resource Statement is an adaptation of a balance sheet; and
➢   the Expanded Value Added Statement is an adaptation of a Value Added Statement.

The Community Social Return on Investment model has been created especially for social organizations, though it too builds upon the input/output logic found in financial accounting.

We note the similarities but also emphasize that each of these approaches includes unpaid labor estimates and estimates of non-monetized social outputs not normally found in conventional accounting statements. The Socioeconomic Impact Statement indicates, in the same manner as the Statement of Activities or profit and loss statement, that (in our given case study) Junior Achievement of Rochester's expenses for the year exceeded its revenues by $3,110. However, the Statement of Activities gives no indication of the value that the organization has created, including the important contribution of the many volunteers that the agency mobilizes. Similarly, the Socioeconomic Resource Statement, like the Statement of Financial Position or balance sheet undertaken by that organization, illustrates that financial liabilities exceeded financial assets by $90,669. However, the Statement of Financial Position does not include the net balance of intellectual capital shown in the Socioeconomic Resource Statement. Junior Achievement can make its service available because it carries forward an important resource of intellectual capital (including paid staff and volunteers) with a net value of $597,986. While the Statement of Financial Position or balance sheet involves dynamics similar to the Socioeconomic Resource Statement, it misses an important part of the story.

Even though most social accounting builds upon traditions in financial accounting and adapts them to a broader range of information, there are risks. Social accounting is still in its early stages of development, and new methods are open to intense scrutiny and criticism. Although this is healthy for the development of new tools, it may limit their use. Initially, it is possible that social accounting may be attempted only by those organizations that have the best track records. This could result in benchmarks based on uncharacteristically high standards of organizational performance.

However, there are limits to this risk. First, because social accounting takes the context of each organization into consideration, it restricts comparisons. Second, because social accounting is in its early stages, there is a lack of common indicators that allow for comparison among organizations. At the same time, this makes it difficult to set benchmarks.

Another risk arises from the difficulty of building upon one social accounting process to the next because methods are refined each time they are applied. This also holds true for the qualitative forms of social accounting, as the methods have been altered with continued use. A lack of consistency can result in using more resources in further applications instead of fewer, as would be expected with repetition. However, as more sophisticated social accounting methods are developed, this risk may be offset by the value of the new information that can be uncovered. New information on an organization's value may attract partners and investors.

At a consultation on social accounting, members of nonprofit organizations pointed out another potential danger. As with the push for outcomes' measurement, there was concern that, if funders began to demand it, social accounting could become a new norm for social organizations and lead to greater work demands. Taken along with the trend toward greater accountability for nonprofits, this is a valid concern. However, by applying social accounting methods at this early stage, organizations may be able to influence their development in ways that meet their needs. Notwithstanding the risks, social accounting can assist nonprofits and cooperatives to demonstrate their value to their communities.

To realize the goal of demonstrating their value, there is a major problem that needs to be solved. At present, there are limits on the process of calculating social inputs and outputs—the examples cited in this book merely scratch the surface. Social outputs are far broader than can currently be captured and include such factors as health and well-being, impact on the environment, inclusiveness of minorities, and many other criteria. To the extent that more organizations become involved in social accounting, the demand will increase to create templates that determine the value of a broader array of social variables.

In addition, the demand will grow to create templates that not only assess value added but also value subtracted. Such a category might be pertinent for such variables as the environment, where citizens, through taxes paid to government, have to bear the costs of cleaning up pollution; or for layoffs, where government bears the cost of social assistance and training. Social accounting opens the door for looking at issues that are not considered in conventional financial statements.

The discussion of social accounting in this book has focused on social organizations, but there is no reason why social accounting cannot be adapted to both government organizations and private sector firms. Government organizations audit social variables, but they segregate them from their financial statements. It would be only a small step to combine the two. By using, for example, an Expanded Value Added Statement, private sector firms can also broaden their financial data to include social variables and to highlight the impact that their business has on its key stakeholders. Thus, social accounting has the potential to help corporations determine the impact of donations—often corporations donate to either the most highly profiled foundations or the safest because they are not sure what other criteria to use. Detailing the value added by a donation can make philanthropy into a more rational process. Similarly, profit-oriented businesses have in-house departments such as legal, marketing, and customer service. If a social accounting framework were applied to these departments, it could demonstrate their contribution to the firm's bottom line.

Social accounting statements that combine social and financial outputs have the potential for creating organizational insights that go beyond the bottom line of conventional financial statements. As the world about us changes, it is incumbent upon accounting to modify its practices. Leading accounting organizations increasingly recognize the limitations of the industrial paradigm of accounting. However, the crux of the problem goes beyond the transition from the industrial to the information paradigm. The central issue is the concept of the organization—whether it is an entity unto itself or is part of a context that influences its results and which, in turn, it influences. For social organizations, measuring social impact is a central issue and, amazingly, conventional accounting statements ignore it.

Related to a contextualized view of the organization is whether there is one stakeholder only (the shareholders in a business corporation and the members in a social organization) or whether there are multiple stakeholders who are of sufficient importance that their contribution to the organization needs to be included in the financial statements. A contextualized view of the organization that characterizes it as impacting on the community and that sees the community as a source of its sustenance recognizes the many stakeholders who are related to the results. Although organizational leaders will acknowledge that this viewpoint is rational, there is a giant gap between the theory and the practice. This book and its practical applications are offered to help bridge that gap.

This book joins with the many movements that are attempting to change what counts. Our piece of this overall objective is the creation of social accounting statements for use by social organizations. We have interpreted this role within the goal of building bridges between the various forms of nonprofits and cooperatives (the social economy framework) and building bridges to the movements for social accountability, social investment, and the movements to reinterpret what is valued. Whereas accounting can be viewed as a technical exercise to measure an organization's results, we view it as part of a historical context that is currently changing. As accounting organizations attempt to adapt themselves to the information age, it is essential they also remember that social organizations have unique characteristics that accounting frameworks should take into consideration. The Jane/Finches of this world are not simply users of others' resources; they generate value that accounting statements must measure. Moreover, this value comes about from the contributions of many stakeholders:

➢ dedicated staff;
➢ volunteers who give generously of their time;
➢ clients in the surrounding community (people on the margins of society who are desperately trying to create a better life for themselves and their families);
➢ taxpayers and donors who provide their financing;
➢ residents of a broader society who value social progress; and
➢ the natural environment that sustains their efforts.

If accounting simply reports that Jane/Finch is living within its means (or, perhaps, even spending a bit too much), it is missing the main part of the story. In its struggle to improve the lives of the residents of the surrounding community, are Jane/Finch centers generating a social return for the investment? Are they adding value? Are they mobilizing the resources needed to serve their community in the coming year? Are they having an impact? These are some of the questions that accounting must address in order to measure what counts.

QUESTIONS FOR DISCUSSION

1. The case studies presented in this book involve financial statements that broaden the domain of accounting and include items normally excluded from financial statements. After reviewing these case studies, do you feel that it is reasonable to broaden the domain of accounting? Why or why not?
2. Accountability is usually viewed as involving a hierarchical relationship. Do you feel that is avoidable? If it isn't, what are the implications for social accounting if one stakeholder tends to dominate? Is it possible to have a multi-stakeholder approach to accounting if one stakeholder dominates?
3. In light of the failure of past attempts at broadening accounting statements that better fit the mission of social organizations, some argue that social accounting should go its own way. Others argue that it would be better to convince accounting governing bodies that a new approach is needed. Discuss.
4. Is the reinterpretation of the gross domestic product (GDP) consistent with social accounting or is it an entirely different phenomenon? Why or why not?

5. In which ways can social accounting inform the social investment movement (for example, ethical funds)?

6. In this book it was argued that presenting information on social and environmental impact (positive or negative) in an integrated accounting statement has more possibilities for influencing decision making than presenting it only in a supplemental report. Discuss.

7. Three of the social accounting statements presented in this book are adaptations of existing financial accounting statements and one is distinct. Do you prefer one approach over another? Why or why not?

8. What are the risks and benefits of social accounting?

9. "The difficulties in creating social accounting statements for social organizations that do not sell their services in the market (that is, they rely totally on unearned revenues) are so great that they do not outweigh the benefits—therefore, well enough should be left alone." Discuss.

10. This book constitutes an initial effort to count things that are important but not yet considered in conventional accounting. What are some ways that this work can go forward?

Afterword

Generally, books about accounting are not exciting to read. However, *What Counts* is an eye-opener and raises issues that have the potential to change practice for nonprofits, cooperatives, and other organizations with a social mission.

As Director of Finance and Administration at Frontier College, a nonprofit that mobilizes large numbers of volunteers across Canada—5,000 in the past year—for adult literacy programs, and as a Certified Management Accountant with many years' experience, my training had not prepared me to address the need for information on all aspects of our program, particularly accounting for volunteer and other social contributions to our organization. After I attended an Accounting for the Value Added by Volunteer workshop and read the book *What Counts* (upon which the workshop was based), I recognized that it is possible to present the contributions of volunteers and other social contributions of our organization within an accounting framework and that social accounting opens the door for addressing such issues as the impact on the community brought about by organizations such as ours.

I decided to use the Expanded Value Added Statement, as presented in *What Counts*, to tell our performance story better and to supplement our existing accounting statements. However, the question I faced after the workshop (one that readers of this book may face) was how to implement these methods in our organization. No matter how interesting, nobody wants to commit to another project with an already extended workload. I knew that to sell this idea, it had to be framed as a solution to our existing issues.

In our case, looking at the value added by volunteers helped us address some of the requests for measures from our Board. The information that we obtained was very useful for communications and fund-raising.

I started with our management team and got the buy-in at that level, which was crucial for this accounting innovation to go ahead. Next I presented the ideas at a staff meeting. The staff found the subject interesting, and the information required (volunteer hours and tasks) was already being collected and so it did not appear to be an extra burden on them. Our staff members generally believe that the finance is concerned only with dollars and cents and does not take account of volunteers and programs. Having the idea of assessing the value added by volunteers presented by the finance department helped to improve our image within the organization, and brought our departments closer together.

We already had systems in place to account for the hours of program volunteers, but there are other volunteers who donate time that are not in programs, the most obvious being the Board. Although we had not documented these hours, it was easy to go through the attendance at Board meetings. We learned too that we had not considered other meetings such as committees of the Board and fund-raising and awareness events. We are now collecting this information on a regular basis on all of our volunteers so that we can present a total picture of their value added.

Once I had gone through the process and calculated the numbers, I made a presentation to the Board. One fact that stood out was that volunteer contributions amounted to 40 percent of all contributions to Frontier College. This was the largest percentage of all contributions including government, and it would never have been recognized without looking at value added in this way.

An important activity of Frontier College is to donate books to children. Through building the data for the Expanded Value Added Statement, we were able to tell people the value of these books. Amazingly, this information had never been communicated either to the general public or even to the Board.

In addition, we were able to put a value on the training we deliver to our volunteers and on the workshops we give in local communities. Frontier College makes a large investment in training volunteers, and it was important to see this recognized.

Upon hearing the facts, the Board's reaction was very positive. One issue they addressed is standards. While they found the information interesting, Board members had many questions on where some of the numbers came from and if there were some sort of established standard. There is more work to be done with standards, but it is clear that accounting for value added is a much better way to show how nonprofit organizations are meeting their mission. Creating and influencing standards and creating public policy require a concerted effort from the nonprofit sector, but I feel that there is the potential for this happen over the coming years.

It is important to make clear that accounting for the value added by volunteers is a measurement that can help tell the organization's story. In no way does it replace the qualitative measurements and stories that we currently collect. However, it does make the picture of what we do much more clear.

Eric Plato
Director of Finance and Administration
Frontier College
Toronto, Canada

References

Abt and Associates Inc. 1974. The Abt model. In *Social auditing: Evaluating the impact of corporate programs*, David Blake, William Frederick, and Mildred Meyers, 149–157. New York: Praeger.

Accounting Standards Steering Committee (ASSC). 1975. *The corporate report*. London: ASSC.

Akingbola, Kunle. 2002. Government funding and staffing in the nonprofit sector: A case study of the Canadian Red Cross, Toronto Region. Master's thesis, Ontario Institute for Studies in Education, University of Toronto.

American Accounting Association. 1971. Report of the Committee on Non-Financial Measures of Effectiveness. *The Accounting Review* Supplement to Vol. XLVI: 165–211.

———. 1972a. Report of the Committee on Concepts of Accounting Applicable to the Public Sector, 1970–71. *The Accounting Review* Supplement to Vol. XLVII (October): 75–108.

———. 1972b. Report of the Committee on the Measures of Effectiveness of Social Programs. *The Accounting Review* Supplement to Vol. 47: 337–396.

———. 1973. Report on the Committee on Environmental Effects of Organizational Behavior. *The Accounting Review* Supplement 48: 76–119.

———. 1989. Report of the Committee on Nonprofit Entities Performance Measures, American Accounting Association Government and Nonprofit Section. *Measuring the performance of nonprofit organizations: The state of the art*. Sarasota, FL: American Accounting Association.

———. 1991. Report of the Committee on Accounting and Auditing Measurement 1989–1990. *Accounting Horizons* (September): 81–105.

American Association of Retired Persons (AARP). 2000. Notes to the Financial Statements. www.aarp.org/ar/2000/graphics/pdfs/fin_full.pdf (9 June 2002).

American Institute of Certified Public Accountants (Accounting Principles Board). 1970. *Basic concepts and accounting principles underlying financial statements of business enterprises*. New York: American Institute of Certified Public Accountants.

———. 1977. *The measurement of corporate social performance*. New York: American Institute of Certified Public Accountants.

———. 1978. *Statement of position. No. 78–10: Accounting principles and reporting practices for certain nonprofit organizations*. New York: American Institute of Certified Public Accountants.

American Red Cross. 2005. Annual report. Washington, DC: American Red Cross.

Amnesty International. 2001. Facts and figures about Amnesty International. www.amnesty.org (19 July 2006).

Andreoni, James. 1990. Impure altruism and donations to public goods: A theory of warm-glow giving. *The Economic Journal* 100 (June): 464–477.

Anthony, Robert N., and David W. Young. 1988. *Management control in nonprofit organizations*. 2d ed. Burr Ridge, IL: Irwin.

Association of Chartered Accountants in the United States (ACAUS). 1999. "Why Study Accounting?" www.acaus.org/history/index.html (13 March 2000).

Barber, Benjamin. 1998. *A place for us: How to make society civil and democracy strong*. New York: Hill and Wang.

Bauer, Raymond, and Dan H. Fenn, Jr. 1973. What is a corporate social audit? *Harvard Business Review* January–February: 37–48.

Baym, Nancy K. 1996. Agreements and disagreements in computer-mediated discussion. *Research on Language and Social Interaction* 29 (4): 315–345.

Bebbington, Jan, Rob Gray, and David Owen. 1999. Seeing the wood for the trees: Taking the pulse of social and environmental accounting. *Accounting, Auditing & Accountability Journal* 12 (1): 47–51.

Becker, Eric, and Patrick McVeigh. 2001. Social funds in the United States: Their history, financial performance and social impacts. In *Working capital: The power of labor's pensions*, ed. Archon Fung, Tessa Hebb, and Joel Rogers, 44–66. Ithaca, NY: Cornell University Press.

Belkaoui, Ahmed. 1984. *Socio-economic accounting*. Westport, CT: Quorum Books.

Benson, Dennis. 1999. Return on investment: Public dollars, private dollars, charitable contributions, voluntarism. Paper presented at the 1999 Conference of the National Association of Community Action Agencies, Chicago. www.roma1.org/documents/ROI/nacaa99.pdf (17 July 2006).

Bilodeau, Marc, and Al Slivinski. 1996. Volunteering nonprofit entrepreneurial services. *Journal of Economic Behavior & Organization* 31: 117–127.

Blake, David, William Frederick, and Mildred Meyers. 1976. *Social auditing: Evaluating the impact of corporate programs*. New York: Praeger.

Blum, Fred. 1958. Social audit of the enterprise. *Harvard Business Review* March–April: 77–86.

Bowen, Howard R. 1953. *Social responsibilities of the businessman*. New York: Harper.

Boyce, Gordon. 1998. Public discourse and decision-making: An exploration of possibilities for financial, social, and environmental accounting. Paper presented at the APIRA conference, Osaka, Japan. www3.bus.osaka-cu.ac.jp/ARIRA98/archives/htmls/51.htm (21 March 2000).

Boyle, David. 2000. *The tyranny of numbers: Why counting can't make us happy*. London: HarperCollins.

Brenner, Harvey. 1976. *Achieving the goals of the Employment Act of 1946—Thirtieth anniversary review*. Washington, DC: U.S. Government Printing Office.

Brinkirhoff, Robert, and Dennis Dressler. 1990. *Productivity measurement: A guide for managers and evaluators*. Newbury Park, CA: Sage.

Brown, Eleanor. 1999, May. Assessing the value of volunteer activity. *Nonprofit and Voluntary Sector Quarterly* 28 (1): 3–17.

Brown, Leslie. 2000. The cooperative difference? Social auditing in Canadian credit unions. *Journal of Rural Cooperation* 28 (2): 87–100.

———. 2001. Social auditing and community cohesion: The co-operative way. Halifax: Mount Saint Vincent University. Photocopy.

Brudney, Jeffrey. 1990. *Fostering volunteer programs in the public sector*. San Francisco: Jossey-Bass.

Brunsting, Suzanne, and Tom Postmes. 2002. Social movement participation in the digital age. Predicting offline and online collective action. *Small Group Research* 33 (5): 525–54.

Burchell, Stuart, Colin Clubb, and Anthony G. Hopwood. 1985. Accounting in its social context: Towards a history of value added in the United Kingdom. *Accounting, Organizations and Society* 10 (4): 381–413.

Business Ethics. 2006. Best corporate citizens—methodology. www.business-ethics.com/media/100_Best_Corp_Citizens_Methodology_Detail.pdf (14 July 2006).

Calabrese, Michael. 2001. In *Working capital: The power of labor's pensions*, ed. Archon Fung, Tessa Hebb, and Joel Rogers, 93–127. Ithaca, NY: Cornell University Press.

Cameron, Michael. 1991. *Transportation efficiency: Tackling Southern California's air pollution and congestion.* Los Angeles: Environmental Defense Fund.

Campbell, Kathryn. 1998. When even your accountant betrays you. *CAUT Bulletin ACPPU* 45 (9): 28.

Canadian Crossroads International (CCI). CCI home page. 2002. Introduction to CCI. www.cciorg.ca (16 June 2002).

Canadian Institute of Chartered Accountants (CICA). 1980. *Financial reporting for non-profit organizations.* Toronto: Canadian Institute of Chartered Accountants.

———. 1993a. *Reporting on environmental performance.* Toronto: Canadian Institute of Chartered Accountants.

———. 1993b. *Audits of non-profit organizations: An audit technique study.* Toronto: Canadian Institute of Chartered Accountants.

———. 1996. CICA Handbook, Sections 4400–4460. Toronto: Canadian Institute of Chartered Accountants.

———. Canadian Institute of Chartered Accountants home page. 2000. Canadian performance reporting initiative. www.cica.ca/cica/cicawebsite.nsf/public/SPCPRI (23 June 2002).

Carmichael, Isla. 2005. *Pension power: Unions, pension funds, and social investment in Canada.* Toronto: University of Toronto Press.

Carmichael, Isla, and Jack Quarter, eds. 2003. *Money on the line: Workers' capital in Canada.* Ottawa: Canadian Centre for Policy Alternatives.

CERES (Coalition for Environmentally Responsible Economies). CERES home page. 2002. www.ceres.org (27 June 2002).

Chambers, Robert. *Whose reality counts? Putting the first last. London:* Intermediate Technology.

Cherny, Julius, Arlene Gordon, and Richard Herson. 1992. *Accounting—a social institution: A unified theory or the measurement of the profit and nonprofit sectors.* New York: Quorum Books.

Chrétien, Jean. 2001. An Accord between the government of Canada and the voluntary sector. Ottawa: Secretariat, Voluntary Sector Initiative. www.vsi-isbc.ca (25 June 2002).

Christenson, James. 1994. Themes of community development. In *Community Development in Perspective*, ed. James Christenson and Jerry Robinson, 26–47. Ames, IA: Iowa State University.

City of Toronto. 1993. *Toronto's first state of the city report.* Toronto: City of Toronto.

Clarkson, Max. 1995. A stakeholder framework for analyzing and evaluating corporate social performance. *Academy of Management Review* 20 (1): 92–117.

Cleveland, Gordon, and Michael Krashinsky. 1998. *The benefits and costs of good child care: The economic rationale for public investment in young children.* Toronto: University of Toronto, Centre for Urban and Community Studies, Childcare Resource and Research Unit.

Cnaan, Ram, Femida Handy, and Margaret Wadsworth. 1996. Defining who is a volunteer: Conceptual and empirical considerations. *Nonprofit and Voluntary Sector Quarterly* 25 (3): 364–383.

Cohen, Bronwen, and Neil Fraser. 1991. *Childcare in a modern welfare system: Towards a new national policy.* London: Institute of Policy Research.

Committee of Planning and Co-ordinating Organizations. 1992. *Social report for Metro.* Toronto: Toronto: Metro Toronto.

Community Literacy of Ontario. 1998. *The economic value of volunteers in community literacy agencies in Ontario.* Barrie, Ontario: Community Literacy of Ontario.

Computer Training Center. 1995. Brochure. Toronto: Computer Training Center.

Cooper, Gerry. 2000. Online assistance for problem gamblers. Ph.D. diss., University of Toronto.

Co-operatives Secretariat. 2005. *Co-operatives in Canada (2003).* Ottawa: Government of Canada.

Co-operative Union of Canada. 1985. *Social auditing: A manual for co-operative organizations.* Ottawa: Co-operative Union of Canada.

Cornell Cooperative Extension. 1995. Financial operations resource manual, code 817. www.cce.cornell.edu/admin/fhar/form/code0800/817.htm (10 June 2002).

Craig, Jack. 1993. *The nature of co-operation.* Montreal: Black Rose.

Crawford, Cameron. 2004. *Improving the odds: Employment, disability and public programs in Canada.* Toronto: Roeher Institute.

Crutchfield, James. 1962. Valuation of fishing resources. *Land Economics* May: 145–154.

Cutt, James, and Vic Murray. 2000. *Accountability and effectiveness: Evaluation in non-profit organizations.* London: Routledge.

Dahl, Robert. 1970. *After the revolution: Authority in a good society.* New Haven: Yale University Press.

Daly, Herman, and John Cobb Jr. 1994. *For the common good: Redirecting the economy toward community, the environment and a sustainable future.* 2d ed. Boston: Beacon Press.

Davidson, James, Margaret Cole, and Anthony Pogorlec. 1997. The economic impact of religions organizations: Results from two recent studies. In *Independent sector, the changing social contract: Measuring the interaction between the independent sector and society,* 93–112. Washington, DC: The Independent Sector.

Day, Kathleen, and Rose Anne Devlin. 1996. Volunteerism and crowding out: Canadian econometric evidence. *Canadian Journal of Economics* XXIX (1): 37–53.

———. 1997. The Canadian nonprofit sector. In *The emerging sector: In search of a framework,* ed. R. Hirschhorn, 61–71. Ottawa: Renouf.

———. 1998. The payoff to work without pay: Volunteer work as an investment in human capital. *Canadian Journal of Economics* 31 (5): 1179–1191.

Dees, Gregory. 1998. Enterprising nonprofits. *Harvard Business Review* January–February: 55–67.

Defourny, Jacques. 1999. *The emergence of social enterprises in Europe.* EMES European Networks, Brussels.

Defourny, Jacques, and José L. Monzon Campos, eds. 1992. *The third sector: Co-operative, mutual and nonprofit organizations.* Brussels: CIRIEC and DeBoeck University.

Deibert, Ronald. 2000. International plug'n play? Citizen activism, the Internet, and global public policy. *International Studies Perspectives* 1 (3): 255–72.

Devlin, Rose Anne. 2000. Labour-market responses to volunteering: Evidence from the 1997 SGVP. Ottawa: Human Resources Development Canada.

———. 2001. Volunteers and paid labour market. *Canadian Journal of Policy Research* 2 (2): 62–68.

Dzinkowski, Ramona. 1998. *The measurement and management of intellectual capital: An introduction.* New York: International Federation of Accountants (IFAC).

Eakin, Lynn. 2001. *Myths, money and service provision: An overview of the funding of Canada's voluntary sector.* Ottawa: Voluntary Sector Initiative.

Ekins, Paul, ed. 1986. *The living economy: A new economics in the making.* London: Routledge and Kegan Paul.

Ellerman, David. 1990. *The democratic worker-owned firm*. Boston: HarperCollins.

Estes, Ralph. 1972. Socio-economic accounting and external diseconomies. *The Accounting Review* April: 284–290.

———. 1976. *Corporate social accounting*. New York: John Wiley.

Eurosif (European Sustainable and Responsible Investment Forum). 2003. *Socially responsible investment among European institutional investors: 2003 report*. Paris: Author.

Evans, Richard. 1997. Accounting for ethics: Traidcraft plc, U.K. In *Building corporate accountability*, ed. Simon Zadek, Peter Pruzan, and Richard Evans, 84–101. London: Earthscan.

Eysenbach, Gunther, John Powell, Marina Englesakis, Carlos Rizo, and Anita Stern. 2004. Health related virtual communities and electronic support group: Systematic review of the effects of online peer to peer interactions. *British Medical Journal* 328 (7449): 1166–1171.

Federal Transit Administration. 1995. TransitChek® in the New York City and Philadelphia Areas. www.fta.dot.gov/library/program/tchek/TransitChek.htm (23 June 2002).

Ferguson, Tom. 1997. Health care in cyberspace: Patients lead a revolution. *The Futurist* 31 (6): 29–33.

Ferris, James M. 1984. Coprovision: Citizen time and money donation in public service provision. *Public Administration Review* 44 (4): 324–333.

Financial Accounting Standards Board (FASB). 1978. *Statement of financial accounting concepts No. 1 Objectives of financial reporting by business enterprises*. Norwalk, CT: FASB.

———. 1980. *Concepts statement No. 4 objectives of financial reporting by nonbusiness organizations*. Norwalk, CT: FASB.

———. 1993. *Statement of financial accounting standards No. 116: Accounting for contributions received and contributions made*. www.fasb.org/st/summary/stsum116.shtml (5 June 2002).

———. 2002. *Disclosure of information about intangible assets not recognized in financial statements*. www.fasb.org/project/intangibles.shtml (14 July 2002).

Finkler, Steven A. 2005. *Financial management: For public, health, and not-for-profit organizations,* 2nd ed. Upper Saddle River, NJ: Prentice-Hall.

Flamholtz, Eric. 1974. *Human resource accounting*. Encino, CA.: Dickenson Pub. Co.

———. 1985. *Human resource accounting*. 2d ed. San Francisco: Jossey-Bass.

———. 1999. *Human resource accounting*: *Advances in concepts, methods, and applications*. 3d ed. Boston: Kluwer Academic Pub.

Flinders, Mathew. 2001. *The politics of accountability in the modern state*. Aldershot, U.K.: Ashgate.

Fountain, Jay. 2001. Using performance measures in K–12. *School Business Affairs*. www.asbointl.org (11 June 2002).

Freeman, R. Edward. 1984. *Strategic management: A stakeholder approach*. Boston: Harper Collins.

Freeman, Richard. 1997. Working for nothing: The supply of volunteer labor. *Journal of Labor Economics* 15 (1): S140–S166.

Friedman, Milton. 1970. Social responsibility of business is to increase its profits. *The New York Times Magazine* (September 13): 32–33.

Gagne, R. L. 1996. Accountability and public administration. *Canadian Public Administration* 39 (2): 213–225.

Garner, William C. 1991. Accounting and budgeting in public and nonprofit organizations. San Francisco: Jossey-Bass.

Garrison, Ray, George Chesley, and Raymond Carroll. 1993. *Managerial accounting.* Homewood, IL: Irwin.

Gaskin, Katharine. 1999. Valuing volunteers in Europe: A comparative study of the Volunteer Investment and Value Audit *Voluntary Action: The Journal of Active Volunteering Research* 2 (1): 35–48.

Gaskin, Katharine, and Barbara Dobson. 1997. The economic equation of volunteering. www.jrf.org.uk/knowledge/findings/socialpolicy/SP110.asp (24 May 2002*).*

Global Reporting Initiative. 2000. Sustainability reporting guidelines on economic, environmental, and social performance. Boston: Interim Secretariat, Global Reporting Initiative. www.globalreporting.org (5 June 2002).

———. 2005. G3 guidelines. www.grig3.org/guidelines/overview.html (14 June 2006).

Goodman, Patti. 1997. *Report on a national survey of home-delivered meals programs in Canada.* Ottawa: The Canadian Association for Community Care.

Government of Ontario. 1996. *Greater Toronto Area Task Force Report.* Toronto: Queen's Printer for Ontario.

Goyder, George. 1961. *The responsible company.* Oxford: Basil Blackwell.

Gray, Rob. 1992. Accounting and environmentalism: An exploration of the challenge of gently accounting for accountability, transparency and sustainability. *Accounting, Organizations and Society* 17 (5): 399–425.

———. 1998. Imagination, a bowl of petunias and social accounting. *Critical Perspectives on Accounting* 9: 205–216.

Gray, Rob, Dave Owen, and K. T. Maunders. 1987. *Corporate social reporting: Accounting and accountability.* London: Prentice Hall.

Gray, Rob, Dave Owen, and Carol Adams. 1996. *Accounting and accountability: Changes and challenges in corporate social and environmental reporting.* London: Prentice Hall.

———. 1997. Struggling with the praxis of social accounting: Stakeholders, accountability, audits and procedures. *Accounting, Auditing & Accountability Journal* 10 (3): 325–364.

Gray, Rob, and Jan Bebbington. 1998. Accounting and the soul of sustainability: Hyperreality, transnational corporations and the United Nations. Paper presented at the 1998 APIRA conference, Osaka, Japan.www3.bus.osaka-cu.ac.jp/APIRA98/archives/paper24.htm (21 March 2000).

Green, David. 1993. *Reinventing civil society: The rediscovery of welfare without politics.* London: IEA Health and Welfare Unit.

Greider, William. 1997. *One world, ready or not: The manic logic of global capitalism.* New York: Simon & Schuster.

Grojer, Jan-Erik, and Agneta Stark. 1977. *Accounting, Organizations and Society* 2 (4): 349–386.

Gross, Malvern J. Jr., and William Warshauer, Jr. 1979. *Financial and accounting guide for nonprofit organizations.* New York: John Wiley.

Guba, Egon, and Yvonna Lincoln. 1989. *Fourth generation evaluation.* Newbury Park, CA: Sage.

Gunderson, Morley. 2001. Multipliers and volunteer activity. Toronto: Centre for Industrial Relations, University of Toronto. Photocopy.

Guthrie, James, Richard Petty, and Ulf Johanson. 2001. Sunrise in the knowledge economy: Managing, measuring and reporting intellectual capital. *Accounting, Auditing and Accountability Journal* 14 (4): 365–382.

Hall, John, ed. 1995. *Civil society: Theory, history, comparison.* Cambridge: Polity Press.

Hall, Michael, David Lashby, Glenn Gulmulka, and Kathryn Tyron. 2006. *Caring Canadians, involved Canadians: Highlights from the 2004 Canada survey of giving, volunteering and participating.* Ottawa: Statistics Canada.

Hall, Michael, and Paul Reed. 1995. Shifting the burden: How much can government download to the nonprofit sector. Paper presented at the annual conference of ARNOVA, Cleveland.

Hall, Michael, and Keith Banting. 2000. The nonprofit sector in Canada. In *The nonprofit sector in Canada: Roles and relationships*, ed. Keith Banting, 1–28. Kingston: Queen's School of Policy Studies.

Hall, Michael, Larry McKeown, and Karen Roberts. 2001. *Caring Canadians, Involved Canadians: Highlights from the 2000 National Survey of Giving, Volunteering and Participating.* Ottawa: Minister of Industry.

Hall, Michael H. et al. (2005). *Cornerstones of community: Highlights of the national survey of nonprofit and voluntary organizations.* Ottawa: Statistics Canada.

Haller, Axel. 1997. About the decision-usefulness of a value added statement as part of financial statements. Paper presented at the annual congress of the European Accounting Association, Graz, Austria, April 23–25.

Handy, Charles. 1984. *The future of work.* Oxford: Basil Blackwell.

Handy, Femida, and Hans Srinivasan. 2002. Volunteers in hospitals: Scope and value. Toronto: York University. Photocopy.

Handy, Femida, Ram A. Cnaan, Jeffrey L. Brudney, Ugo Ascoli, Lucas C. Meijs, and Shree Ranade. 2000. Public perception of "who is a volunteer": An examination of the net-cost approach from a cross-cultural perspective. *International Journal of Voluntary and Nonprofit Organizations* 11 (1): 45–65.

Hatry, Harry P. 1999. *Performance measurement: Getting results.* Washington, DC: Urban Institute Press.

Harte, G. F., and Dave L. Owen. 1987. Fighting de-industrialisation: The role of local government social audits. *Accounting, Organizations and Society* 12 (2): 123–141.

Henderson, Helen. 1981. *The politics of the solar age: Alternatives to economics.* New York: Doubleday.

Henke, Emerson O. 1972. Performance evaluation for not-for-profit organizations. *The Journal of Accountancy* 133 (June): 51–55.

———. 1989. *Accounting for nonprofit organizations.* 2d ed. Boston: PWS-Kent Publishing.

Henriques, Adrian. 2001. Civil society and social auditing. *Business Ethics: A European Review* 10 (1): 40–44.

Heritage Credit Union. 1998. Social audit of Heritage Credit Union Limited. Dartmouth, Nova Scotia: Heritage Credit Union. Photocopy.

Hines, Ruth. D. 1988. Financial accounting: In communicating reality, we construct reality. *Accounting, Organizations and Society* 13 (3): 251–261.

Hirshhorn, Ronald, ed. 1997. *The emerging sector: In search of a framework.* Ottawa: Canadian Policy Research Networks Inc.

Hodgkinson, Virginia, and Murray S. Weitzman. 1988. *Giving and volunteering in the United States: Findings from a national survey.* Washington, DC: Independent Sector.

Hope, Jeremy, and Tony Hope. 1997. *Competing in the third wave: The ten key management issues of the information age.* Boston: Harvard Business School.

Hopkins, Bruce R. 1987. *The law of tax-exempt organizations.* 5d ed. New York: Wiley.

Human Resources and Social Development. 2006. National Occupational Classification (NOC). www.labourmarketinformation.ca/standard.asp?ppid=43&lcode=E (17 July 2006).

IBM. 2002. Takes Top Spot Among 650 Leading U.S. Public Companies. www-916.ibm.com/press/prnews.nsf/jan/7060868835295644852568BA30049DEC8 (21 May 2002).

Independent Sector. 1997. *Nonprofit almanac: Dimensions of the independent sector*. San Francisco: Jossey-Bass.

————. 2001a. Giving and volunteering in the United States: Key Findings. www.independentsector.org/PDFs/GV01keyfind.pdf (12 June 2002).

————. Independent Sector home page. 2001b. www.independentsector.org/media/ voltimePR. htm (22 June 2001).

————. 2002. *Nonprofit almanac in brief*. www.independentsector.org (1 June 2002).

————. 2006. Independent Sector. Volunteer value calculation. www.independentsector.org/programs/research/volunteer_time.html (17 June 2006).

Institute of Chartered Accountants in England and Wales (ICAEW). 1992. *Business, accountancy and the environment: A policy and research agenda*. London: ICAEW.

Institute of Social and Ethical AccountAbility (ISEA). 2000. AccountAbility 1000: Standards guidelines and professional qualifications. London: ISEA. www.accountability.org.uk/ (23 May 2002).

————. 2001. *What is social and ethical accounting, auditing and reporting*. London: ISEA. www.accountability.org.uk (23 May 2002).

Intel. 2002. Intel home page. 2002. Intel ranked #11 in Business Ethics 2002 List of 100 Best Corporate Citizens. www.intel.com/intel/finance/social.htm (21 May 2002).

Internal Revenue Service. 2001. Revised 2001 tax rate schedules. www.irs.gov/graphics/ estimatepaynts.gif (23 June 2002).

International Accounting Standards Committee (IASC). 1996. Presentation of financial statements. Exposure draft E 53. London: IASC.

International Co-operative Alliance (ICA). 1998. ICA Rules: Section 1 and 2. Geneva: ICA. www.ica.coop/ica/ica/rules/rules1.html (4 June 2002).

————. 2001. Statement on the co-operative identity. Geneva: ICA. www.ica.coop/ica/ica/ica-intro.html (2 July 2002).

International Federation of Red Cross and Red Crescent Societies home page. 2006. www.ifrc.org (14 July 2006).

James, Estelle. 1987. The nonprofit sector in comparative perspective. In *The nonprofit sector: A research handbook*, Walter W. Powell ed., 397–415. New Haven, CT: Yale University Press.

Jawahar, I. M., and Gary L. McLaughlin. 2001. Toward a descriptive stakeholder theory: An organizational life cycle approach. *Academy of Management Review* 26 (3): 397–414.

Jeantet, Thierry. 1991. Économie sociale et coopératives. Paris: n.p. Photocopy.

Jonsson, Bo, and Jonathan Rosenbaum, eds. 1993. *Health economics of depression*. Toronto: Wiley.

Jordan, John. 1989. The multi-stakeholder concept of organization. In *Partners in enterprise: The worker ownership phenomenon*, ed. Jack Quarter and George Melnyk, 113–131. Montreal: Black Rose.

Junior Achievement. 2006 Worldwide statistics for the 2004–2005 program year. www.ja.org/about/about_who_stats.shtml (14 July 2006).

Junior Achievement of Rochester (JAR). 2001. Audited Financial Statements. Rochester: Junior Achievement of Rochester.

Kaplan, Robert, and Anthony Atkinson. 1989. *Advanced management accounting*. Englewood Cliffs, NJ: Prentice Hall.

Karn, G. Neil. 1983. Money talks: A guide to establishing the true dollar value of volunteer time, Part 1. *Journal of Volunteer Administration* 1 (Winter): 1–19.

Keane, John. 1998. *Civil society: Old images, new visions*. Stanford, CA.: Stanford University Press.

Keaveny, David. David's domain: The Tom Lehrer pages. 2001. www.keaveny.demon.co.uk/ lehrer (6 July 2002).

Kendall, Jeremy, and Stephen Almond. 1999. United Kingdom. In *Global Civil Society: Dimensions of the nonprofit sector*, ed. Lester Salamon et al., 179–200. Baltimore: The Johns Hopkins University Press.

Kenyon, Ron. 1976. *To the credit of the people*. Toronto: Ontario Credit Union League.

Kinder, Peter, and Amy Domini. 1997. Social screening: Paradigms old and new. *Journal of Investing* (Winter): 12–19.

Lager, Fred. 1994. *Ben & Jerry's: The inside scoop*. New York: Crown.

Land, Kenneth. 1996. Social indicators for assessing the impact of the independent, not-for-profit sector on society. Paper presented at a meeting of Independent Sector, Washington, DC.

Larson, Kermit, Paul Miller, Michael Zin, and Morton Nelson. 1999. *Financial accounting principles*. Homewood, IL: Irwin.

Lévesque Benoît, and Marguerite Mendell. 2004. *L'économie sociale: Diversité des approches et des pratiques. Proposition pour le nouveau programme des ARUC en économie sociale*. Working paper for the Chair, Social Sciences and Humanities Research Council.

Lewin, Kurt. 1935. *A dynamic theory of personality; selected papers*. New York: McGraw-Hill.

Linowes, David. 1972. An approach to socio-economic accounting. *Conference Board Record* 9 (11): 58–61.

———. 1973. Getting a handle on social audit. *Business & Society Review* 4: 39–42.

Lohmann, Roger. 1992. *The commons*. San Francisco: Jossey-Bass.

Macintosh, John C. 1995. Finding the right fit. *CA Magazine* 128 (2): 34–38.

———. "Accounting for Nonprofit Organizations in Canada." Atkinson Faculty of Liberal and Professional Studies, York University, Toronto, 2000. Photocopy.

Macintosh, John C., Henry Bartel, and Kim Snow. 1999. The accounting requirements for nonprofit organizations. Paper presented at the International Atlantic Economic Conference, Montreal, Quebec, October 8–10.

MacPherson, Ian. 1979. *A history of the co-operative movement in English-Canada: 1900–1945*. Toronto: MacMillan.

Mandel, Ernest. 1968. *Marxist economic theory*. London: Merlin Press.

Mansbridge, Jayne, 1982. Fears of conflict in face-to-face democracies. In *Workplace democracy and social change*, ed. Frank Lindenfeld and Joyce Rothschild Whitt, 125–137. Boston, MA: Porter Sargent Publishers.

Martin, Lawrence, and Peter Kettner. 1996. *Measuring the performance of human programs*. Thousand Oaks, CA: Sage.

Martin, Samuel. 1985. *An essential grace: Funding Canada's health care, education, welfare, religion and culture*. Toronto: McClelland and Stewart.

Mathews, M. Reg. 1997. Twenty-five years of social and environmental accounting research: Is there a silver jubilee to celebrate? *Accounting, Auditing & Accountability Journal* 10 (4): 481–531.

Mathews, M. Reg, and M. H. B. Perera. 1995. *Accounting theory and development*. 3d ed. Melbourne: Thomas Nelson.

Mayne, John. 1999. Addressing attribution through contribution analysis, a discussion paper. Ottawa: Office of the Auditor General.

McLean, Rob. 1995. Performance measures in the new economy. cpri.matrixlinks.ca/ Archive/PMNE/PerfMeasNE5.html (23 January 2001).

Meals on Wheels Association of America. 2001. A brief history of Meals on Wheels. Alexandria, Virginia: Meals on Wheels Association of America. Photocopy.

Medawar, Charles. 1976. The social audit: A political view. *Accounting, Organisations and Society* 1 (4): 389–394.

Meek, Gary K., and Sidney J. Gray. 1988. The value-added statement: An innovation for U.S. companies? *Accounting Horizons* 2 (2): 73–81.

Meigs, Walter, Robert Meigs, and Wai Lam. 1988. *Accounting: The basis for business decisions*. Toronto: McGraw-Hill Ryerson.

Metro Credit Union. 1996. *Social audit*. Toronto: Metro Credit Union.

———. 1997. *Credit union social audits*. Toronto: Metro Credit Union.

———. 1998. *Credit union social audits*. Toronto: Metro Credit Union.

———. 2000. *Credit union social audits*. Toronto: Metro Credit Union.

———. 2001. *Credit union social audits*. Toronto: Metro Credit Union.

———. 2003. *Credit union social audits*. Toronto: Metro Credit Union.

Meuller, Gerhard, Helen Gernon, and Gary Meek. 1994. *Accounting: An international perspective*. Burr Ridge, IL: Richard D. Irwin.

Mies, Maria. 1986. *Patriarchy and accumulation on a world scale: Women in the international division of labour*. London: Zed Books.

Milofsky, Carl. 1987. Neighbourhood-based organizations: A market analogy. In *The nonprofit sector: A research handbook*, ed. Walter W. Powell, 277–295. New Haven, CT: Yale University Press.

Monahan, Patrick, with Elie Roth. 2000. *Federal regulation of charities: A critical assessment of recent proposals legislative and regulatory reform*. Toronto: Canadian Centre for Philanthropy.

Mook, Laurie, and Jack Quarter. 2006. Accounting for the social economy: The Socioeconomic Impact Statement. *Annals of Public and Cooperative Economics* 77 (2): 247–269.

Morgan, Gareth. 1988. Accounting as reality construction: Towards a new epistemology for accounting practice. *Accounting, Organizations and Society* 13 (5): 477–485.

Morley, Michael F. 1981. Value added reporting. In Thomas Alexander Lee, *Developments in Financial Reporting*, pp. 251–269. Oxford: Philip Allan.

National Council of Voluntary Organisations. 2002. The Compact. www.ncvo-vol.org.uk/main/gateway/compact.html (14 July 2002).

New Economics Foundation. 1998. *Briefing paper on social auditing*. London: New Economics Foundation.

New York State Office of Tax Policy Analysis. 2002. Handbook of New York State and Local Taxes. New York: New York State Department of Taxation and Finance. www.tax.state.ny.us/Statistics/Policy-Special/Tax%20Handbook/Handbook_2_2002_Personal_Income_Tax.htm (23 June 2002).

Newman's Own. Newman's Own home page. 2002. Shameless exploitation in pursuit of the common good. www.newmansown.com (12 June 2002).

Nozick, Marcia. 1992. *No place like home: Building sustainable communities*. Ottawa: Canadian Council on Social Development.

Olson, Mancur. 1969. *Toward a social report*. Washington, DC: U.S. Department of Health, Education and Welfare.

Ontario Community Support Association. 1993. *Meals on Wheels History*. Toronto: Ontario Community Support Association. Photocopy.

Ontario Network of Employment Skills Training Projects (ONESTEP). 2001. Consolidating a sector: Sustainability and development of human resources in the Ontario community-based training sector. Toronto: ONESTEP.

_____. 2006. About us.www.onestep.on.ca/aboutus/whatiscbt.cfm (17 July 2006).

Oregon Department of Human Services. 2002. The DHS mission, goals and outcomes. www.hr.state.or.us/mission.html (11 June 2002).

Panel on Accountability and Governance in the Voluntary Sector. 1999. *Building on strength: Improving governance and accountability in Canada's voluntary sector.* Ottawa: Secretariat on Accountability and Governance in the Voluntary Sector.

Parker, Allan. 1997. The expert view: Ben & Jerry's Homemade Inc. U.S.A. In *Building corporate accountability*, ed. Simon Zadek, Peter Pruzan and Richard Evans, 129–142. London: Earthscan.

Pearce, John, Peter Raynard, and Simon Zadek. 1995. *Social auditing for small organizations: A workbook for trainers and practitioners.* London: New Economics Foundation.

Phillips, Susan. 2001. *A federal government-voluntary sector accord: Implications for Canada's voluntary sector.* Ottawa: Voluntary Sector Initiative Secretariat.

Pietilä, Hilkka. 1993. A new picture of human economy—a woman's perspective. Paper presented at a meeting of the International Interdisciplinary Congress on Women, San Jose, Costa Rica.

Policy Research Initiative. 2005. *What we need to know about the social economy: A Guide for Policy Research.* Ottawa: Author.

Power, Michael. 1997. *The audit society: The rituals of verification.* Oxford: Oxford University Press.

Pruzan, Peter. 1997. The ethical dimensions of banking: Sbn Bank, Denmark. In *Building corporate accountability*, ed. Simon Zadek, Peter Pruzan, and Richard Evans, 63–83. London: Earthscan.

Putnam, Robert. 1993. *Making democracy work: Civic traditions in modern Italy.* Princeton, NJ: Princeton University Press.

_____. 1995. Bowling alone: America's declining social capital. *Journal of Democracy* 6 (1): 65–78.

_____. 1996. The decline of civil society: How come? So what? Ottawa: John L. Manion Lecture.

_____. 2000. *Bowling alone: The collapse and revival of American community.* New York: Simon & Schuster.

Pyle, William, Kermit Larson, and Michael Zin. 1984. *Fundamental accounting principles.* Homewood, IL: Irwin.

Quarter, Jack. 1992. *Canada's social economy: Co-operatives, non-profits, and other community enterprises.* Toronto: James Lorimer and Company.

_____. 2000. *Beyond the bottom line: Socially innovative business owners.* Westport, CT: Quorum Books.

Quarter, Jack, Laurie Mook, and B.J. Richmond. What is the social economy? *Research Bulletin 13*, Centre for Urban and Community Studies, University of Toronto.

Quarter, Jack, Jorge Sousa, Isla Carmichael, and Betty Jane Richmond. 2001a. Comparing member-based organizations within a social economy framework. *Nonprofit and Voluntary Sector Quarterly* 29 (2): 351–375.

Quarter, Jack, Betty Jane Richmond, Jorge Sousa, and Shirley Thompson. 2001b. An analytic framework for classifying the organizations of the social economy. In *The Nonprofit Sector in Canada*, ed. Keith Banting, 63–100. Kingston: Queen's University School of Policy Studies/McGill-Queen's University Press.

Ramanathan, Kavasseri. 1976. Toward a theory of corporate social accounting. *The Accounting Review* 51 (3): 516–528.

Rans, Sara. 1989. *Community-based training: A field guide*. Toronto: The Ontario Network of Employment Skills Training Projects.

Razek, Joseph, Gordon Hosch, and Martin Ives. 2004. *Introduction to governmental and not-for-profit accounting*. 5d ed. Upper Saddle River, NJ: Prentice Hall.

REDF (Roberts Enterprise Development Fund). 2000. CVE Training Businesses: SROI Report. REDF. www.redf.org/download/sroi/CVETrain.pdf (8 June 2002).

———. 2001. SROI Methodology. REDF. www.redf.org/methodology (8 June 2002).

———. 2005. A Report from the good ship SROI. www.redf.org/download/sroi/goodshipsroi2.doc (17 July 2006).

Riahi-Belkaoui, Ahmed. 1999. *Value added reporting and research: State of the art*. Westport, CT: Quorum Books.

Rice, Dorothy P., and Leonard S. Miller. 1995. The economic burden of affective disorders. *British Journal of Psychiatry* Supplement 27: 34–42.

Richmond, Betty Jane. 1998. *Counting on nonprofits: Final report of the Social Accounting Framework Project*. London: United Way of London and Middlesex.

———. 1999. Counting on each other: A social audit model to assess the impact of nonprofit organizations. Ph.D. diss., University of Toronto.

Richmond, Betty Jane, and Laurie Mook. 2001. Social audit for Waterloo Co-operative Residence Incorporated (WCRI). Toronto: Report to WCRI.

Roeher Institute. 1992. On target? *Canada's employment-related programs for persons with disabilities*. Toronto: Roeher Institute.

Rose, Sanford. 1970. The economics of environmental quality. *Fortune* February: 120–123, 184–186.

Roslender, Robin. 1992. *Sociological perspectives on modern accountancy*. London: Routledge.

Roslender, Robin, and Robin Fincham. 2001. Thinking critically about intellectual capital accounting. *Accounting, Auditing and Accountability Journal* 14 (4): 383–398.

Ross, David. 1986. Making the informal economy visible. In *The living economy: A new economics in the making*, ed. Paul Ekins, 155–166. London: Routledge.

———. 1994. *How to estimate the economic contribution of volunteer work*. Ottawa: Department of Canadian Heritage.

Ross, David, and Richard Shillington. 1989. *A profile of the Canadian volunteer: A guide to the 1987 survey of volunteer activity in Canada*. Ottawa: National Voluntary Associations.

———. 1990. *Economic dimensions of volunteer work in Canada*. Ottawa: Secretary of State.

Rothschild-Whitt, Joyce. 1982. The collective organization: An alternative to bureaucratic models. In *Workplace democracy and social change*, ed. Frank Lindenfeld and Joyce Rothschild Whitt, 23–49. Boston, MA: Porter Sargent Publishers.

Salamon, Lester. 1987. Partners in public service: The scope and theory of government-nonprofit relations. In *The nonprofit sector: A research handbook*, ed. Walter W. Powell, 99–117. New Haven: Yale University Press.

———. 1995. *Partners in public service: Government-nonprofit relations in the modern welfare state*. Baltimore: The Johns Hopkins University Press.

Salamon, Lester, and Helmut K. Anheier. 1997. *Defining the nonprofit sector: A cross-national analysis*. Manchester: Manchester University Press.

Salamon, Lester, Helmut Anheier, Regina List, Stefan Toepler, S. Wojciech Sokolowski, and Associates. 1999. *Global civil society: Dimensions of the nonprofit sector*. Baltimore: The Johns Hopkins University Press.

Salamon, Lester M., S. Wojciech Sokolowski, and Regina List. 2004. Global civil society: An overview. In *Global civil society: Dimensions of the nonprofit sector, Volume two*, Lester M. Salamon, S. Wojciech Sokolowski, and Associates, 3–60. Bloomfield, CT: Kumarin Press, Inc.

Schumacher, Ernst Fritz. 1973. *Small is beautiful*. New York: Harper and Row.

Seetharaman, A., Hadi Helmi Bin Zaini Sooria, and A. S. Saravanan. 2002. Intellectual capital accounting and reporting in the knowledge economy. *Journal of Intellectual Capital* 3 (2): 128–148.

Seidler, Lee. 1973. Dollar values in the social income statement. In *Socio-economic accounting*, Ahmed Belkaoui, 167. Westport, CT: Quorum Books, 1984.

Seligman, Adam. 1998. Between public and private: Towards a sociology of civil society. In *Democratic civility*, ed. Robert Hefner, 79–111. New Brunswick, NJ: Transaction.

Sharpe, David. 1994. *A portrait of Canada's charities*. Toronto: Canadian Centre for Philanthropy.

Shiva, Vandana. 1989. *Staying alive: Women, ecology and development*. London: Zed Books.

Shoup, Donald C. 1997. Evaluating the effects of cashing out employer-paid parking: Eight case studies. *Transport Policy* 4 (4): 201–216.

Shragge, Eric, and Jean-Marc Fontain, eds. 2000. *Social economy: International debates and perspectives*. Montreal: Black Rose.

Shragge, Eric, Peter MacDougall, Elaine Lachance, and Kathryn Church. 2001. Accountability and evaluation: In which direction? Montreal: Concordia University. Photocopy.

Sillanpää, Maria. 1997. Integrated ethical auditing: The Body Shop International, U.K. In *Building corporate accountability*, ed. Simon Zadek, Peter Pruzan, and Richard Evans, 102–129. London: Earthscan.

———. 1998. The Body Shop values report: Towards integrated stakeholder auditing. *Journal of Business Ethics* 17 (13): 1443–1456.

Skinner, Ross M. 1987. *Accounting standards in evolution*. Toronto: Holt, Rinehart and Winston.

Small, Kenneth A., and Kazimi Camilla. 1995. On the costs of air pollution from motor vehicles. *Journal of Transport Economics and Policy* XXIX (1): 7–32.

Smith, David Horton. 1997. The rest of the nonprofit sector: Grassroots associations as the dark matter ignored in the prevailing "flat earth" maps of the sector. *Nonprofit and Voluntary Sector Quarterly* 26 (2): 114–131.

Smith, Steven R., and Michael Lipsky. 1993. *Nonprofits for hire: The welfare state in the age of contracting*. Cambridge, MA: Harvard University Press.

Snaith, Ian. 1991. The économie sociale in the New Europe. In *Yearbook of cooperative enterprise,* 61–75.

Social Accountability 8000 home page. 2002. www.cepaa.org (7 July 2002).

Social Investment Forum. 2006. *2005 report on socially responsible investing trends in the United States: 10-year review*. Washington: Author.

Social Investment Organization. 2005. *Canadian social investment review 2004*. Toronto: Author.

Sokolowski, S. Wojciech, and Lester Salamon. 1999. United States. In *Global Civil Society: Dimensions of the nonprofit sector*, ed Lester Salamon et al., 261–282. Baltimore: The Johns Hopkins University Press.

Statistics Canada. 1995. *Households' unpaid work: Measurement and valuation*. Ottawa: Minister of Industry.

Stein, Beverley. 1996. Oregon benchmarks experience. In Canadian Council on Social Development, *Measuring well-being: Proceedings from a symposium on social indicators*: 10–12. Ottawa: Canadian Council on Social Development.

The Body Shop. 1996. *Social statement 95*. West Sussex, U.K.: The Body Shop.

———. 1998. *Values report 97*. West Sussex, U.K.: The Body Shop.

The Co-operative Bank. 2004. CFS sustainability report 2003. Manchester: Author.

———. 2005. CFS sustainability report 2004. Manchester: Author.

Thompson, Alexander M., and Barbara Bono. 1993. Work without wages: The motivation for volunteer firefighters. *The American Journal of Economics and Sociology* 52 (3): S149–S166.

Tinker, Tony. 1985. *Paper prophets: A social critique of accounting*. New York: Praeger.

Tocqueville, Alexis de. 1969. *Democracy in America*. Garden City, NY: Doubleday Anchor Books.

Townson, Monica. 1986. *The costs and benefits of a national child care system for Canada*. Ottawa: Canadian Day Care Advocacy Association.

Traidcraft. 2000. Traidcraft 1999/2000 social accounts. www.traidcraft.co.uk/sa2000/sindex.html (14 May 2002).

Trainor, John, and Jacques Tremblay. 1992. Consumer/survivor businesses in Ontario challenging the rehabilitation model. *Canadian Journal of Community Mental Health* 11 (2), 65–72.

United Nations Human Development Programme (UNDP). 1995. *United Nations Human Development Report*. New York: Oxford University Press.

United Nations Human Development Report. Human Development Report home page. 2002. hdr.undp.org (26 July 2002).

United Way America. United Way America resources page. 2002. national.unitedway.org/outcomes/resources.htm (14 July 2002).

UNWCED. 1987. *Our common future: A report of the World Commission on Environment and Development*. New York: Oxford University Press.

Upton, Jr., Wayne S. 2001. *Special report: Business and financial reporting, challenges from the new economy*. Norwalk, CT: Financial Accounting Standards Board.

Vaccari, Alessandra. 1997. Constructing the social balance: Consumer Cooperative Italy. In *Building corporate accountability*, ed. Simon Zadek, Peter Pruzan, and Richard Evans, 171–188. London: Earthscan.

Vaillancourt, François. 1994. To volunteer or not: Canada, 1987. *Canadian Journal of Economics* 27 (4): 813–826.

Vaillancourt, Yves. 2002. *Social economy: Health and welfare in four Canadian provinces*. Halifax: Fernwood.

VanCity Credit Union. 1998. *The VanCity social report 1997*. Vancouver: Author.

———. 2000. *The VanCity social report 1998/99*. Vancouver: Author.

———. 2002. *The VanCity social report 2000/01*. Vancouver: Author.

———. 2004. *The VanCity social report 2002/03*. Vancouver: Author.

Verry, Donald. 1990. *An economic framework for the evaluation of child care policy*. Paris: Organisation for Economic Cooperation and Development.

Waring, Marilyn. 1996. *Three masquerades: Essays on equality, work and human rights*. Toronto: University of Toronto Press.

———. 1999. *Counting for nothing: What men value and what women are worth*. Toronto: University of Toronto Press.

WCRI. n.d. WCRI mission statement. Waterloo: WCRI. Photocopy.

WCRI Market Subcommittee. 1998. Market survey. Waterloo: WCRI. Photocopy.

Wheeler, David, and Maria Sillanpää. 2000. *The stakeholder corporation*. Southport, U.K.: Pitman.

W. K. Kellogg Foundation. W. K. Kellogg Foundation evaluation handbook. 1998. www.wkkf.org/pubs/pub770.htm (14 July 2002).

Wilkinson, Kenneth. 1994. The future of community development. In *Community development in perspective*, ed. James Christenson and Jerry Robinson, 337–354. Ames, IA: Iowa State University.

Wolfe, Nancy, Burton Weisbrod, and Edward Bird. 1993. The supply of volunteer labor: The case of hospitals. *Nonprofit Management and Leadership* 4 (1): 23–45.

Worldwide Responsible Apparel Production (WRAP) home page. 2002. www.wrapapparel.org/infosite2 (27 June 2002).

Zadek, Simon. 1998. Balancing performance, ethics, and accountability. *Journal of Business Ethics* 17 (13): 1421–1441.

Zadek, Simon, Peter Pruzan and Richard Evans. 1997. Accountable futures. In *Building corporate accountability*, ed. Simon Zadek, Peter Pruzan, and Richard Evans, 50–60. London: Earthscan.

Zimmerman, Brenda, and Raymond Dart. 1998. *Charities doing commercial ventures: Societal and organizational implications*. Toronto: The Trillium Foundation and Canadian Policy Research Networks Inc.

Index